The New
Naked Poetry

The New Naked Poetry

Recent American poetry
in
open forms

edited by
Stephen Berg and Robert Mezey

The Bobbs-Merrill Company, Inc.
Indianapolis

The Bobbs-Merrill Company, Inc.
4300 West 62nd Street
Indianapolis, Indiana 46268

Designed by Blackstarr

First Printing 1976

Library of Congress Cataloging in Publication Data

Main entry under title:

The new naked poetry.

    1. American poetry—20th century. I. Berg,
Stephen. II. Mezey, Robert.
PS615.M58   811'.5'408   75–12999
ISBN 0–672–61354–9

This book is dedicated to the memory
of the great American poet, Pablo Neruda

CONTENTS

FOREWORD

When our editor suggested that we do a revised edition of *Naked Poetry*, we agreed readily. We had omitted several fine poets from that book and were glad of an opportunity to make amends.

We since have made so many that this book is not simply a new edition but really another anthology, a companion volume to *Naked Poetry*. To make room for new contributors, we decided at the outset to leave out the five dead poets, Roethke, Patchen, Kees, Berryman, and Plath; except for Berryman, we didn't think we could much improve on those selections. We decided also to drop our own work; one exercise of the traditional prerogative was enough.

Two other obvious omissions must be explained.

Robert Creeley asked not to be included this time—his reason, as we understand it, is that he does not approve of anthologies that attempt to represent many diverse tendencies in American poetry. Robert Lowell would certainly have been included again, but the fees his publisher demands are far beyond what we could afford. (When we finished gathering the permissions for the first anthology, we were astonished to find that the fees for Mr. Lowell and Mr. Berryman, both of whom are published by Farrar, Straus & Giroux, exceeded those for all the other poets combined.) So we have reluctantly dropped Mr. Lowell, and have also given up on our plan to add Randall Jarrell and to select more freely from James Wright's last book, also published by Farrar, Straus & Giroux. We are sorry about it, but given our limitations of space and money, we had no choice.

We have added sixteen poets: Hayden Carruth, Robert Duncan, Peter Everwine, Richard Hugo, David Ignatow, Etheridge Knight, Kenneth Koch, John Logan, Thomas McGrath, Frank O'Hara, George Oppen, Adrienne Rich, Jerome Rothenberg, Muriel Rukeyser, Charles Simic, and Louis Simpson. Ten poets who appeared in *Naked Poetry* have been represented again, but by entirely new selections so that the reader who has both books will have some 45 pages of Philip Levine, over 50 pages of Allen Ginsberg, nearly 60 pages of Galway Kinnell, and so on. With one exception, all of the prose statements are new, and all the photographs, and wherever possible, we gave a lot of space to recent, often unpublished, work.

There are of course still other poets we would have liked to include—John Ashberry, Alan Dugan, Donald Hall, Stanley Kunitz, Imamu Amiri Baraka, Donald Justice, Gerald Stern, and John Haines are some of the obvious names that quickly come to mind—but what distinguishes *Naked Poetry* from most other anthologies is the substantial amount of space devoted to each poet, and as we were bound to a limit of approximately 500 pages for this second volume, we have had to pass over a dozen excellent poets who justly should be in it.

In compiling *Naked Poetry*, we made it a condition that no poet or poem be included unless both editors could agree or unless one could persuade the other. This time we have worked with a good deal more freedom. Each of us has added two or three poets and several poems for which the other did not feel equal enthusiasm, yet neither of us is unhappy with the final typescript. Considering how widely our tastes and attitudes have diverged over the years, we are pleasantly surprised by how well we have accorded.

One academic fellow who saw a preliminary version of this book wondered why the editors did not write a long essay defining the "genre" of open form and relating each poet to this "genre." That doesn't seem to be the right word. Listening to the sounds of Etheridge Knight and Robert Duncan, for example, we do not believe it means anything to say they are both working in the "genre" of open form. We would suggest the fellow have a look at "Some Notes on Organic Form" in the first *Naked Poetry*. Organic —the metaphor is of the living and growing thing. The rhythm and shape of the flower cannot be made clear as separate from or meaning anything different from the coming to be of the flower. Denise Levertov puts it better and at great length.

Of course it is possible to theorize about this kind of poetry, to try to discover how its sounds are organized. Some years ago, we used to find this question absorbing and spent many pleasant hours with our learned friend Ronald Goodman looking for abstractions that would somewhat describe what was happening rhythmically in one bit of open verse or another. In "Out of the Cradle Endlessly Rocking," for example, we saw that the simplest musical phrase was the five-syllable /∪∪/∪ which is simply repeated in the first line, that the phrase was a sort of extended amphimacer, and that the rhythm accumulated force by repeating it, by extending it further to seven syllables or nine and by contracting it, like a concertina— damned if it wasn't a genuine aboriginal Variable American Foot (though Kenneth Rexroth claims that this impressive term was just one of Dr. Williams's put-ons). Perhaps this would be interesting to explain to a seminar of graduate students interested in prosody and variable American feet, but how is it any more helpful than our elaborate prosody of traditional verse in explaining the mystery of the poem? Whitman was probably not thinking of that five-syllable unit and how it might be used as a base for a dance of amphibrachs and amphimacers; he was thinking of the boy, the shore, and the midnight song of the mockingbird, and where they might lead him, and his emotion found, without "thought," the music to express itself.

Certainly these new modes will be studied by linguists and prosodists using the most sensitive electronic instruments, and it is possible something of value will be discovered. We have our doubts. The only measure of the sender's accuracy and power is the sensibility of the receiver. It is for the reader, the listener, and not machines and paradigms, to decide if the poem rings true. In any case, we are not theoreticians. We write the stuff, and here, in order to make a little money, to enlarge the audience for poets we love, and to provide an interesting text for ourselves and other teachers, we have collected all these poems, all these genres, into a book.

ROBERT MEZEY
STEPHEN BERG
Salt Lake City—Philadelphia

ACKNOWLEDGMENTS

ROBERT BLY "A Small Bird's Nest Made of White Reed Fiber," "Looking at a Dead Wren in My Hand," "Looking at a Dry Canadian Thistle," and "A Hollow Tree" are from *The Morning Glory,* copyright 1969, 1970 by Robert Bly, and reprinted by permission of the Author and Kayak Books. "Water Under the Earth," copyright © 1973 by Robert Bly, is reprinted by permission of Harper & Row, Publishers, Inc. "Leonardo's Secret," from *Sleepers Joining Hands,* copyright 1973 by Robert Bly is reprinted by permission of Kayak Books. "The Teeth Mother Naked at Last," copyright © 1970 by Robert Bly, is reprinted by permission of City Lights Books. "Written Forty Miles South of a Spreading City," from "On a Farm," appeared in *The New York Times* April 28, 1972, copyright © 1972 by *The New York Times* Company. Reprinted by permission. "Christmas Eve Service at Midnight at St. Michael's," Sceptre Press, copyright 1972 by Robert Bly, and "The Dead Seal Near McClure's Beach," Clear Creek Books and Mudra, copyright 1971 and 1973 by Robert Bly, are reprinted by permission of the Author. "Thinking of 'The Autumn Field'," from *Jumping Out of Bed,* Barre Publishers, Barre, Mass., copyright © 1973 by Robert Bly, and "The Three Brains," Seventies Press, copyright © 1972 by Robert Bly are reprinted by permission of the Author.

HAYDEN CARRUTH "Fear and Anger in the Mindless Universe," "Sonnet," "Once More," "The Insomniac Sleeps Well for Once and," "This Decoration," "Rimrock, Where It Is," "Twilight Comes," and "Emergency Haying" from *From Snow and Rock, From Chaos,* copyright © 1968, 1969, 1971, 1972, 1973 by Hayden Carruth, are reprinted by permission of New Directions Publishing Corporation.

ROBERT DUNCAN "Uprising, *Passages 25*" and "Articulations," from *Bending the Bow,* copyright © 1964, 1966, 1968 by Robert Duncan; "A Poem Beginning with a Line by Pindar," from *The Opening of the Field,* copyright © 1960 by Robert Duncan; and "A New Poem" from *Roots and Branches,* copyright © 1964 by Robert Duncan, are reprinted by permission of New Directions Publishing Corporation.

PETER EVERWINE "The Brother" (appeared originally in *Crazy Horse*); "Drinking Cold Water" (appeared in *The New Yorker*); "The Marsh New Year's Day," "Learning to Speak," and "Someone Knocks" (appeared in *Kayak*); "Perhaps It's As You Say" (appeared in the *Iowa Review*); "The Clearing" (from *In the House of Light,* Stonewall Press); "Going" (originally in *Transpacific*); and "We Meet in the Lives of Animals" (appeared in *Down at the Santa Fe Depot,* Gilgia Press) are all from *Collecting the Animals,* copyright © 1969, 1970, 1971, 1972 by Peter Everwine and reprinted by permission of Atheneum Publishers. "Distance," copyright 1973 by *Antaeus*; "The Burden of Decision," copyright 1975 by the *Ohio Review*; "Routes,"

national Creative Management and the Author. "The Art of Love," Part I, copyright © 1972 by *Poetry Magazine,* is reprinted by permission of International Creative Management and the Author.

DENISE LEVERTOV "Olga Poems" (originally appeared in *Poetry*) from *The Sorrow Dance,* copyright © 1965, 1966 by Denise Levertov Goodman; "Despair," "Adam's Complaint," "Advent 1966" (appeared in *Nation*) and "The Gulf" (appeared in *Mundus Artium* and *Stony Brook*) are from *Relearning the Alphabet,* copyright © 1967, 1968, 1969, 1970 by Denise Levertov Goodman; "The Malice of Innocence," "The Good Dream," and "By Rail Through the Earthly Paradise, Perhaps Bedfordshire," are from *Footprints,* copyright © 1970, 1972 by Denise Levertov Goodman; "Line-breaks, Stanza-spaces, and the Inner Voice," is from *Poet in the World,* copyright © 1973 by Denise Levertov Goodman. All are reprinted by permission of New Directions Publishing Corporation.

PHILIP LEVINE "Salami" (appeared originally in *Iowa Review*), "Autumn," "They Feed They Lion" (appeared in *Kayak*) are from *They Feed They Lion,* copyright © 1970, 1971, 1972 by Philip Levine; "At the Fillmore" (originally in *Transpacific*), "Zaydee" (originally in *Iowa Review*), "The Poem Circling Hamtramck, Michigan All Night in Search of You" (originally in *The New Yorker*), "Uncle" (originally in *Atlantic*), are all from *1933,* copyright © 1972, 1973, 1974 by Philip Levine. All poems listed above are reprinted by permission of Atheneum Publishers, Inc. "To My God in His Sickness," copyright © 1975 by *The New Yorker Magazine,* Inc., is reprinted by permission. "Standing on the Corner" (originally in *Iowa Review*), "New Season" and "Fixing the Foot" (appeared in the *Ohio Review*) are reprinted by permission of the Author. "Red Dust," "In the New Sun," and "How Much Earth" are reprinted by permission of Kayak Books.

JOHN LOGAN "The San Francisco Poem" from *The Zigzag Walk: Poems 1963–1968,* copyright © 1963, 1964, 1965, 1966, 1967, 1968, 1969 by John Logan, are reprinted by permission of the publishers, E. P. Dutton & Co., Inc. "A Century Piece for Poor Heine" and "A Trip to Four or Five Towns" from *Ghosts of the Heart* published by The University of Chicago Press, copyright © 1960 by John Logan are reprinted by permission of the Author. "Spring of the Thief" from *Spring of the Thief,* Alfred A. Knopf, copyright © 1963 by John Logan, is reprinted by permission of the Author. "Saturday Afternoon at the Movies" from *The Anonymous Lover,* copyright © 1969, 1970, 1971, 1972, 1973 by John Logan, is reprinted by permission of Liveright Publishing Corporation. "On Poets and Poetry Today" appeared in *Voyages,* Vol. IV, nos. 3 & 4. Copyright 1972 by Voyages, Inc. Reprinted by permission of the publisher.

THOMAS MCGRATH *Letter to an Imaginary Friend,* Part One: II, 2; VIII, 4; Part Two: II, 2, 3, 4, 5; V, 2; VI, 4, copyright © 1962, 1970 by Thomas McGrath is reprinted by permission of the publisher, the Swallow Press.

"On My Work" originally appeared in *American Poetry Review*, copyright 1974 by Thomas McGrath.

M. S. MERWIN "For a Coming Extinction" (originally appeared in *Southern Review*) and "Fly" (originally in the *Atlantic Monthly*), are from *The Lice*, copyright © 1966, 1967 by W. S. Merwin. "Finding a Teacher," "The Initiate," and "Ballade of Sayings" (appeared first in the *New Yorker*), are from *Writings to an Unfinished Accompaniment*, copyright © 1971, 1972, 1973 by M. S. Merwin. "Voice," "The Black Plateau," "February," "Snowfall," and "The Judgment of Paris" are from *The Carriers of Ladders*, copyright © 1967, 1968, 1969, 1970 by W. S. Merwin and originally appeared in the *New Yorker*. All poems are reprinted by permission of Atheneum Publishers, Inc. "The Vineyard" appeared originally in *Kayak*.

FRANK O'HARA "For James Dean," "Ode: Salute to the French Negro Poets," "Ave Maria," "Personism: A Manifesto," "Answer to Voznesensky and Evtushenko," "Autobiographia Literaria," "A True Account of Talking to the Sun at Fire Island," are copyright © 1956, 1960, 1961, 1964, 1967, 1968 by Maureen Granville-Smith, Administratrix of the Estate of Frank O'Hara. All poems are from *The Selected Poems of Frank O'Hara* and reprinted by permission of Alfred A. Knopf, Inc. "The Hunter," copyright by Folder Editions, is reprinted by permission of the publisher. "Poem," from *Meditations in an Emergency*, copyright © 1957 by James O'Hara, is reprinted by permission of Grove Press, Inc.

GEORGE OPPEN "The Gesture" and "From Virgil" (from "Five Poems About Poetry"); "The Forms of Love" (appeared in *San Francisco Review* and *Poetry*); "Quotations" and "Psalm" (appeared in *San Francisco Review*) are all from *This in Which*, copyright © 1963, 1964, 1965 by George Oppen and reprinted by permission of the New Directions Publishing Corporation. "Sara in Her Father's Arms" (appeared in *San Francisco Review*) is from *The Materials*, copyright © 1962 by George Oppen and reprinted by permission of New Directions Publishing Corporation. "Some San Francisco Poems" from *Seascape: Needle's Eye*, copyright © 1972 by George Oppen is reprinted by permission of Sumac Press and the Author. "The Book of Job," from *Myth of the Blaze*, copyright © 1975 by George Oppen, is reprinted by permission of the Author and New Directions Publishing Corporation.

KENNETH REXROTH "Poems from the Greek Anthology," copyright © 1962 by Kenneth Rexroth, is reprinted by permission of the University of Michigan Press. "The Signature of All Things," "Fish Peddler and Cobbler"; poems from "A Bestiary" ("Fox," "Horse," "Raccoon," "Vulture," "Wolf"); "A Letter to William Carlos Williams," "The Bad Old Days," "On the Eve of the Plebiscite," "For a Masseuse and Prostitute" are from *Collected Shorter Poems*, copyright © 1949, 1963 by Kenneth Rexroth, copyright © 1956 by New Directions Publishing Corporation, and reprinted by permission of New Directions Publishing Corporation. "Poetry Regeneration and D. H. Lawrence," from *Bird in the Bush*, copyright © 1947 by New Directions Publishing Corporation, is reprinted by permission of the publisher. "Introduction to The Collected Longer Poems" from *Collected Longer Poems*, copyright © 1968 by Kenneth Rexroth is reprinted by permission of New Directions Publishing Corporation.

ADRIENNE RICH "The Stranger," from *Necessities of Life*, Poems, 1962–1965, copyright © 1966 by W. W. Norton & Company, Inc.; "From the Prison House," "A Primary Ground," "August," and "The Mirror in Which Two Are Seen as One," from *Diving into the Wreck*, Poems, 1971–1972, copyright © 1973 by W. W. Norton & Company, Inc., are reprinted by permission of the publisher, W. W. Norton & Company, Inc. "From an Old House in America" (first appeared in *Amazon Quarterly*) is reprinted by permission of the Author. From "When We Dead Awaken: Writing as Re-Vision" (original essay appeared in *College English*, October 1972) is reprinted by permission of the National Council of Teachers of English and the Author.

JEROME ROTHENBERG "The Beadle's Testimony," "Soap II," "Esther K Comes to America 1931," "Portrait of a Jew Old Style," "Cokboy, Part Two," from *Poland*, copyright © 1967, 1968, 1969, 1970, 1972, 1973, 1974 by Jerome Rothenberg are reprinted by permission of New Directions Publishing Corporation. "Fifth Hell" and "Sixth Hell," from "The Seven Hells of the Jigoku Zoshi" appearing in *Poems for the Games of Silence*, copyright © 1960, 1971 by Jerome Rothenberg are reprinted by permission of the Author and New Directions Publishing Corporation.

MURIEL RUKEYSER "Gauley Bridge," "George Robinson," copyright © 1938, 1966 by Muriel Rukeyser; "Nuns in the Wind," copyright © 1939, 1966, by Muriel Rukeyser; "Ajanta," copyright 1944, 1972 by Muriel Rukeyser; "Fields Where We Slept," and "No One Ever Walking This Our Only Earth," copyright © 1955, 1963 by Muriel Rukeyser are all from *Waterlily Fire* published by MacMillan Company and reprinted by permission of Monica McCall, ICM. "Looking at Each Other," "Waiting for Icarus," "Myth," "Along History," "Boys of These Men Full Speed," and "Don Baty the Draft Resister" are from *Breaking Open*, published by Random House, copyright © 1973 by Muriel Rukeyser and reprinted by permission of Monica McCall, ICM. Excerpts from *The Life of Poetry*, copyright © 1949 by Muriel Rukeyser, are reprinted by permission of the Author and Monica McCall, ICM.

CHARLES SIMIC "Strictly for Posterity," "Breasts," "Elementary Cosmogony," "Nothing," and "The Story" are from *Return to a Place Lit by a Glass of Milk*, copyright © 1974 by Charles Simic; "The Spoon," "Hunger," "Pastoral," "Poem," "Butcher Shop," "errata," and "Poem Without a Title" are

The New
Naked Poetry

ROBERT BLY

Robert Bly was born in 1926 in western Minnesota, and educated at St. Olaf, Harvard, and Iowa. He is the editor of *The Seventies*, a magazine (formerly *The Sixties*), and a press of the same changing name which has issued several valuable books of translations. His own books include *Silence in the Snowy Fields*, *The Light Around the Body* (for which he won the National Book Award in 1968), *Jumping Out of Bed*, and *Sleepers Joining Hands*. He lives with his wife and children on a farm near Madison, Minnesota.

A SMALL BIRD'S NEST
MADE OF WHITE REED FIBER

It's a white nest! White as the foam thrown up when the sea hits rocks. Some light comes through it, we get the feeling of those cloudy transoms above Victorian doors, or the manless hair of those intense nurses, gray and tangled after long nights in the Crimean wards. It is something made and then forgotten, like our own lives that we will entirely forget in the grave, when we are floating, nearing the shore where we will be reborn, ecstatic and black.

LOOKING AT A DEAD WREN IN MY HAND

Forgive the hours spent listening to radios, and the words of gratitude I did not say to teachers. I love your tiny rice-like legs, like bars of music played in an empty church, and the feminine tail, where no worms of Empire have ever slept, and the intense yellow chest that makes tears come. Your tail feathers open like a picket fence, and your bill is brown, with the sorrow of an old Jew whose daughter has married an athlete. The black spot on your head is your own mourning cap.

LOOKING AT A DRY CANADIAN THISTLE
BROUGHT IN FROM THE SNOW

What is this wonderful thing? Brown and everywhere! It has leaped up on my desk like surf, or like a bull onto a cow! It rushes everywhere in front of me . . . And my sleeping senses are shouted at, called in from the back of my head, to look at it! Well, it is only a broken off bush, a tumble-weed, every branch different, and the whole bush the same, so in that way it is like the sea. Taken in from the deserted shore, it talks of queens sent away to live in cramped farmhouses, living in the dirt, and it talks of coffins and amazing arrows, no it is a love, some love we forget every day, it is my mother.

A HOLLOW TREE

I bend over an old hollow cottonwood stump, still standing, waist high, and look inside. Early spring. Its Siamese temple walls are all brown and ancient. The walls have been worked on by the intricate ones. Inside the hollow walls there is privacy and secrecy, dim light. And yet some creature has died here.

On the temple floor feathers, gray feathers, many of them with a fluted white tip. Many feathers. In the silence many feathers.

WATER UNDER THE EARTH

O yes, I love you, book of my confessions,
when the swallowed begins to rise from the earth again,
and the deep hungers from the wells.
So much is still inside me, like cows eating in a collapsed strawpile
all winter to get out.
Everything we need now is buried,
it's far back into the mountain,
it's under the water guarded by women.
These lines themselves are sunk to the waist in the dusk under the
    odorous cedars,
each rain will only drive them deeper,
they will leave a faint glow in the dead leaves.
You too are weeping in the low shade of the pine branches,
you feel yourself about to be buried too,
you are a ghost stag shaking his antlers in the herony light—
what is beneath us will be triumphant
in the cool air made fragrant by owl feathers.

I am only half-risen,
I see how carefully I have covered my tracks as I wrote,
how well I brushed over the past with my tail.
I enter rooms full of photographs of the dead.
My hair stands up
as a badger crosses my path in the moonlight.

I see faces looking at me in the shallow waters
where I have thrown them down.
Mother and father pushed into the dark.
That shows how close I am to the dust that fills the cracks on the ocean
    floor,
how much I love to fly alone in the rain,
how much I love to see the jellyfish pulsing at the cold borders of the
    universe.

I have piled up people like dead flies between the storm window and
    the kitchen pane.
So much is not spoken!
I stand at the edges of the light, howling to come in.
Then, I follow the wind through open holes in the blood—
So much ecstasy. . . .
long evenings when the leopard leaps up to the stars,
and in an instant we understand all the rocks in the world.
And I am there, prowling like a limp-footed bull outside the circle of
    the fire,
praying, meditating,
full of energy, like a white horse, saddled, alone on the unused fields.

There is a consciousness hovering under the mind's feet,
advanced civilizations under the footsole,
climbing at times up on a shoelace!
It is a willow that knows of water under the earth,
I am a father who dips as he passes over underground rivers,
who can feel his children through all distance and time!

THE TEETH MOTHER NAKED AT LAST

1
Massive engines lift beautifully from the deck.
Wings appear over the trees, wings with eight hundred rivets.

Engines burning a thousand gallons of gasoline a minute sweep over
    the huts with dirt floors.

The chickens feel the new fear deep in the pits of their beaks.
Buddha with Padma Sambhava.

Meanwhile, out on the China Sea,
immense gray bodies are floating,
born in Roanoke,
the ocean on both sides expanding, "buoyed on the dense marine."

Helicopters flutter overhead. The death-
bee is coming. Super Sabres
like knots of neurotic energy sweep
around and return.
This is Hamilton's triumph.
This is the advantage of a centralized bank.
B-52s come from Guam. All the teachers
die in flames. The hopes of Tolstoy fall asleep in the ant heap.
Do not ask for mercy.

Now the time comes to look into the past-tunnels,
the hours given and taken in school,
the scuffles in coatrooms,
foam leaps from his nostrils,
now we come to the scum you take from the mouths of the dead,
now we sit beside the dying, and hold their hands, there is hardly time
      for good-bye,
the staff sergeant from North Carolina is dying—you hold his hand,
he knows the mansions of the dead are empty, he has an empty place
inside him, created one night when his parents came home drunk,
he uses half his skin to cover it,
as you try to protect a balloon from sharp objects. . . .

Artillery shells explode. Napalm canisters roll end over end.
800 steel pellets fly through the vegetable walls.
The six-hour infant puts his fists instinctively to his eyes to keep out
      the light.
But the room explodes,
the children explode.
Blood leaps on the vegetable walls.

Yes, I know, blood leaps on the walls—
Don't cry at that—
Do you cry at the wind pouring out of Canada?
Do you cry at the reeds shaken at the edge of the sloughs?
The Marine battalion enters.
This happens when the seasons change,
This happens when the leaves begin to drop from the trees too early

"*Kill them: I don't want to see anything moving.*"
This happens when the ice begins to show its teeth in the ponds
This happens when the heavy layers of lake water press down on the
fish's head, and send him deeper, where his tail swirls slowly,
and his brain passes him pictures of heavy reeds, of vegetation
fallen on vegetation. . . .
Hamilton saw all this in detail:
"*Every banana tree slashed, every cooking utensil smashed, every mattress cut.*"

Now the Marine knives sweep around like sharp-edged jets; how beautifully they slash open the rice bags,
the mattresses . . .
ducks are killed with $150 shotguns.

Old women watch the soldiers as they move.

2
Excellent Roman knives slip along the ribs.

A stronger man starts to jerk up the strips of flesh.

"*Let's hear it again, you believe in the Father, the Son, and the Holy
Ghost?*"

A long scream unrolls.

More.

"*From the political point of view, democratic institutions are being
built in Vietnam, wouldn't you agree?*"

A green parrot shudders under the fingernails.
Blood jumps in the pocket.
The scream lashes like a tail.

"*Let us not be deterred from our task by the voices of dissent. . . .*"

The whines of the jets
pierce like a long needle.
As soon as the President finishes his press conference, black wings carry
off the words,
bits of flesh still clinging to them.

    *   *   *

The ministers lie, the professors lie, the television lies, the priests
lie. . . .
These lies mean that the country wants to die.

Lie after lie starts out into the prairie grass,
like enormous caravans of Conestoga wagons. . . .

And a long desire for death flows out, guiding the enormous caravans
    from beneath,
stringing together the vague and foolish words.
It is a desire to eat death,
to gobble it down,
to rush on it like a cobra with mouth open

It's a desire to take death inside,
to feel it burning inside, pushing out velvety hairs,
like a clothes brush in the intestines—

This is the thrill that leads the President on to lie
     *   *   *

Now the Chief Executive enters; the press conference begins:
First the President lies about the date the Appalachian Mountains rose.
Then he lies about the population of Chicago, then he lies about the
    weight of the adult eagle, then about the acreage of the Ever-
    glades

He lies about the number of fish taken every year in the Arctic,
    he has private information about which city *is* the capital of
    Wyoming, he lies about the birthplace of Attila the Hun.

He lies about the composition of the amniotic fluid, and he insists
    that Luther was never a German, and that only the
    Protestants sold indulgences,

That Pope Leo X *wanted* to reform the church, but the "liberal ele-
    ments" prevented him,
that the Peasants' War was fomented by Italians from the North.

And the Attorney General lies about the time the sun sets.
     *   *   *

These lies are only the longing we all feel to die.
It is the longing for someone to come and take you by the hand to
    where they all are sleeping:
where the Egyptian pharaohs are asleep, and your own mother,
and all those disappeared children, who used to go around with you in
    the rings at grade school. . . .

Do not be angry at the President—he is longing to take in his hand
the locks of death hair—
to meet his own children dead, or unborn. . . .
He is drifting sideways toward the dusty places

3

This is what it's like for a rich country to make war
this is what it's like to bomb huts (afterwards described as "structures")
this is what it's like to kill marginal farmers (afterwards described as
   "Communists")

this is what it's like to watch the altimeter needle going mad.

Baron 25, this is 81. Are there any friendlies in the area? 81 from 25,
negative on the friendlies. I'd like you to take out as many structures
as possible located in those trees within 200 meters east and west of
my smoke mark.

diving, the green earth swinging, cheeks hanging back, red pins blos-
   soming ahead of us, 20-millimeter cannon fire, leveling off, rice
   fields shooting by like telephone poles, smoke rising, hut roofs
   loom up huge as landing fields, slugs going in, half the huts on
   fire, small figures running, palm trees burning, shooting past, up
   again; . . . blue sky . . . cloud mountains

This is what it's like to have a gross national product.

It's because the aluminum window shade business is doing so well in
   the United States that we roll fire over entire villages
It's because a hospital room in the average American city now costs $90
   a day that we bomb hospitals in the North

It's because the milk trains coming into New Jersey hit the right
   switches every day that the best Vietnamese men are cut in two
   by American bullets that follow each other like freight cars

This is what it's like to send firebombs down from air-conditioned
   cockpits.

This is what it's like to be told to fire into a reed hut with an automatic
   weapon.

It's because we have new packaging for smoked oysters that bomb
   holes appear in the rice paddies

It is because we have so few women sobbing in back rooms,
because we have so few children's heads torn apart by high-velocity
   bullets,
because we have so few tears falling on our own hands
that the Super Sabre turns and screams down toward the earth.

It's because taxpayers move to the suburbs that we transfer popula-
   tions.

ROBERT BLY   7

The Marines use cigarette lighters to light the thatched roofs of huts
because so many Americans own their own homes.

4

I see a car rolling toward a rock wall.
The treads in the face begin to crack.
We all feel like tires being run down roads under heavy cars.

The teen-ager imagines herself floating through the Seven Spheres.
Oven doors are found
open.
Soot collects over the doorframe, has children, takes courses,
goes mad, and dies.

There is a black silo inside our bodies, revolving fast.
Bits of black paint are flaking off,
where the motorcycles roar, around and around,
rising higher on the silo walls,
the bodies bent toward the horizon,
driven by angry women dressed in black.

    *   *   *

I *know* that books are tired of us.
I *know* they are chaining the Bible to chairs.
Books don't want to remain in the same room with us anymore.

New Testaments are escaping . . . dressed as women . . . they go off
    after dark.
And Plato! Plato . . . Plato wants to go backwards. . . .
He wants to hurry back up the river of time, so he can end as some
    blob of sea flesh rotting on an Australian beach.

5

Why are they dying? I have written this so many times.
They are dying because the President has opened a Bible again.
They are dying because gold deposits have been found among the
    Shoshoni Indians.
They are dying because money follows intellect!
And intellect is like a fan opening in the wind—

The Marines think that unless they die the rivers will not move.
They are dying so that the mountain shadows will continue to fall
    east in the afternoon,
so that the beetle can move along the ground near the fallen twigs.

6

But if one of those children came near that we have set on fire,
came toward you like a gray barn, walking,
you would howl like a wind tunnel in a hurricane,
you would tear at your shirt with blue hands,
you would drive over your own child's wagon trying to back up,
the pupils of your eyes would go wild—

If a child came by burning, you would dance on a lawn,
trying to leap into the air, digging into your cheeks,
you would ram your head against the wall of your bedroom
like a bull penned too long in his moody pen—

If one of those children came toward me with both hands
in the air, fire rising along both elbows,
I would suddenly go back to my animal brain,
I would drop on all fours, screaming,
my vocal chords would turn blue, so would yours,
it would be two days before I could play with my own children again.

7

I want to sleep awhile in the rays of the sun slanting over the snow.
Don't wake me.
Don't tell me how much grief there is in the leaf with its natural oils.
Don't tell me how many children have been born with stumpy hands
    all those years we lived in St. Augustine's shadow.

Tell me about the dust that falls from the yellow daffodil shaken in
    the restless winds.
Tell me about the particles of Babylonian thought that still pass
    through the earthworm every day.
Don't tell me about "the frightening laborers who do not read books."

Now the whole nation starts to whirl,
the end of the Republic breaks off,
Europe comes to take revenge,
the mad beast covered with European hair rushes through the mesa
    bushes in Mendocino County,
pigs rush toward the cliff,
the waters underneath part: in one ocean luminous globes float up
    (in them hairy and ecstatic men—)
in the other, the teeth mother, naked at last.

ROBERT BLY   9

Let us drive cars
up
the light beams
to the stars . . .

And return to earth crouched inside the drop of sweat
that falls
from the chin of the Protestant tied in the fire.

WRITTEN FORTY MILES SOUTH OF A SPREADING CITY

It is early dawn. The city forty miles away draws airplanes, as if it
were a Sabbath. They appear and disappear. They are like flakes of
powdered milk that appear in the water an instant, and then disap-
pear. There are still paths that the cows have woven through the
weeds, fences that mark the limits of the 75 × 40 barn the farmer
pushed before him all his life. The barn is now only used for hay, the
stanchions cold, it is like some African trading post, abandoned as
the secrets the Europeans kept caught up with them, and no one
could give a "simple and sincere account of his own life"!

The Germans and Norwegians who opened this land tore it away
from the mother-love of the Sioux. They have sunk back now into
their family Bibles; the great hinges have closed on them, and they
sleep, their knees curiously limber, a coarse sleep—not forgiven—
they know they have done wrong, and they go over and over the
harness-hours, trying to see how they threw on the harness, how
they happened to buckle things in the wrong order. And the souls
of their women float crippled through the hayloft, the floating souls
are missing an arm, or a leg, the missing parts have been sent to
someone as a message, like those hands sent back by kidnappers
in Persia. The feminine dries up early, and is easily torn away by the
wind; pieces of it flying into the gully, or the tree split open, bare
wood showing. The masculine like the windmill from Chicago, re-
placed after the Second World War by a pump set between the
three legs.

In early dawn, sunlight gleaming on the tops of the cars in the
yard, the farm is neither living nor dying. The dolphins go on speak-
ing their high-pitched and playful thoughts, the whale sees himself
less in the wide oceans, the high school girl in the suburbs makes

love, and feels a bit detached, she is surprised to see what the ass of a man looks like; she is drawn to the hair on her arms. I too swim on, like those tortoises nearing a beach, or a coral reef, their great leather wings rising and falling in the friendly ocean, waking after long sleep, I feel secrets being discovered everywhere, thoughts that can save, rising, the sea at dawn littered with schools of live jellyfish, half soul and half body.

CHRISTMAS EVE SERVICE AT MIDNIGHT AT ST. MICHAEL'S

for Father Richter

A cold night, the sidewalk we walk on icy, the dark surrounds the frail wood houses, that were so recently trees. We left my father's house an hour before midnight, carrying boxes of gifts out to the car. My brother, who had been killed six months before, was not there. We had wept sitting near the decorated tree. Now I see the angel on the right of St. Michael's altar praying on his knee, one hand pressed to his chin. The long needled Christmas pine, who is the one inside us, green both summer and winter, is hung with red ribbons of triumph. And it is hung with thirty golden balls, each representing a separate planet on which some needles never fall. Outdoors the snow labors its old Manichean labors to keep the father and his animals in melancholy. We sing. At midnight the priest walks down one or two steps, finds the infant Christ, and puts him into the cradle beneath the altar, where the horses and the sheep have been waiting.

Just after midnight, he turns to face us, lifts up the dry wafer, and breaks it—a clear and terrifying sound. He holds up the two halves . . . frightening . . . for like so many acts, it is permanent. With his arms spread, the cross clear on his white chasuble, he tells us that Christ intended to leave his body behind . . . it is confusing . . . we take our bodies with us when we go. I see oceans dark and lifting near flights of stairs, oceans lifting and torn over which the invisible birds drift like husks over November roads . . . no one sees them. The cups are put down. The ocean now has been stirred and calmed. A large man living and dead is flying over the water with wings spread, a wound on his chest.

LEONARDO'S SECRET

The Virgin is thinking of a child—who will drive the rioters out of the Temple—and her face is smiling. Her smile is full, it reminds you of a cow's side, or a stubble field with water standing in it.

Behind her head, jagged blue rocks. The pointed rocks slope up quietly, and fall back, washed by a blue light, like the light in an octopus's eyes. The rocks, though no one is there, are not empty of people.

The rocks have not been forgotten by the sea either. They are the old brains of the sea. They glow for several seconds every morning, as the old man who lives in a hut on the shore drinks his glass of salt water.

THE DEAD SEAL NEAR McCLURE'S BEACH

1

Walking north toward the point, I come on a dead seal. From a few feet away, he looks like a brown log. The body is on its back, dead only a few hours. I stand and look at him. A quiver in the dead flesh. My God he is still alive. A shock goes through me, as if a wall of my room had fallen away.

His head is arched back, the small eyes closed, the whiskers sometimes rise and fall. He is dying. This is the oil. Here on its back is the oil that heats our houses so efficiently. Wind blows fine sand back toward the ocean. The flipper near me lies folded over the stomach, looking like an unfinished arm, lightly glazed with sand at the edges. The other flipper lies half underneath. The seal's skin looks like an old overcoat, scratched here and there . . . by sharp mussels maybe . . .

I reach out and touch him. Suddenly he rears up, turns over. He gives three cries, like those from Christmas toys. He lunges toward me. I am terrified and leap back, although I know there can be no teeth in that jaw. He starts flopping toward the sea. But he falls over, on his face. He does not want to go back to the sea. He looks up at the sky, and he looks like an old lady who has lost her hair.

He puts his chin back down on the sand, arranges his flippers, and waits for me to go. I go.

2

Today I go back to say goodbye; he's dead now. But he's not—he's
a quarter mile farther up the shore. Today he is thinner, squatting on
his stomach, head out. The ribs show more—each vertebra on the
back under the coat now visible, shiny. He breathes in and out.

He raises himself up, and tucks his flippers under, as if to keep
them warm. A wave comes in, touches his nose. He turns and looks
at me—the eyes slanted, the crown of his head like a leather jacket.
He is taking a long time to die. The whiskers white as porcupine
quills, the forehead slopes, goodbye brother, die in the sound of
waves, forgive us if we have killed you, long live your race, your
innertube race, so uncomfortable on land, so comfortable in the sea.
Be comfortable in death then, where the sand will be out of your
nostrils, and you can swim in long loops through the pure death,
ducking under as assassinations break above you. You don't want
to be touched by me. I climb the cliff and go home the other way.

THINKING OF "THE AUTUMN FIELDS"

1

Already autumn begins here in the mossy rocks.
The sheep bells moving from the wind are sad.
I have left my wife foolishly in a flat country,
I have set up my table looking over a valley.
There are fish in the lake but I will not fish;
I will sit silently at my table by the window.
From whatever appears on my plate,
I will give a little away to the birds and the grass.

2

How easy to see the road the liferiver takes!
Hard to move one living thing from its own path.
The fish adores being in the deep water;
The bird easily finds a tree to live in.
In the second half of life a man accepts poverty and illness;
praise and blame belong to the glory of the first half.
Although cold wind blows against my walking stick,
I will never get tired of the ferns on this mountain.

ROBERT BLY 13

3

Music and chanting help me overcome my faults;
the mountains and woods keep my body fiery.
I have two or three books only in my room.
The sun shining off the empty bookcase warms my back.
Going out I pick up the pine cones the wind has thrown away.
When night comes, I will open a honeycomb.
On the floor-throw covered with tiny red and blue flowers,
I bring my stocking feet close to the faint incense.

THE THREE BRAINS

1

Some recent brain research throws light I think on what we've been talking about. I'll sum up some of the conclusions and speculations made by the American neurologist, Paul MacLean. I first ran into his ideas in Koestler's book, *The Ghost in the Machine,* where he gives about six pages to MacLean's theories, and refers to the neurological journals in which MacLean publishes. The gist of MacLean's thought is that we do not have one brain, but three. MacLean's map of the head isn't psychological, as Freud's Ego, Id, and Superego, but geographical—the three brains are actually in the head, and brain surgeons have known for a long time what they look like. MacLean's contribution has been to suggest that each of these brains is to some extent independent. During evolution, the body often reshaped the body—fins, for example, in us, turned utterly into arms, but the forward momentum in evolution was apparently so great that the brain could not allow itself the time to reform—it simply added.

The reptile brain is still intact in the head. Known medically as the limbic node, it is a horseshoe-shaped organ located in the base of the skull. The job of the reptile brain appears to be the physical survival of the organism in which it finds itself. Should danger or enemies come near, an alarm system comes into play, and the reptile brain takes over from the other brains—it takes what we might call "executive power." In great danger it might hold that power exclusively. It's been noticed, for example, that when mountain climbers are in danger of falling, the brain mood changes—the eyesight intensifies, and the feet "miraculously" take the right steps. Once down the climber realizes he has been "blanked out." This probably means that the reptile brain's need for energy was so great that it withdrew energy even from the memory systems of the mammal and new brains. The presence of fear produces a higher energy input to the reptile brain. The increasing fear in this century means that more and more energy, as a result, is going to the reptile brain: that is the same thing as saying that the military budgets in all nations are increasing.

MacLean himself speculated, in a paper written recently for a philosophical conference, that the persistent trait of paranoia in human beings is due to the inability to shut off the energy source to the reptile brain. In a settled society, if there are no true enemies, the reptile brain will imagine enemies in order to preserve and use its share of the incoming energy. John Foster Dulles represented the reptile brain in the fifties.

When the change to mammal life occurred, a second brain was simply folded around the limbic node. This "cortex," which I will call here the mammal brain, fills most of the skull. The mammal brain has quite different functions. When we come to the mammal brain we find for the first time a sense of community: love of women, of children, of the neighbor, the idea of brotherhood, care for the community, or for the country. "There is no greater love than that of a man who will lay down his life for a friend." Evidently in the mammal brain there are two nodes of energy: sexual love and ferocity. (The reptile brain has no ferocity: it simply fights coldly for survival.) Women have strong mammal brains, and probably a correspondingly smaller energy channel to the reptile brain. They are more interested in love than war. "Make love, not war" means "move from the reptile brain to the mammal brain." Rock music is mammal music for the most part; long hair is mammal hair.

The Viking warrior who went "berserk" in battle may have experienced the temporary capture of himself by the mammal brain. Eye witnesses reported that the face of the "berserk" appeared to change, and his strength increased fantastically—when he "woke up," he sometimes found he had killed twenty or thirty men. The facial expression is probably a union of the concerns of all three brains, so if one brain takes over, it is natural that the shape of the face would change.

What does the third brain, the "new brain," do? In late mammal times, the body evidently added a third brain. Brain researchers are not sure why—perhaps the addition is connected to the invention of tools, and the energy explosion that followed that. In any case, this third brain, which I shall call here the new brain, takes the form of an outer eighth inch of brain tissue laid over the surface of the mammal brain. It is known medically as the neo-cortex. Brain tissue of the neo-cortex is incredibly complicated, more so than the other brains, having millions of neurons per square inch. Curiously, the third brain seems to have been created for problems more complicated than those it is now being used for. Some neurologists speculate that an intelligent man today uses 1/100 of its power. Einstein may have been using 1/50 of it.

The only good speculations I have seen on the new brain, and what it is like, are in Charles Fair's new book, *The Dying Self*, Wesleyan University Press. Fair suggests that what Freud meant by the "Id" was the reptile and mammal brain, and what the ancient Indian philosophers meant by the "self" was the new brain. His book is fascinating. He thinks that the new brain can grow and that its food is wild spiritual ideas. Christ said, "If a seed goes into the ground and dies, then it will grow." The reptile and mammal brains don't understand that sentence at all, both being naturalists, but the new brain understands it, and feels the excitement of it. The Greek mystery religions, and the Essene cult that Christ was a member of, were clear attempts to feed the new brain. The "mysteries" were the religion of the new brain. In Europe it was at its highest energy point about 1500, after knowing the ecstatic spiritual ideas of the Near East for 700 years. Since then, "secularization" means that the other two brains have increased their power. Nevertheless a man may still live if he wishes to more in his new brain than his neighbors do. Many of the parables of Christ, and the remarks of Buddha evidently involve instructions on how to transfer energy from the reptile brain to the mammal brain, and then to the new brain. A "saint" is someone who has managed to move away from the reptile and the mammal brains and is living primarily in the new brain. As the reptile brain power is symbolized by cold, and the mammal brain by warmth, the mark of the new brain is light. The gold light always around Buddha's head in statues is an attempt to suggest that he is living in his new brain. Some Tibetan meditators of the thirteenth century were able to read books in the dark by the light given off from their own bodies.

2

If there is no central organization to the brain, it is clear that the three brains must be competing for all the available energy at any moment. The brains are like legislative committees—competing for government grants. A separate decision on apportionment is made in each head, although the whole tone of the society has weight on that decision. Whichever brain receives the most energy, that brain will determine the tone of that personality, regardless of his intelligence or "reasoning power." The United States, given the amount of fear it generates every day in its own citizens, as well as in the citizens of other nations, is a vast machine for throwing people into the reptile brain. The ecology workers, the poets, singers, meditators, rock musicians and many people in the younger generation in general, are trying desperately to reverse the contemporary energy-flow in the brain. Military appropriations cannot be reduced until the flow of energy in the brain, which has been moving for four or five centuries from the new brain to the reptile brain is reversed. The reptile and the new brains are now trying to make themselves visible. The reptile brain has embodied itself in the outer world in the form of a tank which even moves like a reptile. Perhaps the computer is the new brain desperately throwing itself out into the world of objects so that we'll *see* it; the new brain's spirituality could not be projected, but at least its speed is apparent in the computer. The danger of course with the computer is that it may fall into the power of the reptile brain. Nixon is a dangerous type—a mixture of reptile and new brain, with almost no mammal brain at all.

3

We do not spend the whole day "inside" one brain, but we flip perhaps a thousand times a day from one brain to the other. Moreover we have been doing this flipping so long—since we were in the womb—that we no longer recognize the flips when they occur. If there is no central organization to the brain, and evidently there is not, it means that there is no "I." If your name is John there is no "John" inside you—there is no "I" at all. Oddly, that is the fundamental idea that Buddha had thirteen hundred years ago. "I have news for you," he said, "there is no 'I' inside there. Therefore trying to find it is useless." The West misunderstands "meditation" or sitting because, being obsessed with unity and "identity," it assumes that the purpose of meditation is to achieve unity. On the contrary, the major value of sitting, particularly at the start, is to let the sitter experience the real chaos of the brain. Thoughts shoot in from all three brains in turn, and the sitter does not talk about, but *experiences* the lack of an "I." The lack of an "I" is a central truth of Buddhism (Taoism expresses it by talking of the presence of a "flow"). Christianity somehow never arrived at this idea. At any rate, it never developed practical methods, like sitting, to allow each person to experience the truth himself. Institutional Christianity is in trouble because it depends on a pre-Buddhist model of the brain.

4

Evidently spiritual growth for human beings depends on the ability to transfer energy. Energy that goes normally to the reptile brain can be transferred to the mammal brain, some of it at least; energy intended for the mammal brain can be transferred to the new brain.

The reptile brain thinks constantly of survival, of food, of security. When Christ says, "The lilies do not work, and yet they have better clothes than you do," he is urging his students not to care so much for themselves. If the student wills "not-caring," and that "not-caring" persists, the "not-caring" will eventually cause some transfer of energy away from the reptile brain. Voluntary poverty worked for

St. Francis, and he had so little reptile brain paranoia the birds came down to sit on his shoulders.

If energy has been diverted from the reptile brain, the student, if he is lucky, can then transfer some of it to the mammal, and then to the new brain. Christ once advised his students, "If someone slaps you on the left cheek, point to the right cheek." The mammal brain loves to flare up and to strike back instantly. If you consistently refuse to allow the ferocity of the mammal brain to go forward into action, it will become discouraged, and some of its energy will be available for transfer. Since the mammal brain commits a lot of its energy to sexual love, some students at this point in the "road" become ascetic and celibate. They do so precisely in order to increase the speed of energy transfer. The women saints also, such as Anna of Foligno, experience this same turn in the road, which usually involves an abrupt abandonment of husband and children. Christ remarks in the Gospel of St. Thomas that some men are born eunuchs; and some men make themselves eunuchs in order to get to the Kingdom of the Spirit. However if a man is in the reptile brain at the time he begins his asceticism, then the result is a psychic disaster, as it has been for so many Catholic priests and monks.

The leap from the reptile to the new brain cannot be made directly; the student must go through the mammal brain. St. Theresa's spiritual prose shows much sexual imagery, perhaps because the mammal brain contributed its energy to the spiritual brain.

"Meditation" is a practical method for transferring energy from the reptile to the mammal brain, and then from the mammal to the new brain. It is slow, but a "wide" road, a road many can take, and many religious disciplines have adopted it. The orientals do not call it meditation, but "sitting." If the body sits in a room for an hour, quietly, doing nothing, the reptile brain becomes increasingly restless. It wants excitement, danger. In oriental meditation the body is sitting in the foetal position, and this further infuriates the reptile brain, since it is basically a mammalian position.

Of course if the sitter continues to sit, the mammal brain quickly becomes restless too. It wants excitement, confrontations, insults, sexual joy. It now starts to feed in spectacular erotic imagery, of the sort that St. Anthony's sittings were famous for. Yet if the sitter persists in doing nothing, eventually energy has nowhere to go but to the new brain.

Because Christianity has no "sitting," fewer men and women in Western culture than in oriental civilizations have been able to experience the ecstasy of the new brain. Thoreau managed to transfer a great deal of energy to the new brain without meditation, merely with the help of solitude. Solitude evidently helps the new brain. Thoreau of course willed his solitude and he was not in a reptile city, but in mammal or "mother" nature. Once more the truth holds that the road to the new brain passes through the mammal brain, through "the forest." This truth is embodied in ancient literature by the tradition of spiritual men meditating first in the forest and only after that in the desert. For the final part of the road, the desert is useful, because it contains almost no mammal images. Even in the desert, however, the saints preferred to live in caves—perhaps to remind the reptile brain of the path taken.

5

To return to poetry, it is clear that poets, like anyone else, can be dominated by one of the three brains. Chaucer is a great poet of the mammal brain; clearly St. John of the Cross and Kabir are great poets of the new brain. The reptile brain seems to have no poet of its own, although occasionally that brain will influence poets. Robinson Jeffers is a man with an extremely powerful mammal brain, in whom, nevertheless, the reptile brain had a slight edge. His magnificent poems are not warm towards human beings. On the contrary, he has a curious love for the claw and the most ancient sea rocks. Every once in a while he says flatly that if all human beings died off, and a seal or two remained on earth, that would be all right with him.

Bach makes music of new brain emotions; Beethoven primarily out of mammal brain emotions. Blake is such an amazing poet because he talks of moving from one brain to another. His people in "the state of experience," after all, have been pulled back into the reptile brain.

The invisible worm
That flies in the night,
In the howling storm,
Has found out thy bed
Of crimson joy,
And his dark secret love
Does thy life destroy.

When we are in a state of "innocence," Blake says, we are feeling some of the spiritual ecstasy of the new brain. The industrialists, as Blake saw clearly, are in a state of "experience," trapped by the reptile brain.

I think poetry ought to take account of these ideas. Some biological and neurological speculations are marvellous, and surely that speculation belongs in literary criticism as much as speculation about breath or images or meter. A man should try to feel what it is like to live in each of the three brains, and a poet could try to bring all three brains inside his poems.

ROBERT BLY

HAYDEN CARRUTH

Hayden Carruth was born in 1921 in Waterbury, Connecticut. He was educated at the University of North Carolina and the University of Chicago, and served in Italy during World War II. Among his many books of poetry are *The Crow and the Heart, Journey to a Known Place, The Norfolk Poems, Contra Mortem, For You,* and *From Snow and Rock, From Chaos.* He is also the author of a novel, *Appendix A,* and a book of criticism, *After the Stranger,* and he is the editor of a recent anthology, *The Voice That Is Great Within Us.* For over a decade he has lived on a farm in northern Vermont, supporting himself and his family by free-lance writing, wood-cutting, a little farming, and various other jobs. He is presently poet-in-residence at Johnson State College, and serves as an advisory editor for the Hudson Review.

Thomas Victor

FEAR AND ANGER IN THE MINDLESS UNIVERSE

Evan just had the white birch lined up
   like always

diagonally on the meadow
   at the top of the rise

going to cambridge junction
   the lone birch that made him think

he said
   of his naked daughter

when the stranger from downcountry
   middlebury way

hit the ice patch
   and skidded.

Evan cramped hard left and down
   into the snowbank and sat there

while the snowfields all around turned black-blank
   like a lightbulb burning out

and then turned white again.
   Slowly

(slowly the meteor descending
   bloodspotted feather swimming down the air)

Evan began to curse
   he said

like an oxhandler with a firstyoked team.
   It worked too

for the stranger
   bled to death in ten minutes

though the ice patch weren't his fault
   and Evan begun to feel better—

he even begun to laugh.
    That was last tuesday week in the forenoon

but now
    he tells it without smiling

quicklike
    looking out the corner of his eye.

SONNET

Cry, crow,
caw and caw, clawing
on black wings over hot black pines. What's
one more voice?

This morning the spring gave out,
no water in pipe. Hustled to spring, peered
in and saw three salamanders, very pallid;
saw water-level below pipe-end.

No more syphon. What's that? What? *And*
the brook is polluted.
           Weather going to pot,
each year drier than last, and hotter.

What's the trouble? Long time, 25 years, was I
mad.
    Won through, does anyone know?
    Hey, crow, does anyone know?
I see a chance for peace! What about water?

ONCE MORE

Once more by the brook the alder leaves
turn mauve, bronze, violet, beautiful
after the green of crude summer; galled
black stems, pithy, tangled, twist in the
flesh-colored vines of wild cyclamen.
Mist drifts below the mountaintop
in prismatic tatters. The brook is full,
spilling down heavily, loudly, in silver
spate from the beaver ponds in the high
marshy meadows. The year is sinking:
heavily, loudly, beautifully. Deer move
heavily in the brush like bears, half drunk
on masty acorns and rotten wild apples.
The pileated woodpecker thumps a dead elm
slowly, irregularly, meditatively.
Like a broken telephone a cricket rings
without assertion in dead asters and
goldenrod; asters gone cloudy with seed,
goldenrod burnt and blackened. A gray trout
rests under the lip of glacial stone. One
by one the alder leaves plunge down to earth,
veering, and lie there, glowing, like a shirt
of Nessus. My heart in my ribs does what it
has done occasionally all my life: thumps and
heaves suddenly in irregular rhythm that makes
me gasp. How many times has this season turned
and gone down? How many! I move heavily
into the bracken, and the deer stand still
a moment, uncertain, before they break away,
snorting and bounding heavily before me.

THE INSOMNIAC SLEEPS WELL FOR ONCE AND

rises at five, just when a late moon
rises, huge, out of the snow cloud

at the end of the garden. You sleep.
Coming so tired and worried to middle age,

you'll sleep ten hours if we let you,
yet now, slept nearly out, you lie as if

this moon had brought from far in the east,
Silesia, your old self who you really are

come to inhabit you, girl of the rye fields
silver and green, and here comes another

moon, another, another, the snow gleams,
and each one brings something

so that your eyes smoothen as if for love,
your fine bone rises under your skin,

you move and smile in the sleeping knowledge
of yourself, as the spirit of this house moves

smiling from mirror to mirror in brightness,
and oh my god look at the sky full of moons,

look at the snow, the girl, look at the day!

THIS DECORATION

Blue light, morning
glory color, driven
through green fir boughs,

bright as crow-caw
on the next to last day
of October. You've given

me this decoration
made from dried pasted
flowers inside the cap

of a cottage cheese
carton. Beautiful
flowers, unrecognizable

flowers, at which I stare
with a blue-green feeling,
delighted and ignorant,

until you tell me you
made them up. One
is scales from a pine cone

flattened, with a tuft
of silverrod seedfluff
in the center. Another

from a dried panicle
of millet with petals
of mapleseed. Now

I see burrs, bark, a
snip of duck feather. How
exquisite, flowers

of imagination from this
real world, made and given
for lovingkindness. I

go out, wordless, walking
the stubble rows; and here,
high, comes this black

crow, above the furrows
high and straight, flapping,
as if from a great

distance, from eternity.
Caw, caw, loudly. And back
from beyond the firs comes

the answer, caw, way off, far
although near too, and wordless,
as real things always are.

RIMROCK, WHERE IT IS

Ruined, time ruined, all these once good things.
The structure of many rooms built in the sun,

a refuge from sun; but its parts have gone
wandering, there down the hillside in flowers.

A few doorways remain, arched gently, open
to a white-hot sky, but through them the spirits

long since ceased to pass. Ladders mount the walls
rung by rung to nowhere. The city of desolation,

creviced for the scorpion, is pierced everywhere
by sun, whose mindless immitigable command

beats down with the same force as when its liege folk
listened: generate, generate. Only scorpions hear,

the female eating the male's head while they couple.
Nearby in a refuge of poured concrete and glass

a small woman, small as a girl, black with time,
lies and lies, always raising her head, her charred face,

always raising her knees in a mock of childbirth,
always opening her mouth that is gagged with dust,

always screaming. It reverberates, wave on wave,
the desert's pulse. And the blind albino

fish, relic of a once vast species, that swims
in the lake at the bottom of the deepest cave

in Arizona, in darkness or in glittering rays
of flashlights, goes round and round and round.

TWILIGHT COMES

(after Wang Wei)

Twilight comes to the little farm
At winter's end. The snowbanks
High as the eaves, which melted
And became pitted during the day,
Are freezing again, and crunch
Under the dog's foot. The mountains
From their place behind our shoulders
Lean close a moment, as if for a
Final inspection, but with kindness,
A benediction as the darkness
Falls. It is my fiftieth year. Stars
Come out, one by one with a softer
Brightness, like the first flowers
Of spring. I hear the brook stirring,
Trying its music beneath the ice.
I hear—almost, I am not certain—
Remote tinklings; perhaps sheepbells
On the green side of a juniper hill
Or wineglasses on a summer night.
But no. My wife is at her work,
There behind yellow windows. Supper
Will be soon. I crunch the icy snow
And tilt my head to study the last
Silvery light of the western sky
In the pine boughs. I smile. Then
I smile again, just because I can.
I am not an old man. Not yet.

EMERGENCY HAYING

Coming home with the last load I ride standing
on the wagon tongue, behind the tractor
in hot exhaust, lank with sweat,

my arms strung
awkwardly along the hayrack, cruciform.
Almost 500 bales we've put up

this afternoon, Marshall and I.
And of course I think of another who hung
like this on another cross. My hands are torn

by baling twine, not nails, and my side is pierced
by my ulcer, not a lance. The acid in my throat
is only hayseed. Yet exhaustion and the way

my body hangs from twisted shoulders, suspended
on two points of pain in the rising
monoxide, recall that greater suffering.

Well, I change grip and the image
fades. It's been an unlucky summer. Heavy rains
brought on the grass tremendously, a monster crop,

but wet, always wet. Haying was long delayed.
Now is our last chance to bring in
the winter's feed, and Marshall needs help.

We mow, rake, bale, and draw the bales
to the barn, these late, half-green,
improperly cured bales; some weigh 100 pounds

or more, yet must be lugged by the twine
across the field, tossed on the load, and then
at the barn unloaded on the conveyor

and distributed in the loft. I help—
I, the desk-servant, word-worker—
and hold up my end pretty well too; but God,

the close of day, how I fall down then. My hands
are sore, they flinch when I light my pipe.
I think of those who have done slave labor,

less able and less well prepared than I.
Rose Marie in the rye fields of Saxony,
her father in the camps of Moldavia

and the Crimea, all clerks and housekeepers
herded to the gaunt fields of torture. Hands
too bloodied cannot bear

even the touch of air, even
the touch of love. I have a friend
whose grandmother cut cane with a machete

and cut and cut, until one day
she snicked her hand off and took it
and threw it grandly at the sky. Now

in September our New England mountains
under a clear sky for which we're thankful at last
begin to glow, maples, beeches, birches

in their first color. I look
beyond our famous hayfields to our famous hills,
to the notch where the sunset is beginning,

then in the other direction, eastward,
where a full new-risen moon like a pale
medallion hangs in a lavender cloud

beyond the barn. My eyes
sting with sweat and loveliness. And who
is the Christ now, who

if not I? It must be so. My strength
is legion. And I stand up high
on the wagon tongue in my whole bones to say

woe to you, watch out
you sons of bitches who would drive men and women
to the fields where they can only die.

ANALOGIES ARE HELPFUL, AND MUSIC IS THE BEST

If anyone had given me a choice in the matter I'd have spent my life in some corner of New York with Sid Catlett, Vic Dickenson, Benny Carter, and a few others, playing the blues. Funky blues; but the real good funk, no schmaltz or corn, no antiquarianism, nor any kind of far-out estheticism either; I mean in the main line of human feeling, at the limit of individual imagination. What makes the old forms good? Because good men and women made them. If I couldn't hear something of that good woman Bessie Smith—yes, and something of Scott Joplin too—in the music of John Coltrane, I wouldn't care for Coltrane, and I do. The same with poetry.

Of course no one did give me a choice, and the other principal element of my selfhood, psychopathic illness, drove me away from the city, into isolation and the Green Mountains, where the color is Anglo-Saxon, the speech old-fashioned and twangy, and what music we have is mostly the wind in the spruce trees. How all this mixes with the blues I don't exactly know, but it does. In spontaneity, provided the great tradition comes through, anything is possible, and above all in the throes of vision. As I wrote once in a poem about music, "Freedom and discipline concur/only in ecstasy"; and Bill Basie used to say, "Four to the bar and no cheatin'." That's the way I've tried to play it.

I get tired of the terms used in discussions of poetry—free-form, traditional, open, shut, organic, etc., etc.—not because they are wrong but because they are right; all of them, every one of them. Every good poem is a poem to which they can all be applied with equal justice. It is the combination, the *composition*, that counts. Now I've spent thirty years trying to think how this combination works, and I still can't say it, not objectively. I can only point to good poems, so many and so various. But analogies are helpful, and music is the best. Let the beat rock and be steady, but not too loud, reticence is the soul of expression, and let the syntax ride over in its limitless variety, including the rests. H.D.: ". . . in the sequence of the musical phrase." Jelly Roll Morton: "Man, you gotta keep the melody going somewhere *all* the time." That's the ideal. But I fear I have approached it only rarely and distantly.

HAYDEN CARRUTH

Thomas Victor

ROBERT DUNCAN

Robert Duncan was born in 1919. His poetic works include *Bending the Bow, The Opening of the Field,* and *Roots and Branches.* He is also the author of *The Sweetness and Greatness of Dante's Divine Comedy,* and his essays on myth and poetry are unique in contemporary thought. At present he is living in San Francisco.

A POEM BEGINNING WITH A LINE BY PINDAR

1
The light foot hears you and the brightness begins
god-step at the margins of thought,
    quick adulterous tread at the heart.
Who is it that goes there?
    Where I see your quick face
notes of an old music pace the air,
torso-reverberations of a Grecian lyre.

In Goya's canvas Cupid and Psyche
have a hurt voluptuous grace
bruised by redemption. The copper light
falling upon the brown boy's slight body
is carnal fate that sends the soul wailing
up from blind innocence, ensnared
    by dimness
into the deprivations of desiring sight.

But the eyes in Goya's painting are soft,
diffuse with rapture absorb the flame.
Their bodies yield out of strength.
    Waves of visual pleasure
wrap them in a sorrow previous to their impatience.

A bronze of yearning, a rose that burns
    the tips of their bodies, lips,
ends of fingers, nipples. He is not wingd.
His thighs are flesh, are clouds
    lit by the sun in its going down,
hot luminescence at the loins of the visible.
    But they are not in a landscape.
    They exist in an obscurity.

The wind spreading the sail serves them.
The two jealous sisters eager for her ruin
    serve them.
That she is ignorant, ignorant of what Love will be,
    serves them.
The dark serves them.
The oil scalding his shoulder serves them,
serves their story. Fate, spinning,
    knots the threads for Love.

Jealousy, ignorance, the hurt . . . serve them.

2
This is magic. It is passionate dispersion.
What if they grow old? The gods
   would not allow it.
   Psyche is preserved.

In time we see a tragedy, a loss of beauty
   the glittering youth
of the god retains—but from this threshold
   it is age
that is beautiful. It is toward the old poets
   we go, to their faltering,
their unaltering wrongness that has style,
   their variable truth,
   the old faces,
words shed like tears from
a plenitude of powers time stores.

A stroke.   These little strokes.   A chill.
   The old man, feeble, does not recoil.
Recall. A phase so minute,
   only a part of the word in- jerrd.

   The Thundermakers descend,

damerging a nuv. A nerb.
   The present dented of the U
nighted stayd.   States.   The heavy clod?
   Cloud.   Invades the brain.   What
   if lilacs last in *this* dooryard bloomd?

Hoover, Roosevelt, Truman, Eisenhower—
where among these did the power reside
that moves the heart? What flower of the nation
bride-sweet broke to the whole rapture?
Hoover, Coolidge, Harding, Wilson
hear the factories of human misery turning out commodities.
For whom are the holy matins of the heart ringing?
Noble men in the quiet of morning hear
Indians singing the continent's violent requiem.

Harding, Wilson, Taft, Roosevelt,
idiots fumbling at the bride's door,
hear the cries of men in meaningless debt and war.
Where among these did the spirit reside
that restores the land to productive order?
McKinley, Cleveland, Harrison, Arthur,
Garfield, Hayes, Grant, Johnson,
dwell in the roots of the heart's rancor.
How sad "amid lanes and through old woods"
    echoes Whitman's love for Lincoln!

There is no continuity then.   Only a few
    posts of the good remain.   I too
that am a nation sustain the damage
    where smokes of continual ravage
obscure the flame.
                    It is across great scars of wrong
    I reach toward the song of kindred men
    and strike again the naked string
old Whitman sang from.   Glorious mistake!
    that cried:
    "The theme is creative and has vista."
    "He is the president of regulation."

    I see always the under side turning,
fumes that injure the tender landscape.
    From which up break
lilac blossoms of courage in daily act
    striving to meet a natural measure.

3
for Charles Olson

                        Psyche's tasks—the sorting of seeds
wheat   barley   oats   poppy   coriander
anise   beans   lentils   peas   —every grain
                    in its right place
                                before nightfall;

gathering the gold wool from the cannibal sheep
(for the soul must weep
    and come near upon death);

harrowing Hell for a casket Proserpina keeps
                              that must not
     be opend . . . containing beauty?

no!   Melancholy coild like a serpent
                              that is deadly sleep
     we are not permitted
                    to succumb to.

     These are the old tasks.
     You've heard them before.

     They must be impossible. Psyche
must despair, be brought to her
                              insect instructor;
must obey the counsels of the green reed;
saved from suicide by a tower speaking,
     must follow to the letter
     freakish instructions.

In the story the ants help. The old man at Pisa
     mixd in whose mind
(to draw the sorts) are all seeds
          as a lone ant from a broken ant-hill
had part restored by an insect, was
     upheld by a lizard

          (to draw the sorts)
the wind is part of the process
                    defines a nation of the wind—

     father of many notions,
                    Who?
let the light into the dark?   began
the many movements of the passion?
                              West
from east   men push.
                    The islands are blessd
(cursed)   that swim below the sun,

     man upon whom the sun has gone down!

38 ROBERT DUNCAN

There is the hero who struggles east
widdershins to free the dawn   and must
                    woo Night's daughter,
sorcery, black passionate rage, covetous queens,
so that the fleecy sun go   back from Troy,
    Colchis, India . . . all the blazing armies
spent, he must struggle alone toward the pyres of Day.

                    The light that is Love
rushes on toward passion. It verges upon dark.
    Roses and blood flood the clouds.
    Solitary first riders advance into legend.

    This land, where I stand, was all legend
in my grandfathers' time: cattle raiders,
    animal tribes, priests, gold.
It was the West. Its vistas painters saw
    in diffuse light, in melancholy,
in abysses left by glaciers as if they had been the sun
    primordial carving empty enormities
                    out of the rock.

                    Snakes lurkd
guarding secrets.   Those first ones
                    survived solitude.

    Scientia
holding the lamp, driven by doubt;
Eros naked in foreknowledge
smiling in his sleep;   and the light
spilld, burning his shoulder—the outrage
    that conquers legend—
passion, dismay, longing, search
    flooding up where
the Beloved is lost.   Psyche travels
life after life, my life, station
    after station,
to be tried

    without break, without
news, knowing only—but what did she know?
    The oracle at Miletus had spoken

truth surely: that he was Serpent-Desire
   that flies thru the air,
a monster-husband. But she saw him fair
whom Apollo's mouthpiece said spread
   pain
beyond cure   to those
   wounded by his arrows.

Rilke torn by a rose thorn
blackened toward Eros.   Cupidinous Death!
   that will not take no for an answer.

4
   Oh yes!   Bless the footfall where
step by step   the boundary walker
(in Maverick Road   the snow
thud by thud   from the roof
circling the house—another tread)

   that foot   informd
by the weight of all things
    that can be elusive
no more than a nearness to the mind
    of a single image

     Oh yes!   this
most dear
   the catalyst force that renders clear
the days of a life from the surrounding medium!

     Yes, beautiful rare wilderness!
wildness that verifies strength of my tame mind,
   clearing held against indians,
health that prepared to meet death,
   the stubborn hymns going up
into the ramifications of the hostile air

   that, deceptive, gives way.

Who is there?   O, light the light!
   The Indians give way,   the clearing falls.
Great Death gives way   and unprepares us.

Lust gives way.   The Moon gives way.
Night gives way.   Minutely,   the Day gains.

She saw the body of her beloved
    dismemberd in waking . . . or was it
in sight?   *Finders Keepers* we sang
    when we were children   or were taught to sing
before our histories began   and we began
    who were beloved   our animal life
toward the Beloved,   sworn to be Keepers.

    On the hill before the wind came
the grass moved toward the one sea,
    blade after blade dancing in waves.

There the children turn the ring to the left.
There the children turn the ring to the right.
    Dancing . . . Dancing . . .

And the lonely psyche goes up thru the boy to the king
    that in the caves of history dreams.
Round and round the children turn.
    London Bridge that is a kingdom falls.

We have come so far that all the old stories
whisper once more.
Mount Segur, Mount Victoire, Mount Tamalpais . . .
    rise to adore the mystery of Love!

(An ode? Pindar's art, the editors tell us, was not a statue but a
mosaic, an accumulation of metaphor. But if he was archaic, not
classic, a survival of obsolete mode, there may have been old voices
in the survival that directed the heart. So, a line from a hymn came
in a novel I was reading to help me. Psyche, poised to leap—and
Pindar too, the editors write, goes too far, topples over—listened to
a tower that said, *Listen to me!* The oracle had said, *Despair! The
Gods themselves abhor his power.* And then the virgin flower of
the dark falls back flesh of our flesh from which everywhere . . .

    the information flows
        that is yearning. A line of Pindar
    moves from the area of my lamp
        toward morning.

In the dawn that is nowhere
  I have seen the willful children
clockwise and counter-clockwise turning.

A NEW POEM

for Jack Spicer

You are right. What we call Poetry is the boat.
The first boat, the body—but it was a bed.
  The bed, but it was a car.
And the driver or sandman, the boatman,
  the familiar stranger, first lover,
is not with me.

            You are wrong.
What we call Poetry is the lake itself,
the bewildering circling water way—
having our power in what we know nothing of,
in this having neither father nor son,

our never having come into it,
our never having left it,
our misnaming it, our
giving it the lie so that it lies.

I would not be easy
calling the shadowy figure who refuses to guide the boat
but crosses and recrosses the heart . . .

—He breaks a way among the lily pads.
He breaks away from the directions
  we cannot give—

I would not be easy calling him
  the Master of Truth,
but Master he is of turning right and wrong.

I cannot make light of it.
The boat has its own light.

The weight of the boat
is not in the boat. He will not
give me images but I must
give him images.
He will not give me his name
but I must give him . . .

name after name I give him.
But I will not name the grave easily,
the boat of bone
so light it turns as if earth
were wind and water.

Ka, I call him. The shadow
wavers and wears my own face.

Kaka, I call him. The
whole grey cerement replaces itself and shows
a hooded hole.

From what we call Poetry a cock crows
away off there at the break of something.

Lake of no shores I can name,
Body of no day or night I can account for,
snoring in the throws of sleep I came
sleepless to the joint of this poem,
as if there were a hinge in the ways.

Door opend or closed,
knuckled down where faces of a boat join,
Awake Asleep
from the hooded hold of the boat
join in. The farthest shore is so near
crows fly up and we know it is America.

No crow flies. It is not America.
From what we call Poetry
a bird I cannot name crows.

Now Johnson would go up to join the great simulacra of men,
    Hitler and Stalin, to work his fame
    with planes roaring out from Guam over Asia,
all America become a sea of toiling men
    stirrd at his will, which would be a bloated thing,
    drawing from the underbelly of the nation
    such blood and dreams as swell the idiot psyche
    out of its courses into an elemental thing
    until his name stinks with burning meat and heapt honors

And men wake to see that they are used like things
    spent in a great potlatch, this Texas barbeque
        of Asia, Africa, and all the Americas,
And the professional military behind him, thinking
    to use him as they thought to use Hitler
    without losing control of their business of war,

But the mania, the ravening eagle of America
    as Lawrence saw him "bird of men that are masters,
    lifting the rabbit-blood of the myriads up into—"
    into something terrible, gone beyond bounds, or
As Blake saw figures of fire and blood raging,
    —in what image?   the ominous roar in the air,
the omnipotent wings, the all-American boy in the cockpit
    loosing his flow of napalm, below in the jungles
        "any life at all or sign of life" his target, drawing now
            not with crayons in his secret room
the burning of homes and the torture of mothers and fathers and
                children,
    their hair a-flame, screaming in agony, but
in the line of duty, for the might and enduring fame
    of Johnson, for the victory of American will over its victims,
    releasing his store of destruction over the enemy,
in terror and hatred of all communal things, of communion,
    of communism;

has raised from the private rooms of small-town bosses and business
    men,
from the council chambers of the gangs that run the great cities,
    swollen with the votes of millions,

44 ROBERT DUNCAN

from the fearful hearts of good people in the suburbs turning the savory
    meat over the charcoal burners and heaping their barbeque plates
    with more than they can eat,
from the closed meeting-rooms of regents of universities and sessions
    of profiteers—

back of the scene: the atomic stockpile; the vials of synthesized
    diseases eager biologists have developed over half a century
    dreaming of the bodies of mothers and fathers and children and
    hated rivals swollen with new plagues, measles grown enormous,
    influenzas perfected; and the gasses of despair, confusion of the
    senses, mania, inducing terror of the universe, coma, existential
    wounds, that chemists we have met at cocktail parties, passed daily
    and with a happy "Good day" on the way to classes or work, have
    workt to make war too terrible for men to wage.

raised this secret entity of America's hatred of Europe, of Africa,
    of Asia,
the deep hatred for the old world that had driven generations of
    America out of itself,
and for the alien world, the new world about him, that might have been
    Paradise
but was before his eyes already cleard back in a holocaust of burning
    Indians, trees and grasslands,
reduced to his real estate, his projects of exploitation and profitable
    wastes,

this specter that in the beginning Adams and Jefferson feard and knew
would corrupt the very body of the nation
    and all our sense of our common humanity,
this black bile of old evils arisen anew,
takes over the vanity of Johnson;
and the very glint of Satan's eyes from the pit of the hell of America's
    unacknowledged, unrepented crimes that I saw in Goldwater's eyes
now shines from the eyes of the President
    in the swollen head of the nation.

ARTICULATIONS

The artist, after Dante's poetics, works with all parts of the poem as *polysemous,* taking each thing of the composition as generative of meaning, a response to and a contribution to the building form. The old doctrine of correspondences is enlarged and furthered in a new process of responses, parts belonging to the architecture not only by the fittings—the concords and contrasts in chronological sequence, as in a jigsaw puzzle—by what comes one after another as we read, but by the resonances in the time of the whole in the reader's mind, each part as it is conceived as a member of every other part, having, as in a mobile, an interchange of roles, by the creation of forms within forms as we remember.

But this putting together and rendering anew operates in our apprehension of emerging articulations of time. Every particular is an immediate happening of meaning at large; every present activity in the poem redistributes future as well as past events. This is a presence extended in a time we create as we keep words in mind.

The immediate event—the phrase within its line, the adjoining pulse in silence, the new phrase—each part is a thing in itself; the junctures not binding but freeing the elements of configuration so that they participate in more than one figure. A sign appears—" • "—a beat syncopating the time at rest; as if there were a stress in silence. He strives not for a disintegration of syntax but for a complication within syntax, overlapping structures, so that words are freed, having bounds out of bound.

So, the artist of abundancies delights in puns, interlocking and separating figures, plays of things missing or things appearing "out of order" that remind us that all orders have their justification finally in an order of orders only our faith as we work addresses. Were all in harmony to our ears, we would dwell in the dreadful smugness in which our mere human rationality relegates what it cannot cope with to the "irrational," as if the totality of creation were without ratios. Praise then the interruption of our composure, the image that comes to fit we cannot account for, the juncture in the music that appears discordant.

In a blast, the poem announces the Satanic person of a president whose lies and connivings have manoeuvred the nation into the pit of an evil war. What does it mean? It is a mere political event of the day, yet it comes revealed as an eternal sentence. Polysemous—not only the nation but the soul and the poem are involved in the event. In these days again the last day, the final judgment, in a form that knows only what the here and now knows of first days or last days. What is out of joint with the times moves as this poetry moves towards a doubling of the joint in time, until, multiphasic, we would imagine the figure we had not seen in which the joining is clear where we are.

For these discords, these imperatives of the poem that exceed our proprieties, these interferences—as if the real voice of the poet might render unrecognizable to our sympathies the voice we wanted to be real, these even artful, willful or, it seems to us, affected, psycho-pathologies of daily life, touch upon the living center where there is no composure but a life-spring of dissatisfaction in all orders from which the restless ordering of our poetry comes.

ROBERT DUNCAN

PETER EVERWINE

Peter Everwine was born in Detroit in 1930 and grew up in the mountains of western Pennsylvania. He was educated at Northwestern, Iowa, and Stanford. He has published three books, *The Broken Frieze, In the House of Light,* and *Collecting the Animals,* which won the Lamont in 1972. He teaches at Fresno State University. He is also a professional musician and has performed widely throughout the Western United States.

Micha Langer

THE BURDEN OF DECISION

Late night, with my bundle of new straws,
weighing each one with my headaches, my inverted stars,
my solemn pencils at their ends. . . . .

In this way, sorting the yes and the no,
I arrive. My train
enters a snowy region of firs,

I close my eyes,
the wheels slow and deepen their voices
over the first bridge. . . .

It is then that one knocks
and enters. A man puts down his bag
and slaps dust from his coat.

In silence he crosses the room, nods
and holds out to me
his two closed hands.

I know him by his frayed sleeves.
He knows me by the little song I start to sing,
shifting from foot to foot.

THE BROTHER

When morning came
I rose and made tea
and sent off my brother.
In the quiet house
I sat down to wait.

The day knocked on my door
with its sack of wares. The evening
looked in my window
with its inconsolable gray eyes.
On the table the lamp was lit.

My brother came home then,
white dust on his shoes
and a tiny blue flower in his cap,
weary
as if he'd danced a long time
or met a girl in the fields.

When I touched his sleeve
my fingers brought away
a fragrance of mint and grass.

Now my brother wants sleep
and moons foolishly at my bed.
What I want
is to wash his feet
and send him off again, tomorrow,
with a stone in each shoe
and one for each hand
and no bread in his pocket.

NIGHT

In the lamplight falling
on the white tablecloth
my plate,
my shining loaf of quietness.

I sit down.
Through the open door
all the absent who I love enter
and we eat.

WE MEET IN THE LIVES OF ANIMALS

In Mexico a red flag signifies fresh
meat at the market. "Maggie's
Drawers" is a red flag flown on
army firing ranges.

1
The red flag is up.
The beasts who came to market
from the high fields of light
sprawl heavily from hooks—yellow
with fat, spread-legged,
still beaded with blood.
Having been gentle,
they came easily.
Having opened their breasts,
they give up everything—heart, kidneys,
flecked lungs, the frothy dark rivers of organs,
self-stink of panic and shit—
shameless, without malice.
Even the flies enter them like hives.

2
In the dirt yard next door
the widow Tomasa has fired-up
her black kettle. She calls out,
and my son goes running.
"Here," she says, cradling
a cow's bloody head from which she scrapes
its stringy flesh. "Here,
hold open its eyes.
It will see our hunger."
And my son's eyes fill, as he touches
those milky ones.

They're poor, I tell him later.

3
He weeps and has bad dreams.
It will pass. He will eat meat
as his father does, will come to hunger

and boast like other men: *I'll tear the asshole*
out of skunk! Murder the beaver's balls!
Chew knuckles! Gnaw on the goose's glands,
the peacock's gristle!
The red flag is up, is waving.
Maggie's drawers fill with blood.
The angel in the *Wehrmacht* helmet
goes down on her, eating the ripe lips.
We bang our empty bowls
and come before the lives of animals,
greeting them with nails and empty palms
as they come marching, marching
in their bloody rags.

And still he weeps.

4
At the jaw's hinge
my son has a soft blond down I love to touch.
It is the delicate grass
in which a lion sleeps, the silken weeds
where the crow comes to walk.
A man comes from his own murders
and enters a pasture
in which the grass is filling with light.
He hears a quiet footfall and turns.
And it is something like love.

THE CLEARING

Flowers have fenced-in
The clearing of moss
The clearing of butterflies

The earth is a blend of so many colors
Your song is diffused your word
Diffused

But there my father
You rumble and flash with light
You through whom everything lives

Number upon number of red butterflies
In the midst of them
You are
You speak

after the Nahuatl

GOING

The road climbs, villages
fall away. There are small hawks tightened
on the wires. By the road,
in spiny weeds, a dead cow swells—
her ribs pushing outward
as a wind rises in the eye of her belly.
Her legs, as I pass,
point up like an overturned table.

The road runs straight for evening
and I'm there, the shadows falling
below the first fires.
The holy places at the crossroads
cover their hands,
and the fields close themselves
as my lights touch them.

They speak of ditches running full with meat,
of funeral flowers in profusion.
Behind me in the dark
the cow is a black globe.

DISTANCE

The light pulling away from trees,
the trees speaking in shadows
to whatever listens. . . .

Something as common as water
turns away from our faces
and leaves.

The stars rise out of the hills
—old kings and animals
marching in their thin tunnels of light.

Once more I find myself
standing as on a dark pier, holding
an enormous rope of silence.

ROUTES

1
Sun drops below the elms
Moon comes along
and freezes the wheels of the street.
In her room my mother shakes out
her road of dark colors
and knits the first step.

My window faces the funeral home.
When the exhaust fan
starts to hum
something is flying, something
is leaving at the level of the trees.

2
I enter a street
where the sun is falling.

I look over my shoulder
and follow a thread that was my coat.
At its end is a vacant room
and a little bench of sleep.

I sit down quietly.
A few others arrive,
their eyelashes shining like crystals.
One coughs in a cloud of incense.
One closes his silver telescope.

A lost town circles overhead in the dark.
The houses hang out their lanterns.
On a blue bike
I race the shadows of the trees.

DRINKING COLD WATER

Almost twenty years
since you put on your one good dress
and lay down in the shale hills of Pennsylvania.
What you expected from life was nothing much,
and it came
and so it was.
In California I mourned and then forgot,
though sometimes, in a mirror,
I saw someone walk from the weeds,
stepping from a shine of water,
and it was you, shining.

Tonight I brought my bundle of years
to an empty house.
When I opened it, a boy walked out—
drinking cold water, watching the
moon rise slim and shining over your house.
Whatever it was I wanted
must have come and gone.

Twenty years, grandmother.
Here I stand
in the poverty of my feet,
and I know what you'd do:
you'd enter your black shawl,
step back into the shadows of your hair.
And that's no help tonight.
All I can think of is your house—
the pump at the sink
spilling a trough of clear
cold water from the well—
and you, old love,
sleeping in your dark dress
like a hard, white root.

THE MARSH, NEW YEAR'S DAY

for Zack, among others

The slow, cold breathing.
Black surf of birds lifting away.
The light rising in the water's skin.
How many times now, on a day like this,
I've entered the celebrations of the reeds—
waking by the wren's broken house,
the frosty, burst phallus of the cat-tail.
In the marsh a door slams and slams.
I want to open my throat
and sing the crystal song of the goose.
Wherever I look
I see the old men
of my boyhood, wifeless and half-wild,
in stained coats, dying like rainbows
from the feet up.
I am becoming them.

IN THE END

—I can't stand it, said the old man
and carefully shut the door
behind him.

The boy, still barely visible,
was growing smaller
at the end of the alley.

—Everything goes, said the old man.
—In the end, pain has its way.
He turned then and slept.

And only one little finger,
preparing to set out, whispered to itself
—So much and so much and so much more!

But the cockroach spat
and said in its bitter tongue
—What's done is done.

after Natan Sach

SOMEONE KNOCKS

Someone knocks on the door of your forehead
and you say to yourself, No
it's the flicker hammering the dead trunk,
it's the carpenter building the next day's coffin.

Something drops into the palm of your hand.
You think of journeys hidden
in the pockets of overcoats;
of cities that have not yet fallen.

Somebody enters your bed at night.
It's what I wanted, you say,
and lean into the dark, cradling
the dry hair of your father.

And it goes on and on
as silence waits in the mountains
and the stone gathers you to its breast
and your father sleeps in his own name.

PERHAPS IT'S AS YOU SAY

Perhaps it's as you say
That nothing stays lost forever

How many times have I said No No
There is a darkness in the cell

And opened my hands to cup emptiness
Tasting its bitten face

I do not know if our loves survive us
Waiting through the long night for our step

Or if they will know us then
Entering our flesh with the old sigh

I do not know
But I think of fields that stretch away flat

Beneath the stars their dry grasses
Gathering a light of honey

The few houses wink and go out
Across the fields an asphalt road darkens

And disappears among the cottonwoods by the dry creek
It is so quiet so quiet

Meet me there

LEARNING TO SPEAK

I have nothing against prose that addresses itself to the subject of poetry. The language, however, is not likely to be very interesting unless one has either passionate opinions or radical approaches. Re-reading the essay I first wrote for this anthology, I decided I sounded something like a semi-mystical IBM. Who needs it?

I think that a poet's most personal notion of poetry is often re-vealed in poems rather than in prose—poems that are not *about* poetry but which, in pursuit of a subject, become commentaries on the sources of, and relationships between, language and experience.

LEARNING TO SPEAK

As a child running loose,
I said it this way: *Bird.*
Bird, a startled sound at field's edge.
The sound my mouth makes, pushing away the cold.
So, at the end of this quiet afternoon,
wanting to write the love poems I've never written,
I turn from the shadow in the cottonwood
and say *blackbird,* as if to you.
There is the blackbird. Black bird, until its darkness
is the darkness of a woman's hair falling
across my upturned face.
And I go on speaking into the night.
The oriole, the flicker,
the gold finch. . . .

PETER EVERWINE

ALLEN GINSBERG

Allen Ginsberg was born in 1926 in Paterson, New Jersey, son of
the poet Louis Ginsberg. Educated at Columbia University, he
worked for a time as a market analyst. The publication of his first
book, *Howl*, made him famous overnight; since then he has pub-
lished *Kaddish*, *The Empty Mirror*, *Reality Sandwiches*, *Wichita
Vortex Sutra*, *Planet News*, and *The Fall of America*. He has set
Blake's songs to music and recorded them on two albums. He has
traveled and given readings all over the world. In 1974, he shared the
National Book Award for *The Fall of America*. He lives on a com-
munal farm in Cherry Valley, New York.

THIS FORM OF LIFE NEEDS SEX

I will have to accept women
        if I want to continue the race,
    kiss breasts, accept
    strange hairy lips behind
             buttocks,
Look in questioning womanly eyes
        answer soft cheeks,
bury my loins in the hang of pearplum
    fat tissue
        I had abhorred
before I give godspasm Babe leap
  forward thru death—
Between me and oblivion an unknown
        woman stands;
Not the Muse but living meat-phantom,
a mystery scary as my fanged god
      sinking its foot in its gullet &
vomiting its own image out of its ass
—This woman Futurity I am pledge to
      born not to die,
but issue my own cockbrain replica Me-Hood
    again—For fear of the Blot?
Face of Death, my Female, as I'm sainted
      to my very bone,
I'm fated to find me a maiden for
       ignorant Fuckery—
flapping my belly & smeared with Saliva
  shamed face flesh & wet,
—have long droopy conversations
    in Cosmical Duty boudoirs,
        maybe bored?
Or excited New Prospect, discuss
  her, Futurity, my Wife
    My Mother, Death, My only
      hope, my very Resurrection
Woman
    herself, why have I feared
      to be joined true
embraced beneath the Panties of Forever

in with the one hole that repelled me 1937 on?
—Pulled down my pants on the porch showing
    my behind to cars passing in rain—
& She be interested, this contact
                        with Silly new Male
    that's sucked my loveman's cock
in Adoration & sheer beggary romance-awe
    gulp-choke Hope of Life come
and buggered myself innumerably boy-yangs
        gloamed inward so my solar plexus
    feel godhead in me like an open door—

Now that's changed my decades body old
tho admiring male thighs at my brow,
    hard love pulsing thru my ears,
        stern buttocks upraised
                    for my masterful Rape
    that were meant for a private shit
                if the Army were All—
But no more answer to life
                than the muscular statue
        I felt up its marbles
envying Beauty's immortality in the
                museum of Yore—
You can fuck a statue but you cant
        have children
You can joy man to man but the Sperm
        comes back in a trickle at dawn
    in a toilet on the 45th Floor—
& Can't make continuous mystery out of that
        finished performance
                        & ghastly thrill
    that ends as began,
                    stupid reptile squeak
    denied life by Fairy Creator
        become Imaginary
    because he decided not to incarnate
        opposite—Old Spook
who didn't want to be a baby & die,
    didn't want to shit and scream
            exposed to bombardment on a
                    Chinese RR track

and grow up to pass his spasm on
      the other half of the Universe—
Like a homosexual capitalist afraid of
           the masses—
and that's my situation, Folks—

          4/12/61

WHO BE KIND TO

Be kind to yourself, it is only one
    and perishable
of many on the planet, thou art that
one that wishes a soft finger tracing the
    line of feeling from nipple to pubes—
one that wishes a tongue to kiss your armpit,
    a lip to kiss your cheek inside your
    whiteness thigh—
Be kind to yourself Harry, because unkindness
    comes when the body explodes
napalm cancer and the deathbed in Vietnam
is a strange place to dream of   trees
    leaning over and angry American faces
grinning with sleepwalk terror over your
    last eye—
Be kind to yourself, because the bliss of your own
    kindness will flood the police tomorrow,
because the cow weeps in the field and the
    mouse weeps in the cat hole—
Be kind to this place, which is your present
    habitation, with derrick and radar tower
    and flower in the ancient brook—
Be kind to your neighbor who weeps
    solid tears on the television sofa,
he has no other home, and hears nothing
    but the hard voice of telephones
Click, buzz, switch channel and the inspired
    melodrama disappears

and he's left alone for the night, he disappears
    in bed—
Be kind to your disappearing mother and
    father gazing out the terrace window
    as milk truck and hearse turn the corner
Be kind to the politician weeping in the galleries
    of Whitehall, Kremlin, White House
    Louvre and Phoenix City
aged, large nosed, angry, nervously dialing
    the bald voice connected to
electrodes underground converging thru
    wires vaster than a kitten's eye can see
on the mushroom shaped fear-lobe under
    the ear of Sleeping Dr. Einstein
crawling with worms, crawling with worms, crawling
    with worms the hour has come—
Sick, dissatisfied, unloved, the bulky
    foreheads of Captain Premier President
    Sir Comrade Fear!
Be kind to the fearful one at your side
    Who's remembering the Lamentations
    of the bible
the prophesies of the Crucified Adam   Son
    of all the porters and char men of
                    Bell   gravia—
Be kind to your self who weep under
    the Moscow moon and hide your bliss hairs
    under raincoat and suede Levis—
For this is the joy to be born, the kindness
    received thru strange eyeglasses on
    a bus thru Kensington,
the finger touch of the Londoner on your thumb,
    that borrows light from your cigarette,
the morning smile at Newcastle Central
    station, when longhair Tom blond husband
    greets the bearded stranger of telephones—
the boom bom that bounces in the joyful
    bowels as the Liverpool Minstrels of
    CavernSink
raise up their joyful voices and guitars
    in electric Africa hurrah
    for Jerusalem—

The saints come marching in, Twist &
    Shout, and Gates of Eden are named
    in Albion again
Hope signs a black psalm from Nigeria,
    and a white psalm echoes in Detroit
    and reechoes amplified from Nottingham to Prague
and a Chinese psalm will be heard, if we all
    live our lives for the next 6 decades—
Be kind to the Chinese psalm in the red transistor
    in your breast—
Be kind to the Monk in the 5 Spot who plays
    lone chord-bangs on his vast piano
lost in space on a bench and hearing himself
    in the nightclub universe—
Be kind to the heroes that have lost their
    names in the newspaper
and hear only their own supplication for
    the peaceful kiss of sex in the giant
    auditoriums of the planet,
nameless voices crying for kindness in the orchestra,
screaming in anguish that bliss come true
    and sparrows sing another hundred years
    to white haired babes
and poets be fools of their own desire—O Anacreon
    and angelic Shelley!
Guide these new-nippled generations on space
    ships to Mars' next universe
The prayer is to man and girl, the only
    gods, the only lords of Kingdoms of
    Feeling, Christs of their own
    living ribs—
Bicycle chain and machine gun, fear sneer
    & smell cold logic of the Dream Bomb
have come to Saigon, Johannesberg,
    Dominica City, Pnom-Penh, Pentagon
    Paris and Lhasa—
Be kind to the universe of Self that
    trembles and shudders and thrills
    in XX Century,
that opens its eyes and belly and breast
    chained with flesh to feel
    the myriad flowers of bliss

that I Am to Thee—
A dream! a Dream! I don't want to be alone!
    I want to know that I am loved!
I want the orgy of our flesh, orgy
    of all eyes happy, orgy of the soul
    kissing and blessing its mortal-grown
    body,
orgy of tenderness beneath the neck, orgy of
    kindness to thigh and vagina
Desire given with meat hand
    and cock, desire taken with
    mouth and ass, desire returned
    to the last sigh!
Tonite let's all make love in London
    as if it were 2001 the years
    of thrilling god—
And be kind to the poor soul that cries in
    a crack of the pavement because he
    has no body—
Prayers to the ghosts and demons, the
    lackloves of Capitals & Congresses
    who make sadistic noises
    on the radio—
Statue destroyers & tank captains, unhappy
    murderers in Mekong & Stanleyville,
That a new kind of man has come to his bliss
    to end the cold war he has borne
    against his own kind flesh
    since the days of the snake.

WALES VISITATION

White fog lifting & falling on mountain-brow
    Trees moving in rivers of wind
                    The clouds arise
    as on a wave, gigantic eddy lifting mist
    above teeming ferns exquisitely swayed
                        along a green crag
    glimpsed thru mullioned glass in valley raine—

Bardic, O Self, Visitacione, tell naught
　　but what seen by one man in a vale in Albion,
　　　of the folk, whose physical sciences end in Ecology,
　　　　the wisdom of earthly relations,
　　of mouths & eyes interknit ten centuries visible
　　　orchards of mind language manifest human,
of the satanic thistle that raises its horned symmetry
　flowering above sister grass-daisies' pink tiny
　　　　bloomlets angelic as lightbulbs—

Remember 160 miles from London's symmetrical thorned tower
　　& network of TV pictures flashing bearded your Self
　the lambs on the tree-nooked hillside this day bleating
heard in Blake's old ear, & the silent thought of Wordsworth in
　　　　　　eld Stillness
　clouds passing through skeleton arches of Tintern Abbey—
　　Bard Nameless as the Vast, babble to Vastness!

All the Valley quivered, one extended motion, wind
　　　　undulating on mossy hills
　a giant wash that sank white fog delicately down red runnels
　　　　on the mountainside
　whose leaf-branch tendrils moved asway
　　　　in granitic undertow down—
and lifted the floating Nebulous upward, and lifted the arms of the
　　　　　　　　　trees
　　　and lifted the grasses an instant in balance
　　　and lifted the lambs to hold still
　and lifted the green of the hill, in one solemn wave

A solid mass of Heaven, mist-infused, ebbs thru the vale,
　a wavelet of Immensity, lapping gigantic through Llanthony
　　　　　　Valley,
　the length of all England, valley upon valley under Heaven's ocean
　　　　　tonned with cloud-hang,
　　　Heaven balanced on a grassblade—
Roar of the mountain wind slow, sigh of the body,
　One Being on the mountainside stirring gently
　　Exquisite scales trembling everywhere in balance,
one motion thru the cloudy sky-floor shifting on the million
　　　　　feet of daisies,

one Majesty the motion that stirred wet grass quivering
to the farthest tendril of white fog poured down
through shivering flowers on the mountain's
head—

No imperfection in the budded mountain,
Valleys breathe, heaven and earth move together,
daisies push inches of yellow air, vegetables tremble,
green atoms shimmer in grassy mandalas,
sheep speckle the mountainside, revolving their jaws with empty
eyes,
horses dance in the warm rain,
tree-lined canals network through live farmland,
blueberries fringe stone walls
on hill breasts nippled with hawthorn,
pheasants croak up meadow-bellies haired with fern—

Out, out on the hillside, into the ocean sound, into delicate
gusts of wet air,
Fall on the ground, O great Wetness, O Mother, No harm on
thy body!
Stare close, no imperfection in the grass,
each flower Buddha-eye, repeating the story,
the myriad-formed soul
Kneel before the foxglove raising green buds, mauve bells drooped
doubled down the stem trembling antennae,
& look in the eyes of the branded lambs that stare
breathing stockstill under dripping hawthorn—
I lay down mixing my beard with the wet hair of the mountainside,
smelling the brown vagina-moist ground, harmless,
tasting the violet thistle-hair, sweetness—
One being so balanced, so vast, that its softest breath
moves every floweret in the stillness of the valley floor,
trembles lamb-hair hung gossamer rain-beaded in the grass,
lifts trees on their roots, birds in the great draught
hiding their strength in the rain, bearing same weight,

Groan thru breast and neck, a great Oh! to earth heart
Calling our Presence together
The great secret is no secret
Senses fit the winds,
Visible is visible,

rain-mist curtains wave through the bearded vale,
grey atoms wet the wind's Kaballah
Crosslegged on a rock in dusk rain,
rubber booted in soft grass, mind moveless,
breath trembles in white daisies by the roadside,
Heaven breath and my own symmetric
Air wavering thru antlered green fern
drawn in my navel, same breath as breathes thru Capel-Y-Ffn,
Sounds of Aleph and Aum
through forests of gristle,
my skull and Lord Hereford's Knob equal,
All Albion one.

What did I notice? Particulars! The
vision of the great One is myriad—
smoke curls upward from ash tray,
house fire burned low,
The night, still wet & moody black heaven
starless
upward in motion with wet wind.

July 29, 1967 (LSD)—August 3, 1967 (London)

BAYONNE TURNPIKE TO TUSCARORA

Grey water tanks in Grey mist,
grey robot
towers carrying wires thru Bayonne's
smog, silver
domes, green chinaworks steaming,
Christmas's leftover lights hanging
from a smokestack—
Monotone grey highway into the grey West—
Noon hour, the planet smoke-covered
Truck wheels roaring forward
spinning past the garbagedump
Gas smell wafting thru Rahway overpass
oiltanks in frozen ponds, cranes' feederladders &
Electric generator trestles, Batteries open under
heaven

Anger in the heart—
        hallucinations in the car cabin, rattling
        bone ghosts left and right
    by the car door—the broken icebox—
On to Pennsylvania turnpike
                  Evergreens in Snow
   Laundry hanging from the blue bungalow
Mansfield and U Thant ask halt Bombing North Vietnam
    State Department says "Tit For Tat."
       Frank Sinatra with negro voice
            enters a new phase—
   Flat on his face 50 years "I've been a beggar & a
                        clown
     a poet & a star, roll myself in July
          up into a ball and die."
               Radio pumping
     artificial rock & roll, Beach Boys
& Sinatra's daughter overdubbed microphone
     antennae'd car dashboard vibrating
   False emotions broadcast thru the Land
   Natural voices made synthetic,
      pflegm obliterated
   Smart ones work with electronics—
      What are the popular songs on the Hiway?
"Home I'm Coming Home I am a Soldier—"
     "The girl I left behind . . .
I did the best job I could
     Helping to keep our land free
I am a soldier"
     Lulled into War
   thus commercial jabber Rock & Roll Announcers
False False False
    "Enjoy this meat—"
    Weak A&P Superright ground round
    Factories building, airwaves pushing . . .
Trees stretch up parallel into grey sky
Yellow trucks roll down lane—
    Hypnosis of airwaves
  In the house you can't break it
    unless you turn off yr set

In the car it can drive yr eyes inward
from the snowy hill,
withdraw yr mind from the birch forest
make you forget the blue car in the ice,
Drive yr mind down Supermarket aisles
looking for cans of Save-Your-Money
Polishing-Glue
made of human bones manufactured in N. Vietnam
during a mustard gas hallucination:
The Super-Hit sound of All American Radio.

Turnpike to Tuscarora
Snow fields, red lights blinking in the broken car
Quiet hills' genital hair black in Sunset
Beautiful dusk over human tinyness
Pennsylvanian intimacy,
approaching Tuscarora Tunnel
Quiet moments off the road, Tussie Mountains'
snowfields untouched.
A missile lost Unprogrammed
Twisting in flight to crash 100 miles
south of Cuba into the
Blue Carib!
Diplomatic messages exchanged
"Don't Worry it's only the Setting Sun—"
(Western correspondents assembling in Hanoi)
"perfect ball of orange in its cup of clouds"
Dirty Snowbanks pushed aside from Asphalt thruway-edge—
Uphill's the little forests where the boyhoods grow
their bare feet—

Night falling, "Jan 4 1967, The Vatican Announces Today
No Jazz at the Altar!"
Maybe in Africa
maybe in Asia they got funny music
& strange dancing before the Lord
But here in the West No More Jazz at the Altar,
"It's an alien custom—"
Missa Luba crashing thru airwaves with Demonic Drums
behind Kyrie Eleison—
Millions of tiny silver Western crucifixes for sale
in the Realms of King Badouin—

color TV in this year—weekly
    the Pope sits in repose & slumbers to classical music
        in his purple hat—
Gyalwa Karmapa sits in Sikkim
    & yearly shows his most remarkable woven
                    dakini-hair
                black Magic Hat
      Whose very sight is Total Salvation—
Ten miles from Gangtok—take a look!

        *   *   *   *   *

Mary Garden dead in Aberdeen,
    Jack Ruby dead in Dallas—
      Sweet green incense in car cabin.
    (Dakini sleeping head bowed, hair braided
                over her Rudraksha beads
                driving through Pennsylvania.
    Julius, bearded, hasn't eaten all day
        sitting forward, pursing his lips, calm.)
Sleep, sweet Ruby, sleep in America, Sleep
    in Texas, sleep Jack from Chicago,
    Friend of the Mafia, friend of the cops
        friend of the dancing girls—
      Under the viaduct near the book depot
        Under the hospital Attacked by Motorcades,
        Under Nightclubs under all the
                groaning bodies of Dallas,
           under their angry mouths
        Sleep Jack Ruby, rest at last,
          bouquet'd with cancer.
Ruby, Oswald, Kennedy gone
New Years' 1967 come,
      Reynolds Metals up a Half
    Mary Garden, 92, sleeping tonite in Aberdeen.

Three trucks adorned with yellow lights crawl uproad
    under winter network-shade, bare trees, night fallen.
Under Tuscarora Mountain, long tunnel,
          WBZ Boston coming thru—
    "Nobody needs icecream nobody *needs* pot nobody
                needs movies."
. . . "Public Discussion."

Is sexual Intercourse any Good? Can the kids handle it?
                out the Tunnel,
The Boston Voice returning: "controlled circumstances . . ."
        Into tunnel, static silence,
        Trucks roar by in carbon-mist,
                Anger falling asleep at the heart.
White Rembrandt, the hills—
        Silver domed silo standing above house
        in the White Reality Place
                farm up the road,
        Mist Quiet on Woods,
        Silent Reality everywhere.
Till the eye catches the billboards—
        Howard Johnson's Silent Diamond Reality
        "makes the difference."
Student cannon fodder prepared for next Congress session
    Willow Hill, Willow hill, Cannon Fodder, Cannon fodder—
And the Children of the Warmakers're exempt from fighting
                their parents' war—
Those with intellectual money capacities who go to college
                till 1967—
Slowly the radio war news
                steals o'er the senses—
Negro photographs in Rochester
                axe murders in Cleveland,
        Anger at heart base
        all over the Nation—
Husbands ready to murder their wives
        at the drop of a hat-statistic
I could take an axe and split Peter's skull with
                        pleasure—
Great trucks crawl up road
        insect-lit with yellow bulbs outside Pittsburgh,
    "The Devil with Blue Dress" exudes over radio,
        car headlights gleam on motel signs in
                        blackness,
        Satanic Selfs covering nature
        spiked with trees.
Crash of machineguns, ring of locusts, airplane roar,
        calliope yell, bzzzs.

MEMORY GARDENS

covered with yellow leaves
in morning rain

—Quel Deluge
he threw up his hands
& wrote the Universe dont exist
& died to prove it.

Full Moon over Ozone Park
Airport Bus rushing thru dusk to
Manhattan,
Jack the Wizard in his
grave at Lowell
for the first nite—
That Jack thru whose eyes I
saw
smog glory light
gold over Mannahatta's spires
will never see these
chimneys smoking
anymore over statues of Mary
in the graveyard

Black misted canyons
rising over the bleak
river
Bright doll-like ads
for Esso Bread—
Replicas multiplying beards
Farewell to the Cross—
Eternal fixity, the big headed
wax painted Buddha doll
pale resting incoffined—
Empty-skulled New
York streets
Starveling phantoms
filling city—
Wax dolls walking park
Ave,

Light gleam in eye glass
Voice echoing thru Microphones
Grand Central Sailor's
        arrival 2 decades later
                feeling melancholy—
Nostalgia for Innocent World
        War II—
A million corpses running
        across 42'd street
Glass buildings rising higher
                transparent
                        aluminum—
artificial trees, robot sofas,
        Ignorant cars—
One Way Street to Heaven.

. . . .

Grey Subway Roar

A wrinkled brown faced fellow
                with swollen hands
leans to the blinking plate glass
        mirroring white poles, the heavy car
        sways on tracks uptown to Columbia—
Jack no more'll step off at Penn Station
        anonymous erranded, eat sandwich
        & drink beer near New Yorker Hotel or walk
under the shadow of Empire State.
Didn't we stare at each other length of the car
        & read headlines in faces thru Newspaper Holes?
Sexual cocked & horny bodied young, look
        at beauteous Rimbaud & Sweet Jenny
                riding to class from Columbus Circle.
"Here the kindly dopefiend lived."

and the rednecked sheriff beat the longhaired
                boy on the ass.
—103d street Broadway, me & Hal abused for sidewalk
                        begging twenty-five years ago.
Can I go back in time & lay my head on a teenage
        belly upstairs on 110th Street?
or step off the iron car with Jack
        at the blue-tiled Columbia sign?

at last the old brown station where I had
a holy vision's been rebuilt, clean ceramic
over the scum & spit & come of quarter century.

Saki Wani Choey Bhaki/Cupbearing kid where's the wine?

Flying to Maine in a trail of black smoke
Kerouac's obituary conserves *Time's*
                    Front Paragraphs—
Empire State in Heaven Sun Set Red,
              White mist in old October
          over the billion trees of Bronx—
              There's too much to see—
Jack saw sun set red over Hudson horizon
          Two three decades back
thirtynine fourtynine fiftynine
              sixtynine
John Holmes pursed his lips,
              wept tears.
Smoke plumed up from oceanside chimneys
          plane roars toward Montauk
              stretched in red sunset—
Northport, in the trees, Jack drank
      rot gut & made haikus of birds
          tweetling on his porch rail at dawn—
Fell down and saw Death's golden lite
          in Florida garden a decade ago.
Now taken utterly, soul upward,
          & body down in wood coffin
              & concrete slab-box.
I threw a kissed handful of damp earth
          down on the stone lid
              & sighed
          looking in Creeley's one eye,
Peter sweet holding a flower
      Gregory toothless bending his
          knuckle to Cinema machine—
and that's the end of the drabble tongued
          Poet who sounded his Kock-rup
              throughout the Northwest Passage.
Blue dusk over Saybrook, Holmes
              sits down to dine Victorian—

& *Time* has a ten-page spread on
            Homosexual Fairies!

Well, while I'm here I'll
            do the work—
and what's the Work?
            To ease the pain of living.
Everything else, drunken
            dumbshow.
                                    October 22–29, 1969

FRIDAY THE THIRTEENTH

Blasts rip Newspaper Grey Mannahatta's mid day Air Spires,
Plane roar over cloud, Sunlight on blue fleece-mist,
I travel to die, fellow passengers silk-drest & cocktailed burn oil NY
            to Chicago—
Blasting sky with big business, billion bodied Poetry Commerce,
all Revolution & Consumption, Manufacture & Communication
Bombburst, vegetable pie, rubber donut sex accessory & brilliant TV
            Jetplane CIA Joke Exorcism Fart Mantra
or electronic war Laos to AID Gestapo training in Santo Domingo
equally massacre grass, exhaust flower power in coal factory smoke-
            dust
—O how beautiful snowy fields earth-floored below cloudholes
glimpsed from air-roads smogged thru heavens toward Illinois—
What right have I to eat petrol guns & metal from earth heart
What right have I to burn gas air, screech overground rubber tired
            round midnight stoplight corners in Peoria, Fort Wayne,
            Ames—
What prayer restores freshness to eastern meadow, soil to cindered
            acres, hemlock to rusty hillside,
transparency to Passaic streambed, Blue whale multitudes to coral
            gulfs—
What mantra bring back my mother from Madhouse, Private Brake-
            field from Leavenworth, Neal from the Street of Hades,
Hampton, King, Gold, murdered suicided millions from the War-torn
            fields of Sheol

where bodies twitch arm from leg torn heart beat spasmed brainless
       in dynamite Napalm rubble Song-My to West 11th Street
       Manhattan
as war bomb-blast burns along neckbone-fused nations Hanoi to
       Chicago Tu-Do to Wall Street,
Dynamite metastasis heading toward earth-brain cankering human
       world forms—
Banks burn, boys die bullet-eyed, mothers scream realization the vast
       tonnage of napalm
rolling down Grand Concourse, Fragmentation nails bounced off
       Haiphong walls
rattling machine-gunned down Halstead, the Karma of State Violence
washing terror-waves round earth-globe back to suburb TV home
       night kitchens
The image 3 years ago, prophetic shriek of electric screen dots burst-
       ing thru bathroom walls,
tile & pipes exploded in NY as on Saigon's Embassy Street
—"Northrop is favorite in hot bidding on a jet fighter for a fat market
       overseas,"   —*Business Week* March 7, 1970

Earth pollution identical with Mind pollution, consciousness Pollution
       identical with filthy sky,
dirty-thoughted Usury simultaneous with metal dust in water courses
murder of great & little fish same as self besmirchment short hair
       thought control,
mace-repression of gnostic street boys identical with DDT extinction
       of Bald Eagle—
Mother's milk poisoned as fathers' thoughts, all greed-stained over
       the automobile-body designing table—

What can Poetry do, how flowers survive, how man see right mind
       multitude, hear his heart's music, feel cockjoys, taste
ancient natural grain-bread and sweet vegetables, smell his own baby
       body's tender neck skin
when 60% State Money goes to heaven on gas clouds burning off
       War Machine Smokestacks?

When Violence floods the State from above, flowery land razed for
       robot proliferation
metal rooted & asphalted down 6 feet below topsoil,

then when bombcarrying children graduate from Grammar-school's
     sex-drenched gymnasia
terrified of Army Finance Meatbones, busted by cops for grassy hair,
Who can prophesy Peace, or vow Futurity for any but armed insects,
steeltip Antennaed metal soldiers porting white eggbombs where
     genitals were,
Blue-visor'd spray-bugs, gasmasked legions in red-brick Armory
     Nests—
(bearded spiders ranged under attick & roof with homebrew Arsenic
     mercury dung plastic readied for the Queen Bee's Immola-
     tion
in Sacramento, Trenton, Phoenix, Miami?)
The State set off a plague of bullets bombs & burning words
two decades back, & seeded Asia with Mind-thoughts excreted in
     Washington bathrooms—
now the Great Fear's rolled round the world & washes over News-
     paper Grey air
rolling waved through cloud-smogbanks in Heaven
as the gas-burning TWA Jet house crashes thru sound barriers over
     Manhattan.

Chicago Chicago Chicago Trials, screams, tears, Mace, coalgas, Mafia
     highways—old Massacres in suburb garages!
Autos turn to water City Halls melt in Aeon-flood,
Police & revolutionaries pass as gas cloud by eagle wing.
"What's your name?" asks badge-man as machines eat all Name &
     Form,
History's faster than thought, poetry obsolete in tiny decades tho
     maybe slow tunes dance eternal—
war language comes, bombblasts last a minute, coalmines exhaust
     earth-heart,
Chicago suburb blocks stretch new-bared earthskin under suneye,
autos speed myriad thru grey air to jet port.
Slaves of Plastic! Leather-shoe chino-pants prisoners! Haircut junkies!
     Dacron-sniffers!
Striped tie addicts! short hair monkeys on their backs! Whiskey freaks
     bombed out on 530 billion cigarettes a year—
twenty Billion dollar advertising Dealers! lipstick skin-poppers &
     syndicate Garbage telex-Heads!
Star-striped scoundrelesque flag-dopers! Car-smog hookers Fiendish
     on superhighways!

Growth rate trippers hallucinating Everglade real estate! Steak swal-
lowers zonked on Television!
Old ladies on Stockmarket habits—old Wall Street paper Money-
pushers!
Central Intelligence cutting Meo opium fields! China Lobby copping
poppies in Burma!
How long this Addict government support our oil-burner matter-habit
shooting gasoline electric speed before the blue light blast & eternal
Police-roar Mankind's utter bust?
Robot airfields soulless Market electronic intelligence business sky-
scraper streets
empty-soul'd, exploding.
Sheer matter crackling, disintegrating back to void,
Sunyatta & Brahma undisturbed, Maya-cities blow up like Chinese
firecrackers,
Samsara tears itself apart—Dusk over Chicago, light-glitter along
boulevards,
insect-eyed autos moving slow under blue streetlamps,
plane motor buzz in eardrum, city cloud roof filling with grey gas on
up into clear heaven—planet horizon auroral twilight-
streaked,
blue space above human truck-moil, Empty sky
Empty mind overhanging Chicago, the universe suspended entire
overhanging Chicago.
O Jack thou'st scaped true deluge.
Smart cock, to turn to shade, I drag hairy meat loss thru blood-red sky
down thru cloud-floor to Chicago, sunset fire obliterate in black gas.

THUS CROSSLEGGED ON ROUND PILLOW SAT IN SPACE

for Chögyam Trungpa

I breathed upon the aluminum microphone-stand a body's length
away
I breathed upon the teacher's throne, the wooden chair with yellow
pillow
I breathed further, upon the cup of wine half emptied by the breath-
ing guru
Breathed upon the green sprigged thick-leaved plant in flowerpot
Breathed upon the vast plateglass shining back the assembled sitting

Sangha in the meditation cafeteria
my breath thru nostril floated out to the moth of evening beating
        into the window'd illumination
breathed outward over the aspen twigs trembling September's top
        yellow leaves in twilight at the mountain foot
breathed over the mountain, over the snowpowdered crags ringed
        under slow-breathed cloud-mass white spumes
windy across Tetons to Idaho, grey ranges under blue space swept
with delicate snow flurries, breaths of wind Westward
mountain grass trembling in tiny winds toward Wasatch
Breezes south late autumn in Salt Lake's temple wooden streets,
white salt dust lifted swirling by the thick leaden lake, dust carried
        up over Kennicot's pit onto the massive Unit rig,
out towards Reno's neon, dollar bills skittering downstreet along the
        curb,
up into Sierras the leaves blown down by fall cold chills
over the peaktops the snowy gales beginning,
a breath of prayer down on Kitkitdizze horngreen leaves close to the
        ground
over Gary's tile roof, over temple pillar, over tents and arbors in
        Sierra pine foothills—
a breath falls over Sacramento Valley, a roar of wind down the sixlane
        freeway across Bay Bridge
uproar of papers floating over Montgomery Street, pigeons fluttering
        before sunset down from Washington Park's white church—
Golden Gate waters whitecapped scudding out to Pacific spreads
over Hawaii a balmy wind thru the Hotel palmtrees, a moist warmth
        swept over the airbase, a dank breeze in Guam's rotten
        Customs shed,
clear winds breathe on Fiji's palm & coral shores, by wooden hotels
        in Suva flags flutter, taxis whoosh by Friday night's black
        promenaders under the rock & roll discotheque upstairs
        window beating with English neon—
on a breeze into Sydney, and across hillside grass where mushrooms
        lie low on Cow Flops in Queensland, down Adelaide's alleys
        a flutter of music from Brian Moore's Dobro carried in the
        wind—
up thru Darwin Land, out Gove Peninsula green ocean breeze, clack
        of Yerkalla song sticks by the trembling wave
yea and a wind over mercurial waters of Japan North East, a hollow
        wooden gong echoes in Kyoto's temple hall below the
        graveyard's wavy grass

A foghorn blowing in the China Sea, torrential rains over Saigon,
    bombers floating over Cambodia, visioned tiny from stone
    Avalokiteshvara's many-faced towers Angkor Wat in windy
    night,
a puff of opium out of a mouth yellowed in Bangkok, a puff of hashish
    flowing thick out of a bearded saddhu's nostrils & eyes in
    Nimtallah Burning Ghat,
wood smoke flowing in wind across Hoogley Bridge, incense wafted
    under the Bo Tree in Bodh Gaya, in Benares woodpiles burn
    at Manikarnika returning incensed souls to Shiva,
wind dallies in the amorous leaves of Brindaban, still air on the vast
    mosque floor above Old Delhi's alleys,
wind blowing over Kausani's stone wall, Himalayan peaktops ranged
    hundreds of miles along snowy horizon, over Almora's
    wood brown housetops,
trade winds carry dhows thru Indian Ocean to Mombassa or down to
    Dar 'Sallam's riverside sail port, palms sway & sailors
    wrapped in cotton sleep on the log decks—
a breeze up thru Red Sea to Elat's dry hotels, paper leaflets scatter by
    the Wailing Wall, blown into the Sepulchre,
Mediterranean zephyrs leaving Tel Aviv, over Crete, Lassithi Plains'
    windmills still turning century after century near Zeus'
    birth-cave
Pyraeus wave-lashed, Venice lagoon's waters blown up over the
    floor of San Marco, Piazza flooded and mud on the marble
    porch, gondolas bobbing up & down choppy waters at the
    Zatteree,
chill September fluttering thru Milan's Arcade, cold bones & overcoats
    flapping in St. Peter's Square,
down Appian Way silence by the gravesites, stelae stolid on the
    lonely grass path, the breath of an old man laboring up
    road—
Across Scylla & Charybdis, Sicilian tobacco smoke wafted across the
    boat deck,
into Marseilles coalstacks black fumes float into clouds, and steamer's
    white driftspume down wind all the way to Tangier,
a breath of red-tinged Autumn in Provence, boats slow on the Seine,
    the lady wraps her cloak tight round her bodice on toppa
    Eiffel Tower's iron head—
across the Channel rough black-green waves, in London's Piccadilly
    beer cans roll on concrete neath Eros' silver breast, the
    Sunday Times lifts and settles on wet fountain steps—

over Iona blue day and a balmy Scottish breeze, fog drifts across
Atlantic,
Labrador white frozen blowing cold, down New York's canyons
manila paper bags scurry toward Wall from Lower East
side—
a breath over my Father's head in his apartment on Park Avenue
Paterson,
a cold September breeze down from East Hill, Cherry Valley's maples
tremble red,
out thru Chicago Windy City the vast breath of Consciousness dis-
solves, smokestacks and autos drift their expensive fumes
ribboned across railroad tracks,
Westward, a single breath blows across the plains, Nebraska's fields
harvested & stubble bending delicate in evening airs
up Rockies, from Denver's Cherry Creek another zephyr risen,
across Pike's Peak on icy blast at sunset, Wind River peaktops flowing
toward the Tetons,
a breath returns vast gliding the grass flats cow-dotted into Jackson
Hole, into the corner of the plains,
up the asphalt road and mud parking lot, a breeze of restless Sep-
tember, up wood stairways in the wind
into the cafeteria at Teton Village under the red tram lift
a calm breath, a silent breath, a slow breath breathes outward from
the nostrils.

FROM AN EARLY LETTER

Back to Howl: construction. After sick & tired of shortline free verse
as not expressionistic enough, not swinging enough, can't develop a
powerful enough rhythm. I simply turned aside, accidentally to writing
part I of Howl, in solitude, diddling around with the form, thinking
it couldn't be published anyway (queer content my parents shouldn't
see, etc.) also it was out of my short-line line. But what I did taught
my theory, I changed my mind about "measure" while writing it.
Part one uses repeated base who, as a sort of kithera BLANG, homeric
(in my imagination) to mark off each statement, with rhythmic unit.
So that's experiment with longer & shorter variations on a fixed base
—the principle being, that each line has to be contained within the
elastic of one breath—with suitable punctuatory expressions where
the rhythm has built up enough so that I have to let off steam by
building a longer climactic line in which there is a jazzy ride. All the
ear I've ever developed goes into the balancing of those lines. The
interesting moments when the rhythm is sufficiently powerful pushing
ahead so I can ride out free and drop the key that holds it together.
The method of keeping a long line still all poetic and not prosey is
the concentration and compression of basically imageistic notations
into surrealist or cubist phrasing, like hydrogen jukeboxes. Ideally
anyway. Good example of this is Gregory's great (I swear) Coit Tower
ode. Lines have greater poetic density. But I've tried to keep the
language sufficiently dense in one way or another—use of primitive
naive grammer (expelled for crazy), elimination of prosey articles &
syntactical sawdust, juxtaposition of cubist style images, or hot
rhythm. Well then Part II. Here the basic repeated word is Moloch.
The long line is now broken up into component short phrases with !
rhythmical punctuation. The key repeat BLANG word is repeated in-
ternally in the line (basic rhythm sometimes emerging /—/—) but
the rhythm depends mostly on the internal Moloch repeat. Lines here
lengthened—a sort of free verse prose poetry STANZA form invented
or used here. This builds up to climax (Visions! Omens! etc.) and then
falls off in coda, Part III, perhaps an original invention (I thought so
then but this type of thinking is vain & shallow anyway) to handling
of long line (for the whole poem is an experiment in what you can
do with the long line—the whole book is)—: : : that is, a phrase base
rhythm (I'm with you etc.), followed as in litany by a response of the
same length (Where you're madder etc.), then repeat of base over
and over with the response elongating itself slowly, still contained
within the elastic of one breath till the stanza (for it is a stanza form

there, I've used variations of it since) building up like a pyramid, an emotion crying siren sound, very appropriate to the expressive appeal emotion I felt (a good healthy emotion said my analyst at that time, to dispose once and for all of that idiotic objection)— anyway, building up to the climax where there's a long long long line, pentultimate, too long for one breath, where I open out and give the answer (O starry spangled shock of Mercy the eternal war is here. All this rather like a jazz mass, I mean the conception of rhythm not derived from jazz directly, but if you listen to jazz you get the idea (in fact specifically old trumpet solo on a JATP Can't Get Started side)—well all this is built like a brick shithouse and anybody can't hear the mystic id as I told you—guess I meekly inferred Trilling, who is absolutely lost in poetry, is got a tin ear, and that's so obviously true, I get sick and tired I read 50 reviews of Howl and not one of them written by anyone with enough technical interests to notice the fucking obvious construction of the poem, all the details besides (to say nothing of the various esoteric classical allusions built in like references to Cezanne's theory of composition, etc., etc.)—that I GIVE UP and anybody henceforth comes up to me with a silly look in his eye and begins bullshitting about morals and sociology & tradition and technique & JD—I mean I je ne sais plus parler—the horrible irony of all these jerks who can't *read* trying to lecture me (us) on FORM)

Kerouac has his own specific method of construction of prose which he has persued for a decade now and I have yet to see one piece of criticism taking that into account, or even interested enough to realize he has one & its implications in how it relates to the rhythm of his prose—much less how his method alters and develops chrono- logically from book to book, what phases it goes thru, which changes one would encounter in so prolonged a devoted experiment as his (rather like Gertrude Stein)—but nobody's interested in literature, in technique, all they think about is their goddamn lousy ideas of what they preconceive writing to be about and IM SICK OF LISTEN- ING TO THAT AND READING ABOUT THAT AND UNLESS THERE IS MORE COOPERATION FROM THE SUPPOSEDLY RESPONSIBLE PARTIES IN UNIVERSITIES & MAGAZINES I ABSOLUTELY CUT OUT AND REFUSE TO MY HEART WRUNG POEMS TO THE DIRTY HANDS AND MINDS OF THESE BASTARDS AND THEY CAN TAKE THEIR FUCKING literary tradition AND SHOVE IT UP THEIR ASS—I don't need them and they don't need me and I'm sick of putting myself out and being put down and hit on the head by jerks who have no interest but their ridiculous devilish social careers and MONEY

MONEY MONEY which is the root of the EVIL here in America and I'M MAD.

Footnote to Howl is too lovely & serious a joke to try to explain. The built in rhythmic exercise should be clear, it's basically a repeat of the Moloch section. It's dedicated to my mother who died in the madhouse and it says I loved her anyway & that even in worst conditions life is holy. The exaggerations of the statements are appropriate, and anybody who doesn't understand the specific exaggerations will never understand "Rejoice in the Lamb" or Lorca's "Ode to Whitman" or Mayakovsky's "At the Top of My Voice" or Artaud's "Pour En Finir Avec le Jugement de Dieu" or Apollinaire's "inspired bullshit" or Whitman's madder passages or anything, anything, anything about international modern spirit in poesy to say nothing about the international tradition in prosody which has grown up nor the tradition of open prophetic bardic poetry which 50 years has sung like an angel over the poor soul of the world while all sorts of snippy cats castrates pursue their good manners and sell out their own souls and the spirit of god who now DEMANDS sincerity and hell fire take him who denies the voice in his soul—except that it's all a kindly joke & the universe disappears after you die so nobody gets hurt no matter how little they allow themselves to live and blow on this Earth.

Anyone noticing the construction & series of poems in Howl would then notice that the next task I set myself to was adapting that kind of open long line to tender lyric feelings and short form, so next is Supermarket in Calif. where I pay homage to Whitman in realistic terms (eyeing the grocery boys) and it's a little lyric, and since it's almost prose it's cast in form of prose paragraphs like St. Perse—and has nobody noticed that I was aware enough of that to make that shift there. Nor that I went on in the next poem Transcription of Organ music to deliberately write a combo of prose and poetry some lines indented which are poetic and some lines not but paragraphed like prose to see what could be done with Absolute transcription of spontaneous material, transcription of sensual data (organ) at a moment of near Ecstasy, not, nor has anyone noticed that I have technically developed my method of transcription (as Cezanne developed sketching) so that I could transcribe at such moments & try to bring back to the poor suffering world what rare moments exist, and that technical practice has led to a necessary spontaneous method of transcription which will pass in and out of poetry and so needs a flexible form—its own natural form unchanged—to preserve the moment alive and uncensured by the arbitrary ravenings of conceptual or preconceptual or post-censuring-out-of-embarrassment so called

intelligence? Anyway there is a definite experiment in FOR
FORM and not a ridiculous idea of what form *should* be lik
is an example that has all sorts of literary precedents in Frei
in Hart Crane, in—but this whole camp of FORM is so ridi ˍˍˍˍˍ ˍˍᴧ
I am ashamed to have to use the word to justify what is THERE. (and
only use it in a limited academic context but would not dream of
using this kindergarten terminology in poets from whom I *learn*—
Kerouac, Burroughs or Corso—who start to new worlds of their own
invention with minds so Columbian & holy that I am ashamed of my
own academic Tribe that is so superciliously hung on COLLEGE that
it has lost touch with living creation.)
    The next problem attacked in the book is to build up a rhythmical
drive in long lines without dependence on repetition of any words
and phrases, who's, Moloch's, or Holy's, a drive forward to a climax
and conclusion and to do it spontaneously (well, I've broken my
typewriter on this explanation I continue on Peter's)—a twenty minute
task ("Sunflower") with 15 years practice behind—to ride out on the
breath rhythm without any artificial built in guides or poles or diving
boards or repetition except the actual rhythm, and to do it so that
both long long lines, and lone lines, and shorter 10 word lines all
have the same roughly weight, and balance each other out, and
anybody take the trouble to read Sutra out will see it does that & the
Come of the rhythmic buildup is "You were never no locomotive
Sunflower, you a sunflower, and you locomotive (pun) you
were a locomotive, etc.," And furthermore at this point in the book
I am sick of preconceived literature and only interested in *writing*
the actual process and technique, wherever it leads, and the various
possible experiments in composition that are in my path—and if any-
body still is confused in what literature is let it be hereby announced
once for all in the 7 Kingdoms that that's what it is—Poetry is what
poets write, and not what other people think they should write.

ALLEN GINSBERG

RICHARD HUGO

Richard Hugo was born in Seattle in 1923 and educated at the University of Washington. Formerly on the faculty at the University of Montana, he is now teaching at the University of Colorado. His published works include *Good Luck in Cracked Italian, Death of Kapowsin Tavern,* and *The Lady in Kicking Horse Reservoir,* all poetry, as well as essays and reviews, and he is at present working on an autobiographical novel. He is an expert fly fisherman.

LETTER TO WAGONER FROM PORT TOWNSEND

Dear Dave: Rain five days and I love it. A relief from sandy arroyos, buzzards, and buttes, and a growing season consisting strictly of June. Here, the grass explodes and trees rage black green deep as the distance they rage in. I suppose all said, this is my soul, the salmon rolling in the strait and salt air loaded with cream for our breathing. And around the bend a way, Dungeness Spit. I don't need any guide but the one I've got, the one you threw the world like a kiss of wind ending hot summer, though of course I am seldom called lover these days and in bad moments when I walk the beach I claim the crabs complain. Aside from those momentary failures I am soaring, looping the loop over blackfish schools and millions of candlefish darting in and out of glint. I think because the sea continually divides the world into dark and gleam, the northwest sky relieves us from the pressure of always choosing by being usually gray, but of course that's only theory. No real accounting for calm. The stable chunky ferry is leaving for Keystone. Perch curve around the pilings oblivious in their bulk to porgies and the starfish napping tight to barnacles. They all remind me of Kenny, a boy I fished with from the pier at Seola. When we got older I saw he was subnormal and I saw the space between us grow, and finally we saw each other in passing in White Center and didn't speak. We don't take others by the hand and say: we are called people. The power to make us better is limited even in the democratic sea. Discovery of cancer, a broken back, our inability to pass our final exam—I guess the rain is finally getting me down. What matter? I plan to spend my life dependent on moon and tide and the tide is coming, creeping over the rocks, washing the remains of crippled fish back deep to the source, renewing the driftwood supply and the promise of all night fires on the beach, stars and dreams of girls, and that's as rich as I'll ever get. We are called human. C'iao. Dick.

LETTER TO WELCH FROM BROWNING

Dear Jim: This is as far as I ever chased a girl. She's worth it, but she isn't here. Man, it's a grim pull from Missoula in a car. Had a haircut in Augusta, a drink in Choteau, Bynum, and Depuyer. I wanted to arrive well groomed and confident. I'm in a cheap motel, the walls

are beveled board and painted a faint green that reminds me some-
how of the '30s and a cabin on Lake Meridian. I spent this night, the
only white in the Napi Tavern where the woman tending bar told me
she's your aunt. A scene of raw despair. Indians sleeping on the filthy
floor. Men with brains scrambled in wine. A man who sobbed all
night, who tried in strangled desperation to articulate the reason.
And the bitterest woman I've seen since the depression. Of course.
The '30s never ended here. They started. In the '80s. Some braves
took turns apologizing for a poor demented derelict who stole my
beer and bummed me twice for a quarter. One gave me fishing tips
for a lake on the reservation. What a sharp description. I could see
it as he talked. Grass banks that roll into the water. No trees. Sur-
rounding land as open as the lake. I thanked him like I'd never thank
a white. And I thank a lot of things because tomorrow I'll be pulling
out. When my car points south I hope a waltz by Strauss is on the
radio, the day is sunny and the clouds so vivid in their forms I'll have
the urge to give them names. I'll never see you quite the same. Your
words will ring like always on the page, but when drunk you shrug
away the world, our petty, gnawing bugs, degrees and grades and
money, even sometimes love, I'll simply nod and pour. I hope I find
that girl. I plan to touch her in such ways, tender and direct until she
reaches for me every morning out of instinct. She's up here, when
she's here, doing social work. I'll probably never find her. And while
I'm at it, the food in Browning is not good. Take care, Chief Boiling
Whiskey. Dick.

LETTER TO LOGAN FROM MILLTOWN

Dear John: This a Dear John letter from booze. With you, liver. With
me, bleeding ulcer. The results are the horrific same: as drunks we're
done. Christ, John, what a loss to those underground political move-
ments that count, the Degradationists, the Dipsomaniacists, and that
force gaining momentum all over the world, the Deteriorationists. I
hope you know how sad this is. Once I quit drinking it was clear to
others, including our chairman (who incidentally also had to quit
drinking), that less 40 pounds I look resolute and strong and on the
surface appear efficient. Try this for obscene development: they made
me director of creative writing. Better I'd gone on bleeding getting
whiter and whiter and finally blending into the snow to be found

next spring, a tragedy that surely would increase my poetic reputa-
tion. POET FOUND IN THAW   SNOWS CLAIM MISSOULA BARD
I'm in Milltown. You remember that bar, that beautiful bar run by
Harold Herndon where I pissed five years away but pleasantly. And
now I can't go in for fear I'll fall sobbing to the floor. God, the ghosts
in there. The poems. Those honest people from the woods and mill.
What a relief that was from school, from that smelly student-teacher
crap and those dreary committees where people actually say 'consid-
ering the lateness of the hour.' Bad times too. That depressing sum-
mer of '66 and that woman going—I've talked too often about that.
Now no bourbon to dissolve the tension, to find self love in blurred
fantasies, to find the charm to ask a woman home. What happens to
us, John? We are older than our scars. We have outlasted and sur-
vived our wars and it turns out we're not as bad as we thought. And
that's really sad. But as a funny painter said at a bash in Portland,
and I thought of you then, give Mother Cabrini another Martini. But
not ever again you and me. Piss on sobriety, and take care. Dick.

LETTER TO LEVERTOV FROM BUTTE

Dear Denise: Long way from, long time since Boulder. I hope you and
Mitch are doing OK. I get rumors. You're in Moscow, Montreal.
Whatever place I hear, it's always one of glamor. I'm not anywhere
glamorous. I'm in a town where children get hurt early. Degraded by
drab homes. Beaten by drunken parents, by other children. Mitch
might understand. It's kind of a microscopic Brooklyn, if you can
imagine Brooklyn with open pit mines, and more Irish than Jewish.
I've heard from many of the students we had that summer. Even seen
a dozen or so since then. They remember the conference fondly. So
do I. Heard from Herb Gold twice and read now and then about
Isaac Bashevis Singer who seems an enduring diamond. The mines
here are not diamond. Nothing is. What endures is sadness and long
memories of labor wars in the early part of the century. This is the
town where you choose sides to die on, company or man, and both
are losers. Because so many people died in mines and fights, early in
history man said screw it and the fun began. More bars and whores
per capita than any town in America. You live only for today. Let me
go symbolic for a minute: great birds cross over you any place, here
they grin and dive. Dashiell Hammett based Red Harvest here though
he called it Personville and 'person' he made sure to tell us was

'poison' in the slang. I have ambiguous feelings coming from a place like this and having clawed my way away, thanks to a few weak gifts and psychiatry and the luck of living in a country where enough money floats to the top for the shipwrecked to hang on. On one hand, no matter what my salary is or title, I remain a common laborer, stained by the perpetual dust from loading flour or coal. I stay humble, inadequate inside. And my way of knowing how people get hurt, make my (damn this next word) heart go out through the stinking air into the shacks of Walkerville, to the wife who has turned forever to the wall, the husband sobbing at the kitchen table and the unwashed children taking it in and in and in until they are the wall, the table, even the dog the parents kill each month when the money's gone. On the other hand, I know the cruelty of poverty, the embittering ways love is denied, and food, the mean near insanity of being and being deprived, the trivial compensations of each day, recapturing old years in broadcast tunes you try to recall in bars, hunched over the beer you can't afford, or bending to the bad job you're lucky enough to have. How, finally, hate takes over, hippie, nigger, Indian, anyone you can lump like garbage in a pit, including women. And I don't want to be part of it. I want to be what I am, a writer good enough to teach with you and Gold and Singer, even if only in some conference leader's imagination. And I want my life inside to go on long as I do, though I only populate bare landscape with surrogate suffering, with lame men crippled by more than disease, and create finally a simple grief I can deal with, a pain the indigent can find acceptable. I do go on. Forgive this raving. Give my best to Mitch and keep plenty for yourself. Your rich friend, Dick.

LETTER TO SCANLON FROM WHITEHALL

Dear Dennice: I'm this close but the pass is tough this year. I'm stranded by this rotten winter. My car is ailing and the local mechanic doesn't know what he's doing or he does but never learned clear phrasing. It will take four hours or a week. An odd town. A friendly waitress says the main drag is the old road so I must have been here but I don't remember. It looks like several towns in Montana. Columbus, for one. Even , a little, like the edge of Billings. You know. On one side, stores, cafés, a movie theater you feel certain no one attends. And across the street, the railroad station. Most of all, that desolate feeling you get, young hunger, on a gray sunday afternoon,

when you survive only because the desolation feeds your dying, a
dream of living alone on the edge of a definite place, a desert or the
final house in town with no threat of expansion, or on the edge of a
canyon, coyotes prowling below and a wind that never dies. Girl, you
wouldn't believe the people who live alone, preparing themselves
daily for dying, planning their expenditures to the penny so just when
they die their money is gone and the county must bury them, a final
revenge on a world that says work is good, plan for the future. They
did. And dear Dennice, bring their laughing bones no flowers. Pay
them the honor of ignoring their graves, the standard bird authorities
chip on stones, a magpie designed by the same man you always see
in towns like this, sitting in the station, knowing the trains don't run.
The soup in the café I was lucky enough to pick of the available three,
turned out thick tomato macaroni, and the chicken salad sandwich,
yum. The mechanic says my car is done. He says, if I understand,
it's ready and no charge. He says, if I understand, he just wants to be
friendly and it wasn't anything really wrong. Homestake grade is
sanded. I may even beat this letter to your home. It's saturday and I
suppose there's a dance somewhere in Butte tonight. Would you
please consider? Would you come? I hope it's one of those virtuoso
bands, you know, songs from all the generations, jazz, swing, rock.
And a big crowd. Girls in mini minis, tighter than skin over their
behinds and a friendly bar, a table where we can talk. Think about it.
Say yes. Be nice. Love. Dick.

LETTER TO BELL FROM MISSOULA

Dear Marvin: Months since I left broke down and sobbing
in the parking lot, grateful for the depth
of your understanding and since then I've been treated
in Seattle and I'm in control like Ghengas Khan.
That was a hairy one, the drive west, my nerves so strung
I couldn't sign a recognizable name on credit slips.
And those station attendants' looks. Until Sheridan
I took the most degenerate motels I saw because they seemed
to be where I belonged. I found my way by instinct
to bad restaurants and managed to degrade myself
in front of waitresses so dumb I damn near offered them
lessons in expression of disdain. Now, it's all a blur.

Iowa. South Dakota. Wyoming. Lots of troublesome deja vu
in towns I'd seen or never seen before. It's snowing
in Missoula, has been off and on for days but no fierce winds
and no regrets. I'm living alone in a house I bought,
last payment due 2001. Yesterday, a religious nut
came to the door and offered me unqualified salvation
if I took a year's subscription to Essential Sun Beam.
I told him I was Taoist and he went away. Today,
a funny dog, half dachshund, waddles through my yard.
A neighbor boy, Bud, poor, shovels my walk for a dollar
and on the radio a break is predicted. A voice is saying,
periods of sun tomorrow, a high front from the coast.
For no reason, I keep remembering my first woman
and how I said afterward happy, so that's what you do.
I think of you and Dorothy. Stay healthy. Love. Dick.

LETTER TO REED FROM LOLO

Dear J. D.: One should think of Chief Joseph here, coming soft out
of the Lolo Canyon, turning right at the Don Tripp Truck Stop and
heading south for Wisdom where the white man killed his wife.
Instead, I think of that drunk afternoon, still embarrassing, when you,
Kittredge, and I verbally shot up the Lolo Tavern. I won't go to the
P.O. here for fear I'll see our photos on the wall. Even worse, to find
out what we're wanted for, to find a halfhearted offer of a flimsy
reward. The Lolo vigilantes wouldn't recognize me now, not nearly
so heavy, sober as a sloth and given to civility. Still, I drive by the
tavern with my head down. I see you are teaching with Tate, Cuomo
and Fetler. Give Jim and George my best. Don't know Fetler, but he's
a fine writer. Went icefishing saturday with Yates, Kittredge, and our
Indian poet friend. No luck, as Welch says. Cold though. Jesus. The
others lushed it up in Perma. The Dixon Bar is off personal limits
since they misread our New Yorker poems and found them
derogating, not the acts of love we meant, not necessarily for them,
but all men and the degraded human condition we knew long before
we heard of Dixon. Why name a town Wisdom? Why not because an
Indian wept once over the body of his wife, each tear a ton of resolve
to make the trek that will always fail, even if you cross the border
into Canada, and will always be worth while though it ends a few
miles short of your imagined goal, with you erect in surrender, wind

from the soar of ancient horses blowing your hair, and your words, your words: 'I will fight no more forever' leaving the victorious bent and forgotten, cheap in their success. Across this nation, dying from faith in progress, I send you and Chris and the baby a wordy kiss. I will write some more forever though only poetry and therefore always failure. Dick.

LETTER TO BERG FROM MISSOULA

Dear Steve: As you know I didn't care much for my letter poems and would have thrown them away had it not been for Jeff Marks and Madeline DeFrees, who urged me to stick with them. The popularity of the poems bewilders me, but they are fun to write, and I've done a few new ones recently. Anyway, you asked me to comment on them.

In 1966 I did a short poem called "Letter to Bly from La Push" and published it in Colorado State Review. The lines were of normal length and the rhythm was usual, more or less. I never found a spot for that piece in my next two books, some place where it seemed to fit and I finally forgot about it. Strictly speaking however, it was the first letter poem I tried.

Then, in the spring of 1971, I found myself cracking up in Iowa City, the result of years of accumulated bitterness compounded by grim drinking. I was popular at Iowa, what you might call "a success," but I had taken to dwelling over and over on past painful episodes and somehow the image of myself as "a success" was one I simply couldn't accept. It clashed with the picture I kept replaying every night, where I was despised and rejected by women, a degraded wretch who made fatal mistakes that caused women to turn against me. Finally, as the popularity persisted, in a kind of effort to maintain the negative image of self I had been cultivating for a long time, I started going out with women I liked very much and at some point late in the evening when I was drunk enough, I indulged in some insufferable behavior that would insure their alienation. I would remember none of it the next morning because to turn women I liked against me, I had to be terribly drunk. As you know, I place a high value on friendship, on enjoying good relations with others. You can imagine how twisted I had become to do anything that would deliberately cause people to dislike me, and how depressed and terrified I was when I realized what I was doing.

During that time, Carolyn Kizer called again and again from North

Carolina, begging me to hang on, lecturing me on my drinking, offering to come see me if I felt my desperation was so advanced that I couldn't make it without support. Carolyn, for all her statuesque, witty, blonde, flashy, urbane surface, is an old-fashioned woman, one who puts a premium on loyalty to old friends, and her supportive calls were of tremendous importance.

By the end of that summer, I'd been thrown into the hospital for five days, having lost close to half my blood from a leaking ulcer. I'd diagnosed my dizziness and weakness as the flu for two days, while I bled away, vomited up and shit out thick dark liquid I was too stupid to recognize as blood. Since then, I've given up diagnosing my own illnesses, and am also trying to discourage physicians from writing poems unless the doctor's name is Williams. By the time I was released, I knew 30 years of drinking had come to an end. I had gone five days without booze, so I just continued going without it. I started to write at a rate I'd never experienced before.

The first of the letter poem series was "Letter to Kizer from Seattle." I published it in *Quarry*, a new Mag out of Santa Cruz, and it was written out of deep gratitude to Carolyn. I guess you can say that Carolyn's phone calls to Iowa City resulted in the whole series because had I not written that first poem, I doubt I would have done the others.

Usually, I took a 14-syllable line, propped it up here and there with an anapest and fired away. Maybe a couple I didn't pay that much attention, but for the most part, that's what I was up to. I liked the direct way I could address myself to things, get loads off my mind, and play here and there within the loose rhythm (loose for me, anyway). Also, I found I could get into the public arena now and then, something I seldom did in my other poems. As far as quality is concerned, I think Jim Harrison's Letters to Yesenin are much better poems, more complicated, richer, and far better crafted. In mine I was often deliberately careless, and that's something I can't approve of in myself. It's the only time I ever screwed off on the art.

I've had a lot of feedback on the letter poems. Someone suggested I was name dropping and that hurt. I won't defend myself from the charge because it's possible I was, but I can assure you that if I was, it was unconscious. Another comment, grandiose to be sure, is that the letter poems have changed the course of American poetry. I can't accept that but if in some wild accidental circumstance it could be true, it was the farthest thing from my mind. I've never had literary ambitions like that. My ambition has been to write good poems and hope others would like them, and nothing else (though I'd like to be wealthy). In fact, I don't much care for the attitude that sees poetry as literature, a heritage I suppose from T. S. Eliot, and if so, the result of concentrating on the wrong qualities in his poems. Eliot's poems are honest recordings of personal pain for all the literary devices he had to employ to render them. In most schools, he is not taught right in my opinion, but some of that may be his own fault.

I guess my favorite of all the letter poems is "Letter To Levertov From Butte" because there I tackled head on the problem of many poets in my generation, those of us who were children during the depression and who saw our parents trapped by economic circumstances. Both James Wright and David Wagoner, to name just two, saw their fathers virtually enslaved to bad jobs in a mill or factory, and it has colored their lives. Most of the poets in my generation came from working classes and we grew up to find ourselves in middle class circumstances. Our fears were basic: destitution, dispossession, deprivation; and while the younger poets do not want for suffering, their concerns are different. In some cases, they are almost the reverse of us, middle-class people who have rejected that life and search for values in areas we still find threatening. I think, in the Levertov poem, I got at something basic in me and in many other poets about my age.

Bill Stafford said sometime back that in the letter poems I was forgiving us all. I hope that's true. Time comes to forgive, especially to forgive one's self. Ever since I gave up drinking, almost three years ago, I've been slowly approaching that state of self-acceptance that seems to run through so many of my poems as an obsessive ideal. Thanks to Carolyn, a lot of other poets, a lot of editors, a lot of students, colleagues, weather, a marvelous woman who has come along, damned good luck, and even the letter poems themselves, I find myself thinking often that you and I and a lot of others aren't such bad guys after all.

> Much affection, even if,
> as you would say, I'm
> not Jewish.

DICK HUGO

DAVID IGNATOW

David Ignatow was born in 1914. He ran a bindery for many years and has also worked as a hospital orderly. He is one of the few poets whose experience includes a deep knowledge of the business world. Among his books are *Say Pardon, Rescue the Dead, Figures of the Human, The Gentle Weight Lifter,* and *Facing the Tree.* His collected poems were published in 1970, and in 1974, *The Notebooks of David Ignatow.* He teaches at York College in New York City.

THE DREAM

Someone approaches to say his life is ruined
and to fall down at your feet
and pound his head upon the sidewalk.
Blood spreads in a puddle.
And you, in a weak voice, plead
with those nearby for help;
your life takes on his desperation.
He keeps pounding his head.
It is you who are fated;
and you fall down beside him.
It is then you are awakened,
the body gone, the blood washed from the ground,
the stores lit up with their goods.

THE PROFESSIONAL

She has begun to see men invite themselves.
The flowers and fruit and other gifts pile up.
She wonders, if only she could turn all that
back into cash, how well off she could be.
She must first have had a pride in her abilities.

One man, any, all, each a new subtlety
and overtone that goes to prove an idea
and work supporting it, of which she honestly
has become proud; to be able at a glance
to tell what any amateur would need seclusion for
and a dim light. She has all that
at her fingertips now—starting
from a sincere liking for that kind of knowledge.

Adroit now and live to technique,
she is quick to tell you her main interest
in tones that hardly hurt,
they are so direct and clear—
no longer hers, but of a spirit that demands
to be compensated for its skill.

DAVID IGNATOW 99

THE SKY IS BLUE

Put things in their place,
my mother shouts. I am looking
out the window, my plastic soldier
at my feet. The sky is blue
and empty. In it floats
the roof across the street.
What place, I ask her.

EUROPE AND AMERICA

My father brought the emigrant bundle
of desperation and worn threads,
that in anxiety as he stumbles
tumble out distractedly;
while I am bedded upon soft green money
that grows like grass. Thus,
between my father who lives on a bed of anguish
for his daily bread, and I who tear money
at leisure by the roots,
where I lie in sun or shade,
a vast continent of breezes, storms to him,
shadows, darkness to him, small lakes,
difficult channels to him, and hills,
mountains to him, lie between us.

My father comes of a hell
where bread and man have been kneaded
and baked together. You have heard the scream
as the knife fell; while I have slept
as guns pounded on the shore.

AND THE SAME WORDS

I like rust on a nail,
fog on a mountain.
Clouds hide stars,
rooms have doors,
eyes close,
and the same words
that began love
end it
with changed emphasis.

NO THEORY

No theory will stand up to a chicken's guts
being cleaned out, a hand rammed up
to pull out the wriggling entrails,
the green bile and the bloody liver;
no theory that does not grow sick
at the odor escaping.

FOR ONE MOMENT

You take the dollar
and hand it to the fellow beside you
who turns and gives it to the next one
down the line. The world being round,
you stand waiting, smoking, and lifting
a cup of coffee to your lips, talking
of seasonal weather and hinting
at problems. The dollar returns,
the coffee spills to the ground
in your hurry. You have the money

in one hand, a cup in the other,
a cigarette in your mouth,
and for one moment have forgotten
what it is you have to do,
your hair grey, your legs weakened
from long standing.

THE BUSINESS LIFE

When someone hangs up, having said
to you, "Don't come around again,"
and you have never heard the phone
banged down with such violence
nor the voice vibrate with such venom,
pick up your receiver gently and dial
again, get the same reply; and dial
again, until he threatens. You will
then get used to it, be sick only
instead of shocked. You will live,
and have a pattern to go by, familiar
to your ear, your senses and your dignity.

NIGHT AT AN AIRPORT

Just as the signal tower lights flash
on and off, so the world recedes
and comes on, giving the illusion
of end and beginning. Before light
there was darkness in which the plane
kept roaring in for landing. Particles
of dust rise in the wind's path
and settle obscurely
when the wind has passed.
We have our beginnings

in breeze or storm, dancing or swirling;
and are still when the wind is still.
We have earth and return to it—
everlasting as a thought.

THE SIGNAL

How can I regret my life
when I find the blue-green traffic light
on the corner delightful against the red brick
of my house. It is when the signal turns red
that I lose interest. At night
I am content to watch the blue-green
come on again against the dark
and I do not torture myself
with my shortcomings.

SELF-EMPLOYED

for Harvey Shapiro

I stand and listen, head bowed,
to my inner complaint.
Persons passing by think
I am searching for a lost coin.
You're fired, I yell inside
after an especially bad episode.
I'm letting you go without notice
or terminal pay. You just lost
another chance to make good.
But then I watch myself standing at the exit,
depressed and about to leave,
and wave myself back in wearily,
for who else could I get in my place
to do the job in dark, airless conditions?

A DIALOGUE

I now will throw myself down
from a great height
to express sorrow.
Step aside, please.
I said please step aside
and permit me access
to the building's edge.
How is this, restrained,
encircled by arms,
in front of me a crowd?
I cannot be detained in this manner.
Hear me, I speak with normal emotion.
Release me,
I would express sorrow in its pure form.
I am insane, you say
and will send me away—
and I will go
and die there
in sorrow.

NOTES FOR A LECTURE

I will teach you to become American, my students:
take a turn at being enigmatic, to yourselves especially.
You work at a job and write poetry at night.
You write about working. Married,
you write about love.

I speak of kisses and mean quarrels,
the kiss brings the quarrel to mind,
of differences for their own sakes.

Did I ever think, going to bed,
a woman beside me would be no more uplifting
than a five-dollar raise? Since then

I've been uplifted in bed a hundred times
and but once raised in pay,
and that once has not been forgotten.

Take a broken whiskey bottle,
set it on top of your head
and dance. You have a costume,
you have meaning.

A SUITE FOR MARRIAGE

You keep eating and raising a family
in an orderly, calm fashion
for the sake of the child,
but behind you at your heels
in a humble mass
lies a figure.

Do you own me?
I sense it in your nervous
irritated talk, as for someone
who has become a burden—
when what is possessed
becomes equally demanding
for being possessed.

I am not sure that you wish me to live.
I am not sure that I can.
We circle each other
with the taut courtesy
of two respectful opponents.
Difficult to say what next,
this could be all,
to confront each other
in suspense.

Your eyes are so cold-looking,
rejecting me silently
as I talk in low, cultured tones
to convince you
of my superiority.

So what shall they make of their daughter
who knows nothing of their unhappiness
with each other? She stands between them
like a light of many colors, turning
and dancing.

My daughter, I cry to you from my solitude.
I play the yea-sayer, most bitter,
to spare you with deeds I know can win
good from evil, my despair
a blessing for your life.

SIX MOVEMENTS ON A THEME

for Denise Levertov

Thinking myself in a warm country
of maternal trees under whose shade
I lie and doze, I dream I am weightless.
Magnified faces stare back at me—
of friends wanting me to live
to whom I am dying stretched out
on the ground and barely breathing.
Dead, they say as I hold my breath
to close in and possess myself.

I dream my life to be a plant
floating upon a quiet pool,
gathering nourishment from water
and the sun. I emerge
of my own excess power, my roots
beginning to move like legs,

my leaves like arms,
the pistil the head. I walk
out of the pool
until I reach my utmost weariness
in a dance of the fading power
of my roots—when I lie down
silently to die and find myself
afloat again.

I see no fish crawling
to become man. The mountains
have been standing
without a single effort
to transform themselves
into castles or apartment houses.
Amid silence, I set a statue
in my image.
                    I love you, man,
on my knees. To you
I will address my pleas
for help. You will save me
from myself. From your silence
I will learn to live.

I was shown my only form.
I have no hope
but to approach myself,
palm touching palm.

Tapping on a wall
I feel my humankind,
secretly content
to suffer.
I too am a wall.

The stars are burning overhead.
Excited, I understand
from a distance:
I am fire,
I'll be dumb.

AGAINST THE EVIDENCE

As I reach to close each book
lying open on my desk, it leaps up
to snap at my fingers. My legs
won't hold me, I must sit down.
My fingers pain me
where the thick leaves snapped together
at my touch.

      All my life
I've held books in my hands
like children, carefully turning
their pages and straightening out
their creases. I use books
almost apologetically, I believe
I often think their thoughts for them.
Reading, I never know where theirs leave off
and mine begin. I am so much alone
in the world, I can observe the stars
or study the breeze, I can count the steps
on a stair on the way up or down,
and I can look at another human being
and get a smile, knowing
it is for the sake of politeness.
Nothing must be said of estrangement
among the human race and yet
nothing is said at all
because of that.
But no book will help either.
I stroke my desk,
its wood so smooth, so patient and still.
I set a typewriter on its surface
and begin to type
to tell myself my troubles.
Against the evidence, I live by choice.

ELEGY

I must wait for a stranger to knock on my door.
For one month I have lain on my couch waiting
for a friendly knock. Why has there been none?
Why outside is the sound always of traffic,
the high-pitched impersonal hard rubber?
The sunlight has been a composition,
it poses for me like a cold model.
My presence here has begun to feel like an intrusion.
What have I stirred up to anger that refuses
to talk to me or even to knock? What in my
    behavior
has been offensive, though I recall only
my good humor? When did I last speak to someone?
I cannot recall even, and may be making up
to salvage my pride this being good-natured,
for it is so distant that its reality is like an echo
that I can suspect only as a distortion of my mind.
I shall wait for a stranger,
and if in fact I have not been good to my friends
I will be so now to a stranger.

EACH DAY

Cynthia Matz, with my finger in your cunt
and you sliding back and forth on it,
protesting at the late hour and tiredness
and me with kidneys straining to capacity
with piss I had no chance to release
all night, we got up from the park bench
and walked you home. I left you
at the door, you said something
dispiriting about taking a chance
and settling on me. I had left Janette
to chase after you running out
of the ice cream parlor where the three

of us had sat—I had felt so sorry
and so guilty to have had you find me
with her in the street. You and I
had gone to shows together,
you needed me to talk to and I was glad.
The talk always was about him
whom you still loved and he had jilted
you for someone else. I'm sorry, Cynthia,
that it had to end this way between us too.
I did not return the next day,
after leaving you at the door.
I did not return the following day either.
I went with Janette in whom I felt
nothing standing in the way,
while with you it would have been
each day to listen to your sadness
at having been betrayed by him.
I was not to be trusted either,
I too wanted love pure and simple.

I. from THE NOTEBOOKS OF DAVID IGNATOW

I wonder why my style is as it is, my language. I am after a certain
tone between the learned and the street. I think it is weighted on the
street side, without ignoring the necessary ideas or learning. In other
words, through colloquial language I try to give as broad an
interpretation of my insights as I can. I try to reach as broad a group
of persons as I can, and that is based on the assumption that most
persons speak and think in a colloquial language. It is my contention
that I lose nothing of force or depth writing so. If anything it gains
through a certain authenticity. It also assumes that this broad range
of persons should be addressed and do have the capacity for
understanding and appreciation, that they have in them the capacity
for sensing truth from falsehood, sentimentality from honesty, and
that it is in them to encourage the writer along this path, since it is in
them to desire the same for themselves. I am giving them qualities
that are in me. I project on them my understanding. Now who
exactly is this audience? Is it composed of the middle class lawyer,
doctor, student? Is the working class included, the plumber, the
carpenter, the machinist? No. I know now that they are far from lovers
of modern poetry. I must say the same for the professional classes,
with the exceptions among them far more than among the laboring
classes. Those who I can actually rely on for appreciation are other
poets and even here a select few: students generally, writers of prose,
critics, teachers, but here I come up against a contradiction. Colloquial
writing does not impress them any longer. They too are suspicious
of the laboring classes and of the general population as I am and this
colloquial language—based on educated standards.

There is the difference between street talk and cultivated speech. I
use or try to use cultivated speech. The blab and yawp of Whitman
is a sham. No worker can understand him, once he gets started.
Almost no worker will accept his attitudes, his loves, his freedoms,
his daring. This is all rot and sentiment to them. They're beer drinkers
and TV hounds. This contents them, with a lay every now and then.
If it does not fully satisfy them, then it is the next best thing. In any
case, it beats being depressed and murderous as they might want to
be after a day's monotonous work and pressure from the bosses. They
escape into TV, drinking, gambling. Some buy houses, etc.

But the language of most poetry is not their language. Definitely
not theirs. My appeal then is to other poets and intellectuals who
have other backgrounds and specializations, who think in categories,
who work with systems of ideas as taught them in schools and who

want to hear something of the same from their poets. Not wild loosening of systems, an abandonment of systems. Yes, an abandonment but only for other coherent systems. Thus is the challenge they enjoy, an intellectual challenge. Hardly an emotional or frightening chaotic challenge. Yes, if it is organized for them and accent is on organization. They do not want to see emotions taken at random here and there, thoughts and observations and comments drawn from every place and slapped together freely and bravely, loosely. They don't want to see me work without guide or principle, simply in the pleasure of picking up what pleases me and making something of it that I can like. They don't want to see me wandering everywhere in search of things to see and do, setting no limits to where I go or what I do and holding all things pleasant and sacred because each has its own right and beauty. I am defeating their purpose of organizing things into coherent wholes from which they derive light and guidance which then can give them a sealed-in place, comfort, stability at which they can work efficiently within borders. I am upsetting them. I am setting them adrift when they do not want to be set adrift, when there are systems by which one does not have to drift any longer. Why drift when we can simulate drift by systems and discover things without losing things, losing ourselves especially, especially when it is so easy to lose oneself in a world of so many entities and systems, all at cross-purposes it seems?

I say it must be done. I say that each must be treated and entertained playfully because the human being is beyond any system and is more than all the systems combined. He is himself first.

*   *   *

II. ON WRITING

Obviously, I'm not a confessional poet. I feel no guilt or hatred or consuming love that must be allowed to spill over. Any guilt or love or hatred that I feel is subjected to contemplation. I can't write simply to please myself and I can't write to please others. I can't write simply to give myself something to do, and I can't write simply to give someone something of mine to read. What in hell is writing? I think I could live without it unless it helps me to live without dread. It is when I feel dread coming over me, dread of my existence, dread of myself, in particular, when I become too much for myself, when a hole begins to form in me that is inviting me to fall in or a thickness gathers in me in which I fear I will suffocate as it spreads through me. I write to escape myself in this condition. I write to be distracted from myself that I begin to see is a nothing of huge proportions.

* * *

I don't have to write. I can pretend to write by keeping my door closed to all viewers while I lie on the couch taking it easy, looking up at the trees or debating with myself whether to write—making that enough in itself. Why write when there is nothing to say but that writing is the subject, as now?

* * *

What I also notice about myself is that the angers and despairs of the past that propelled me into writing no longer exist with that force to make me write out of their energies. They are very low keyed in me now and if anything, serve to warn me away from themselves rather than to use them. What am I after? I should ask what is after me. What I just saw frightening me were the folds of a curtain that resembled three fingers hanging down over my hi-fi set. It was as if another nature than human had entered my room, a sacred fright, as if God had just made himself known to me with three holy fingers. But all this is in me. I would not have become scared if I were not disposed to becoming scared. In other words, something in me lies latent and ready to spring up to worship an extranatural event. Unconsciously I must be looking for something to take me out of myself and I write for that event to happen in writing.

DAVID IGNATOW

GALWAY KINNELL

Galway Kinnell was born in Rhode Island in 1927. Educated at
Princeton and Rochester, he has taught in American universities,
and in Grenoble and Teheran. Besides his books of poetry,
which include *What a Kingdom It Was*, *Flower-Herding on Mount
Monadnock*, *Body Rags*, and *The Book of Nightmares*, his works
include a novel, *Black Light*, and four volumes of translation. He has
been poet-in-residence at several schools in recent years and now
lives with his wife and children in New York City and on a farm near
Sheffield, Vermont.

THE BEAR

1
In late winter
I sometimes glimpse bits of steam
coming up from
some fault in the old snow
and bend close and see it is lung-colored
and put down my nose
and know
the chilly, enduring odor of bear.

2
I take a wolf's rib and whittle
it sharp at both ends
and coil it up
and freeze it in blubber and place it out
on the fairway of the bears.

And when it has vanished
I move out on the bear tracks,
roaming in circles
until I come to the first, tentative, dark
splash on the earth.

And I set out
running, following the splashes
of blood wandering over the world.
At the cut, gashed resting places
I stop and rest,
at the crawl-marks
where he lay out on his belly
to overpass some stretch of bauchy ice
I lie out
dragging myself forward with bear-knives in my fists.

3
On the third day I begin to starve,
at nightfall I bend down as I knew I would
at a turd sopped in blood,
and hesitate, and pick it up,
and thrust it in my mouth, and gnash it down,

and rise
and go on running.

4
On the seventh day,
living by now on bear blood alone,
I can see his upturned carcass far out ahead, a scraggled,
steamy hulk,
the heavy fur riffling in the wind.

I come up to him
and stare at the narrow-spaced, petty eyes,
the dismayed
face laid back on the shoulder, the nostrils
flared, catching
perhaps the first taint of me as he
died.

I hack
a ravine in his thigh, and eat and drink,
and tear him down his whole length
and open him and climb in
and close him up after me, against the wind,
and sleep.

5
And dream
of lumbering flatfooted
over the tundra,
stabbed twice from within,
splattering a trail behind me,
splattering it out no matter which way I lurch,
no matter which parabola of bear-transcendence,
which dance of solitude I attempt,
which gravity-clutched leap,
which trudge, which groan.

6
Until one day I totter and fall—
fall on this
stomach that has tried so hard to keep up,
to digest the blood as it leaked in,

to break up
and digest the bone itself: and now the breeze
blows over me, blows off
the hideous belches of ill-digested bear blood
and rotted stomach
and the ordinary, wretched odor of bear,

blows across
my sore, lolled tongue a song
or screech, until I think I must rise up
and dance. And I lie still.

7
I awaken I think. Marshlights
reappear, geese
come trailing again up the flyway.
In her ravine under old snow the dam-bear
lies, licking
lumps of smeared fur
and drizzly eyes into shapes
with her tongue. And one
hairy-soled trudge stuck out before me,
the next groaned out,
the next,
the next,
the rest of my days I spend
wandering: wondering
what, anyway,
was that sticky infusion, that rank flavor of blood, that
    poetry, by which I lived?

from THE BOOK OF NIGHTMARES

I. UNDER THE MAUD MOON

1
On the path,
by this wet site
of old fires—

black ashes, black stones, where tramps
must have squatted down,
gnawing on stream water,
unhouseling themselves on cursed bread,
failing to get warm at a twigfire—

I stop,
gather wet wood,
cut dry shavings, and for her,
whose face
I held in my hands
a few hours, whom I gave back
only to keep holding the space where she was,

I light
a small fire in the rain.

The black
wood reddens, the deathwatches inside
begin running out of time, I can see
the dead, crossed limbs
longing again for the universe, I can hear
in the wet wood the snap
and re-snap of the same embrace being torn.

The raindrops trying
to put the fire out
fall into it and are
changed: the oath broken,
the oath sworn between earth and water, flesh and spirit, broken,
to be sworn again,
over and over, in the clouds, and to be broken again,
over and over, on earth.

2
I sit a moment
by the fire, in the rain, speak
a few words into its warmth—
stone saint smooth stone—and sing
one of the songs I used to croak
for my daughter, in her nightmares.

Somewhere out ahead of me
a black bear sits alone
on his hillside, nodding from side
to side. He sniffs
the blossom-smells, the rained earth,
finally he gets up,
eats a few flowers, trudges away,
his fur glistening
in the rain.

The singed grease streams
out of the words, the one
held note
remains—a love-note
twisting under my tongue, like the coyote's bark,
curving off, into a
howl.

3
A round-
cheeked girlchild comes awake
in her crib. The green
swaddlings tear open,
a filament or vestment
tears, the blue
flower opens.

And she who is born,
she who sings and cries,
she who begins the passage, her hair
sprouting out,
her gums budding for her first spring on earth,
the mist still clinging about
her face, puts
her hand
into her father's mouth, to take hold of
his song.

4
It is all over,
little one, the flipping
and overleaping, the watery

somersaulting alone in the oneness
under the hill, under
the old, lonely bellybutton
pushing forth again
in remembrance,
the drifting there furled in the dark,
pressing a knee or elbow
along a slippery wall, sculpting
the world with each thrash—the stream
of omphalos blood humming all about you.

5
Her head
enters the headhold
which starts sucking her forth: being itself
closes down all over her, gives her
into the shuddering
grip of departure, the slow,
agonized clenches making
the last molds of her life in the dark.

6
The black eye
opens, the pupil
droozed with black hairs
stops, the chakra
on top of the brain throbs a long moment in world light,

and she skids out on her face into light,
this peck
of stunned flesh
clotted with celestial cheesiness, glowing
with the astral violet
of the underlife. And as they cut

her tie to the darkness
she dies
a moment, turns blue as a coal,
the limbs shaking
as the memories rush out of them. When

they hang her up
by the feet, she sucks
air, screams
her first song—and turns rose,
the slow,
beating, featherless arms
already clutching at the emptiness.

7
When it was cold
on our hillside, and you cried
in the crib rocking
through the darkness, on wood
knifed down to the curve of the smile, a sadness
stranger than ours, all of it
flowing from the other world,

I used to come to you
and sit by you
and sing to you. You did not know,
and yet you will remember,
in the silent zones
of the brain, a specter, descendant
of the ghostly forefathers, singing
to you in the nighttime—
not the songs
of light said to wave
through the bright hair of angels,
but a blacker
rasping flowering on that tongue.

For when the Maud moon
glimmered in those first nights,
and the Archer lay
sucking the icy biestings of the cosmos,
in his crib of stars,

I had crept down
to riverbanks, their long rustle
of being and perishing, down to marshes
where the earth oozes up
in cold streaks, touching the world

with the underglimmer
of the beginning,
and there learned my only song.

And in the days
when you find yourself orphaned,
emptied
of all wind-singing, of light,
the pieces of cursed bread on your tongue,

may there come back to you
a voice,
spectral, calling you
sister!
from everything that dies.

And then
you shall open
this book, even if it is the book of nightmares.

II. THE HEN FLOWER

1
Sprawled
on our faces in the spring
nights, teeth
biting down on hen feathers, bits of the hen
still stuck in the crevices—if only
we could let go
like her, throw ourselves
on the mercy of darkness, like the hen,

tuck our head
under a wing, hold ourselves still
a few moments, as she
falls out into her little trance in the witchgrass,
or turn over
and be stroked with a finger
down the throat feathers,
down the throat knuckles,

down over the hum
of the wishbone tuning its high D in thin blood,
down over
the breastbone risen up
out of breast flesh, until the fatted thing
woozes off, head
thrown back
on the chopping block, longing only
to die.

2
When the ax-
scented breeze flourishes
about her, her cheeks crush in,
her comb
grays, the gizzard
that turns the thousand acidic millstones of her fate
convulses: ready or not
the next egg, bobbling
its globe of golden earth,
skids forth, ridding her even
of the life to come.

3
Almost high
on subsided gravity, I remain afoot,
a hen flower
dangling from a hand,
wing
of my wing,
of my bones and veins,
of my flesh
hairs lifting all over me in the first ghostly breeze
after death,

wing
made only to fly—unable
to write out the sorrows of being unable
to hold another in one's arms—and unable
to fly,
and waiting, therefore,
for the sweet, eventual blaze in the genes,

that one day, according to gospel, shall carry it back
into pink skies, where geese
cross at twilight, honking
in tongues.

4

I have glimpsed
by corpse-light, in the opened cadaver
of hen, the mass of tiny,
unborn eggs, each getting
tinier and yellower as it reaches back toward
the icy pulp
of what is, I have felt the zero
freeze itself around the finger dipped slowly in.

5

When the Northern Lights
were opening across the black sky and vanishing,
lighting themselves up
so completely they were vanishing,
I put to my eye the lucent
section of the spealbone of a ram—

I thought suddenly
I could read the cosmos spelling itself,
the huge broken letters
shuddering across the black sky and vanishing,

and in a moment,
in the twinkling of an eye, it came to me
the mockingbird would sing all her nights the cry of the rifle,
the tree would hold the bones of the sniper who chose not to
    climb down,
the rose would bloom no one would see it,
the chameleon longing to be changed would remain the color
    of blood.

And I went up
to the henhouse, and took up
the hen killed by weasels, and lugged
the sucked
carcass into first light. And when I hoisted

her up among the young pines, a last
rubbery egg slipping out as I flung her high, didn't it happen
the dead
wings creaked open as she soared
across the arms of the Bear?

6
Sprawled face down, waiting
for the rooster to groan out
it is the empty morning, as he groaned out thrice
for the disciple
of stone,
he who crushed with his heel the brain out of the snake,

I remember long ago I sowed
my own first milk
tooth under hen feathers, I planted under hen feathers
the hook
of the wishbone,
which had broken itself so lovingly toward me.

For the future.

It has come to this.

7
Listen, Kinnell,
dumped alive
and dying into the old sway bed,
a layer of crushed feathers all that there is
between you
and the long shaft of darkness shaped as you,
let go.

Even this haunted room
all its materials photographed with tragedy,
even the tiny crucifix drifting face down at the center of the earth,
even these feathers freed from their wings forever
are afraid.

IX. THE PATH AMONG THE STONES

1

On the path winding
upward, toward the high valley
of·waterfalls and flooded, hoof-shattered
meadows of spring,
where fish-roots boil
in the last grails of light on the water,
and vipers pimpled with urges to fly
drape the black stones hissing *pheet! pheet!*—land
of quills
and inkwells of skulls filled with black water—

I come to a field
glittering with the thousand sloughed skins
of arrowheads, stones
which shuddered and leapt forth
to give themselves into the broken hearts
of the living,
who gave themselves back, broken, to the stone.

2

I close my eyes:
on the heat-rippled beaches
where the hills came down to the sea,
the luminous
beach dust pounded out of funeral shells,
I can see
them living without me, dying
without me, the wing
and egg
shaped stones, broken
war-shells of slain fighting conches,
dog-eared immortality shells
in which huge constellations of slime, by the full moon,
writhed one more
coat of invisibility on a speck of sand,

and the agates knocked
from circles scratched into the dust

with the click
of a wishbone breaking, inward-swirling
globes biopsied out of sunsets never to open again,

and that wafer-stone
which skipped ten times across
the water, suddenly starting to run as it went under,
and the zeroes it left,
that met
and passed into each other, they themselves
smoothing themselves from the water . . .

3
I walk out from myself,
among the stones of the field,
each sending up its ghost-bloom
into the starlight, to float out
over the trees, seeking to be one
with the unearthly fires kindling and dying

in space—and falling back, knowing
the sadness of the wish
to alight
back among the glitter of bruised ground,
the stones holding between pasture and field,
the great, granite nuclei,
glimmering, even they, with ancient inklings of madness and war.

4
A way opens
at my feet. I go down
the night-lighted mule-steps into the earth,
the footprints behind me
filling already with pre-sacrificial trills
of canaries, go down
into the unbreatheable goaf
of everything I ever craved and lost.

An old man, a stone
lamp at his forehead, squats
by his hell-flames, stirs into
his pot

chopped head
of crow, strings of white light,
opened tail of peacock, dressed
body of canary, robin breast
dragged through the mud of battlefields, wrung-out
blossom of caput mortuum flower—salts
it all down with sand
stolen from the upper bells of hourglasses . . .

Nothing.
Always nothing. Ordinary blood
boiling away in the glare of the brow lamp.

5
And yet, no,
perhaps not nothing. Perhaps
not ever nothing. In clothes
woven out of the blue spittle
of snakes, I crawl up: I find myself alive
in the whorled
archway of the fingerprint of all things,
skeleton groaning,
blood-strings wailing the wail of all things.

6
The witness trees heal
their scars at the flesh fire,
the flame
rises off the bones,
the hunger
to be new lifts off
my soul, an eerie blue light blooms
on all the ridges of the world. Somewhere
in the legends of blood sacrifice
the fatted calf
takes the bonfire into his arms, and *he*
burns *it*.

7
As above: the last scattered stars
kneel down in the star-form of the Aquarian age:
a splash

on the top of the head,
on the grass of this earth even the stars love, splashes of the
    sacred waters . . .

So below: in the graveyard
the lamps start lighting up, one for each of us,
in all the windows
of stone.

X. LASTNESS

1
The skinny waterfalls, footpaths
wandering out of heaven, strike
the cliffside, leap, and shudder off.

Somewhere behind me
a small fire goes on flaring in the rain, in the desolate ashes.
No matter, now, whom it was built for,
it keeps its flames,
it warms
everyone who might wander into its radiance,
a tree, a lost animal, the stones,

because in the dying world it was set burning.

2
A black bear sits alone
in the twilight, nodding from side
to side, turning slowly around and around
on himself, scuffing the four-footed
circle into the earth. He sniffs the sweat
in the breeze, he understands
a creature, a death-creature
watches from the fringe of the trees,
finally he understands
I am no longer here, he himself
from the fringe of the trees watches

a black bear
get up, eat a few flowers, trudge away,
all his fur glistening
in the rain.

And what glistening! Sancho Fergus,
my boychild, had such great shoulders,
when he was born his head
came out, the rest of him stuck. And he opened
his eyes: his head out there all alone
in the room, he squinted with pained,
barely unglued eyes at the ninth-month's
blood splashing beneath him
on the floor. And almost
smiled, I thought, almost forgave it all in advance.

When he came wholly forth
I took him up in my hands and bent
over and smelled
the black, glistening fur
of his head, as empty space
must have bent
over the newborn planet
and smelled the grasslands and the ferns.

3
Walking toward the cliff, I call out
to the stone,
and the stone
calls back, its voice hunting among the rubble
for my ears.

Stop.
As you approach an echoing
cliffside, you sense the line
where the voice calling from stone
no longer answers,
turns into stone, and nothing comes back.

Here, between answer
and nothing, I stand, in the old shoes
flowed over by rainbows of hen-oil,

each shoe holding the bones
which ripple together in the communion
of the step,
and which open out
in front into toes, the whole foot trying
to dissolve into the future.

A clatter of elk hooves.
Has the top sphere
emptied itself? Is it true
the earth is all there is, and the earth does not last?

On the river the world floats by holding one corpse.

Stop.
Stop here.
Living brings you to death, there is no other road.

4
This is the tenth poem
and it is the last. It is right
at the last, that one
and zero
walk off together,
walk off the end of these pages together,
one creature
walking away side by side with the emptiness.

Lastness
is brightness. It is the brightness
gathered up of all that went before. It lasts.
And when it does end
there is nothing, nothing
left,

in the rust of old cars,
in the hole torn open in the body of the Archer,
in river-mist smelling of the weariness of stones,
the dead lie,
empty, filled, at the beginning,

and the first
voice comes craving again out of their mouths.

5

That Bach concert I went to so long ago—
the chandeliered room
of ladies and gentlemen who would never die . . .
the voices go out,
the room becomes hushed,
the violinist
puts the irreversible sorrow of his face
into the opened palm
of the wood, the music begins:

a shower of rosin,
the bow-hairs listening down all their length
to the wail,
the sexual wail
of the back-alleys and blood strings we have lived
still crying,
still singing, from the sliced intestine
of cat.

6

This poem
if we shall call it that,
or concert of one
divided among himself,
this earthward gesture
of the sky-diver, the worms
on his back still spinning forth
and already gnawing away
the silks of his loves, who could have saved him,
this free floating of one
opening his arms into the attitude
of flight, as he obeys the necessity and falls . . .

7

Sancho Fergus! Don't cry!

Or else, cry.

On the body,
on the blued flesh, when it is
laid out, see if you can find
the one flea which is laughing.

from THE POETICS OF THE PHYSICAL WORLD

At the end of *A Season in Hell*, where Rimbaud reaches autumn where his boat turns toward the port of misery, where he surrenders his supernatural claims and knows he has only rough reality to embrace, he says, "It is necessary to be absolutely modern."

How different this is from Ezra Pound's phrase, "Make it new," which suggests that the poem is a technical problem, located outside of us, and subject to decisions of the will. I distrust discussions of poetry which are heavily technical; the source of the poem, and all its worth, lie in what one knows and feels. Yet to approach what it might mean to be "absolutely modern," I would like to touch for a moment on what seems a technical matter, the uses of outward form in English poetry—rhyme, meter, and stanza.

Through the seventeenth century, rhyme and meter act as means of imitating the supernatural harmony; the regular beat, the fore-known ringing of the rhymes, seem to echo a celestial music. In the eighteenth century, when English poetry becomes very worldly, these forms imitate the natural order; outward form is a test of objective truth—for example, if a statement can't be rhymed it can't be true. With the Romantics and the Victorians, when the faith in spiritual beauty and in natural order both crumble, rhyme and meter assume a far more energetic function, which is to call back, in poetry, the grace disappearing from everything else. The poem is erected against chaos. The more disorderly reality appears, the stricter the iambs become, the more grasping the rhymes. It is thought a beautiful achievement, a kind of rescue, to reduce the rhythms of human speech to the iambic foot. So poetry also undertakes the conquest of nature. No nineteenth century poem written in fixed form, unless perhaps something by Clare or Hopkins or Melville, fails to give off the aroma of this nostalgia.

For modern poets—for everyone after Yeats—rhyme and meter amount to little more than mechanical aids for writing. It is probably less difficult to write in rhyme and meter than it is to write without them; or at least, these elements drastically change the nature of the difficulty. In rhyme and meter one has to be concerned with how to say something, perhaps *anything*, which fulfills the formal requirements. It is hard to move into the open that way. If you were walking through the woods in winter, rhyming would be like following those footprints continually appearing ahead of you in the snow. Fixed form tends to bring you to a place where someone has been before. Naturally, in a poem, you wish to reach a new place. That requires pure wandering—that rare condition, when you have no external guides at all, only your impulse to go, or to turn, or to stand still, when each line does not, by the sound of the word on which it ends, force the direction of the next line, when the voice does not subjugate speech, but tries only to conform to the irregular curves of reality, to the rough terrain itself. Robert Frost said writing free verse was like playing tennis with the net down. It is an apt analogy, except that the poem is not like a game, but more resembles a battle or a journey, where there are so many obstacles in the nature of the case that it would be a kind of evasion to invent additional, purely arbitrary ones.

The first poet in English to discard form—to be modern in this sense—is Walt Whitman. There is often a deep anti-intellectualism, a lack of balance and reasonableness, even a certain stupidity, in American writers. What normal person would have thought it possible to write a great book of the soul on the search to kill a white whale? Or who with any sense would have supposed to describe a few months spent in a cabin in the woods could produce a masterpiece of the spirit? I once witnessed in Paris a meeting between William Faulkner and French intellectuals. The meeting was a failure, because whenever anyone turned to Faulkner to ask his opinion on a weighty matter, he would reply, "Oh, I'm not a literary man, I'm just a farmer."

Had Whitman been more clever, conceivably he could have turned out to be as good a poet as Whittier or Longfellow. He was too awkward, too unschooled, too mad. His attempts to write formal poetry failed miserably. And so he gave up the attempt to be a poet like the others and followed his crazy intimations of a poetry which could not be contained in regular form. Halfway through his life he broke free and discovered the absolutely new. Of course, the universities suppressed his discovery for a hundred years, always preferring lesser poets, including, in our time, Ezra Pound and T. S. Eliot, whose work is so much better suited to classrooms. When I was in college I was taught that Whitman was just a compulsive blabber and a nut. . . .

Simone Weil writes: "Keep away from beliefs which fill the emptiness, which sweeten the bitterness. Avoid the belief in immortality, and the belief in the usefulness of sin, and the belief in the guiding hand of Providence." "For," she goes on, "love is not consolation, it is light." And this is also true for poetry. The poetics of heaven agrees to the denigration of pain and death; the poetics of the physical world builds on these stones.

Consider Emily Dickinson's poem on the fly.

I heard a Fly buzz—when I died—
The stillness in the Room
Was like the Stillness in the Air—
Between the Heaves of Storm—

The Eyes around—had wrung them dry—
And Breaths were gathering firm
For that last Onset—when the King
Be witnessed—in the Room—

I willed my Keepsakes—Signed away
What portion of me be
Assignable—and then it was
There interposed a Fly—

With blue-uncertain stumbling Buzz—
Between the light—and me—
And then the Windows failed—and then
I could not see to see—

Those sitting by the bedside awaiting the death have almost become abstractions, solemn, hushed figures prefiguring the beings of the life to come. Into this scene appears a fly—its "blue, uncertain stumbling buzz" the only physical image in the poem—a fly, that creature which disdains the spirit and hungers only for flesh. Of course, it is repulsive that a fly come to you, if you are dying and if it may be a corpse fly, its thorax the hysterical green color of slime. And yet in the illumination of the dying moment, everything the poet knew on earth is transfigured. The fly appears, alive, physical, voracious, a last sign of the earthly life. It is the most ordinary thing, the most despised, which brings the strange brightening, this last moment of increased life. . . .

Theology and philosophy, with their large words, their abstract formulations, their airtight systems which they hope will last forever, deal with eternity. The subject of the poem is the thing which dies. Zeus on Olympus is a theological being; the swan who desires a woman enters the province of poetry. In "*Eloi, Eloi, lama sabacthani,*" so does Jesus. Poetry is the wasted breath. This is why it clings to the imperfect music of a human voice, this is why its verbs are so imitative of bodily motions, why its prepositions pile up like crazed longings, why its nouns reverberate from the past as if they spoke for archetypes of earthly life, this is why the poem depends on adjectives, as if they were its senses, which want only to smell, touch, see, hear, taste, to press themselves to the physical world.

It is part of whatever may be glowing in our lives that we have been able to dream of paradise, that we have glimpsed eternity. It is as much a part of this glory that we are unable to enter paradise or live in eternity. That we endure only for a time, that everyone and everything around us endures only for a time, that we know this, is the thrilling element in every creature, every relationship, every moment.

> The earth is all that lives
> And the earth shall not last.
> We sit on a hillside, by the Greasy Grass,
> And our little shadow lies out in the blades of
>   grass, until sunset.

GALWAY KINNELL

ETHERIDGE KNIGHT

Etheridge Knight was born in 1933 in Corinth, Mississippi. Before finishing high school, he was sent to fight in Korea, where he was badly wounded. In 1960 he was convicted of armed robbery and spent the next six years in Indiana State Prison. Of these experiences he writes, "I died in Korea from a shrapnel wound and narcotics resurrected me. I died in 1960 from a prison sentence and poetry brought me back to life." His published books include *Poems from Prison* and *Belly Song*. *Poems from Prison* has been translated into Italian and published in Italy. The poet is also the editor of an anthology, *Black Voices from Prison,* and is currently working on a novel about the slave revolt led by Denmark Vesey. In 1974 he received a Guggenheim Fellowship.

McGuire Studio

THE IDEA OF ANCESTRY

1

Taped to the wall of my cell are 47 pictures: 47 black
faces: my father, mother, grandmothers (1 dead), grand-
fathers (both dead), brothers, sisters, uncles, aunts,
cousins (1st & 2nd), nieces, and nephews. They stare
across the space at me sprawling on my bunk. I know
their dark eyes, they know mine. I know their style,
they know mine. I am all of them, they are all of me;
they are farmers, I am a thief, I am me, they are thee.

I have at one time or another been in love with my mother,
1 grandmother, 2 sisters, 2 aunts (1 went to the asylum),
and 5 cousins. I am now in love with a 7 yr old niece
(she sends me letters written in large block print, and
her picture is the only one that smiles at me).

I have the same name as 1 grandfather, 3 cousins, 3 nephews,
and 1 uncle. The uncle disappeared when he was 15, just took
off and caught a freight (they say). He's discussed each year
when the family has a reunion, he causes uneasiness in
the clan, he is an empty space. My father's mother, who is 93
and who keeps the Family Bible with everybody's birth dates
(and death dates) in it, always mentions him. There is no
place in her Bible for "whereabouts unknown."

2

Each Fall the graves of my grandfathers call me, the brown
hills and red gullies of mississippi send out their electric
messages, galvanizing my genes. Last yr/like a salmon quitting
the cold ocean—leaping and bucking up his birthstream/I
hitchhiked my way from L.A. with 16 caps in my pocket and a
monkey on my back. and I almost kicked it with the kinfolks.
I walked barefooted in my grandmother's backyard/I smelled the
old
land and the woods/I sipped cornwhiskey from fruit jars with the
men/

I flirted with the women/I had a ball till the caps ran out
and my habit came down. That night I looked at my grandmother
and split/my guts were screaming for junk/but I was almost
contented/I had almost caught up with me.
(The next day in Memphis I cracked a croaker's crib for a fix.)

This yr there is a gray stone wall damming my stream, and when
the falling leaves stir my genes, I pace my cell or flop on my bunk
and stare at 47 black faces across the space. I am all of them,
they are all of me; I am me, they are thee, and I have no sons
to float in the space between.

CELL SONG

Night   Music   Slanted
Light strike the cave
of sleep.   I alone
tread the red circle
and twist the space
with speech.

Come now, etheridge, don't
be a savior; take
your words and scrape
the sky, shake rain

on the desert, sprinkle
salt on the tail
of a girl,

can there anything
good come out of
prison

HARD ROCK RETURNS TO PRISON FROM
THE HOSPITAL FOR THE CRIMINAL INSANE

Hard Rock was "known not to take no shit
From nobody," and he had the scars to prove it:
Split purple lips, lumped ears, welts above
His yellow eyes, and one long scar that cut
Across his temple and plowed through a thick
Canopy of kinky hair.

The WORD was that Hard Rock wasn't a mean nigger
Anymore, that the doctors had bored a hole in his head,
Cut out part of his brain, and shot electricity
Through the rest. When they brought Hard Rock back,
Handcuffed and chained, he was turned loose,
Like a freshly gelded stallion, to try his new status.
And we all waited and watched, like indians at a corral,
To see if the WORD was true.

As we waited we wrapped ourselves in the cloak
Of his exploits: "Man, the last time, it took eight
Screws to put him in the Hole." "Yeah, remember when he
Smacked the captain with his dinner tray?" "He set
The record for time in the Hole—67 straight days!"
"Ol Hard Rock! man, that's one crazy nigger."
And then the jewel of a myth that Hard Rock had once bit
A screw on the thumb and poisoned him with syphilitic spit.

The testing came, to see if Hard Rock was really tame.
A hillbilly called him a black son of a bitch
And didn't lose his teeth, a screw who knew Hard Rock
From before shook him down and barked in his face.
And Hard Rock did *nothing*. Just grinned and looked silly,
His eyes empty like knot holes in a fence.

And even after we discovered that it took Hard Rock
Exactly 3 minutes to tell you his first name,
We told ourselves that he had just wised up,
Was being cool; but we could not fool ourselves for long,
And we turned away, our eyes on the ground. Crushed.
He had been our Destroyer, the doer of things

ETHERIDGE KNIGHT 141

We dreamed of doing but could not bring ourselves to do,
The fears of years, like a biting whip,
Had cut grooves too deeply across our backs.

HE SEES THROUGH STONE

He sees through stone
he has the secret
eyes this old black one
who under prison skies
sits pressed by the sun
against the western wall
his pipe between purple gums

the years fall
like overripe plums
bursting red flesh
on the dark earth

his time is not my time
but I have known him
in a time gone

he led me trembling cold
into the dark forest
taught me the secret rites
to take a woman
to be true to my brothers
to make my spear drink
the blood
of my enemies

now black cats circle him
flash white teeth
snarl at the air
mashing green grass beneath
shining muscles
ears peeling his words

he smiles
he knows
the hunt   the enemy
he has the secret eyes
he sees through stone

2 POEMS FOR BLACK RELOCATION CENTERS

1

Flukum couldn't stand the strain. Flukum
wanted inner and outer order, so
he joined the army where U.S. Manuals made
everything plain—even how to button his shirt,
and how to kill the yellow men. (If Flukum
ever felt hurt or doubt about who his enemy
was, the Troop Information Officer or the Stars
and Stripes straightened him out.)
Plus, we must not forget
that Flukum was paid well to let the Red
Blood. And sin? If Flukum ever thought about sin
or Hell for squashing the yellow men, the good Chaplain
(Holy by God and by Congress) pointed out with
Devilish skill that to kill the colored men was not
altogether a sin.

Flukum marched back from the war, straight and tall,
and with presents for all: a water pipe for daddy,
teeny tea cups for mama, sheer silk for tittee, and
a jade inlaid dagger for me. But, with a smile
on his face in a place just across the bay,
Flukum, the patriot, got shot that same day,
got shot in his great wide chest, bedecked with good
conduct ribbons. He died surprised, he had thought
the enemy far away on the other side of the sea.

(When we received his belongings they took away my dagger.)

2

Dead. He died in Detroit, his beard
was filled with lice; his halo glowed
and his white robe flowed magnificently
over the charred beams and splintered glass;
his stern blue eyes were rimmed with red,
and full of reproach; and the stench: roasted rats
and fat baby rumps swept up his nose that
had lost its arch of triumph. He died outraged,
and indecently, shouting impieties and betrayals.
And he arose out of his own ashes. Stripped.
A faggot in steel boots.

AS YOU LEAVE ME

Shiny record albums scattered over
the livingroom floor, reflecting light
from the lamp, sharp reflections that hurt
my eyes as I watch you, squatting among the platters,
the beer foam making mustaches on your lips.

And, too,
the shadows on your cheeks from your long lashes
fascinate me—almost as much as the dimples:
in your cheeks, your arms and your legs:
dimples . . . dimples . . . dimples . . .

You
hum along with Mathis—how you love Mathis!
with his burnished hair and quicksilver voice that dances
among the stars and whirls through canyons
like windblown snow. sometimes I think that Mathis
could take you from me if you could be complete
without me. I glance at my watch. it is now time.

You rise,
silently, and to the bedroom and the paint:
on the lips red, on the eyes black,
and I lean in the doorway and smoke, and see you

grow old before my eyes, and smoke. why do you
chatter while you dress, and smile when you grab
your large leather purse? don't you know that when you
leave me I walk to the window and watch you? and light
a reefer as I watch you? and I die as I watch you
disappear in the dark streets
to whistle and to smile at the johns.

ON WATCHING POLITICIANS PERFORM
AT MARTIN LUTHER KING'S FUNERAL

Hypocrites shed tears
like shiny snake skins

words rolling
thru the electric air

the scent of flowers
mingles with Jack Daniels
and Cutty Sark

the last
snake skin slithers
to the floor where
black baptist feet
have danced in ecstasy

they turn
away
to begin
again

manicured fingers shuffling
the same stacked deck
with the ante
raised

HUEY

Wel/come back, brother
from . .
the House of many Slams
to
these mean bricks

a poet
sung to me:
lets us
drink wine in the alley
and dance in the streets

everyday people
have found
a prince

bright-eyed
wonder-child

comes
Revolution.

UPON YOUR LEAVING

for Sonia

Night
and in the warm blackness
your woman smell filled the room
and our rivers flowed together. became one
my love's patterns. our sweat/drenched bellies
made flat cracks as we kissed
like sea waves lapping against the shore
rocks rising and rolling and sliding back.

And
your sighs softly calling my name
became love songs child/woman songs
old as a thousand years new as the few
smiles you released like sacred doves. and I
fell asleep, ashamed of my glow, of my halo, and
ignoring them who waited below
to take you away when the sun rose. . . .

Day
and the sunlight playing in the green leaves
above us fell across your face traced the tears
in your eyes and love patterns in the wet grass.
and as they waited inside in triumphant patience
to take you away I begged you to stay.
"but, etheridge," you said, "i don't know what to do."
and the love patterns shifted and shimmered in your eyes.

And
after they had taken you and gone, the day
turned stark white. bleak. barren like
the nordic landscape. I turned and entered
into the empty house and fell on the floor.
laughing. trying to fill the spaces your love had left.
knowing that we would not remain apart long.
our rivers had flowed together.
we are one.
and are strong.

FEELING FUCKED/UP

Lord she's gone done left me done packed/up and split
and i with no way to make her
come back and everywhere the world is bare
bright bone white   crystal sand glistens
dope death dead dying and jiving drove
her away made her take her laughter and her smiles
and her softness and her midnight sighs—

Fuck Coltrane and music and clouds drifting in the sky
fuck the sea and trees and the sky and birds
and alligators and all the animals that roam the earth
fuck marx and mao fuck fidel and nkrumah and
democracy and communism fuck smack and pot
and red ripe tomatoes fuck joseph fuck mary fuck
god jesus and all the disciples fuck fanon nixon
and malcolm fuck the revolution fuck freedom fuck
the whole muthafucking thing
all i want now is my woman back
so my soul can sing

MY LIFE, THE QUALITY
OF WHICH

My life, the quality of which
From the moment
My Father grunted and comed
Until now
As the sounds of my words
Bruise your ears
IS
And can be felt
In the one word: DESPERATION

But you have to feel for it

June 6, 1972

ANOTHER POEM FOR ME

(after recovering from an O.D.)

what now
what now dumb nigger damn near dead
what now

now that you won't dance
behind the pale white doors of death
what now   is   to be
to be what you wanna be
what you spozed to be
or what white/america wants you to be
a lame crawling from nickel bag to nickel bag
be black brother/man be black
and blooming in the night
be black like your fat brother
sweating and straining to hold you
as you struggle against the straps
be black   be black like
your woman   her pained face floating
above you   her hands sliding
                  under the sheets
to take yours   be black like
your mama sitting in a quiet corner
praying to a white/jesus to save her black boy

what now dumb nigger damn near dead
where is the correctness
the proper posture
the serious love of living
now that death has fled these quiet corridors

A POEM TO GALWAY KINNELL

Sat., Apr. 26, 1973
Jefferson City, Mo. 65101
(500 yards, as the crow flies,
from where i am writing you
this letter, lies the Missouri
State Prison—it lies, the prison,
like an overfed bear alongside
the raging missouri river—
the pale prison, out of which,
sonny liston, with clenched fist,

fought his way, out of which,
james earl ray ripped his way
into the hearts of us all . . .)

dear galway,
    it is flooding here, in missouri,
the lowlands are all under water and at night
the lights dance on the dark water,
our president, of late of watergate,
is spozed to fly above the flooded areas
and estimate how much damage has been done
to THE PEOPLES. . . .

dear galway,
    it is lonely here, and sometimes,
THE PEOPLES can be a bitch

dear galway,
    i hear poems in my head
as the wind blows in your hair
and the young brown girl
with the toothpaste smile
who flows freely because she has heard OUR SOUNDS. . . .

dear galway,
    OUR SONGS OF LOVE are still
murmurs among these melodies of madness. . . .
dear galway, and what the fuck are the irish doing/
and when the IRA sends JUST ONE, just one soldier
to fight with say the American Indians, then i'll believe them. . . .

dear galway,
    the river is rising here, and i am
scared and lonely. . . . . .

Mary and the children send their love
to you and yours

                    always

            Imamu Etheridge Knight Soa

ANSWERS TO QUESTIONS ASKED AFTER A READING

More and more poetry is going to be what it used to be—a spoken thing. Poetry is an oral art. Also, I see black poets involved in other things than saying "Hey, white people, get off my back."

Our poetry will always speak mainly to black people, but I don't see it being as narrow in the 70s as it was in the 60s.

My poetry is also important to white people because it invokes feelings. . . The feelings are common, whether or not the situations that create the feelings are common. . . I might feel fear in a small town in Iowa. You might be afraid if you got off the subway in Harlem. It's the same fear, but the situations are different.

You have to be telling people essentially 'I love you' or you have no basis for your art.

I pay attention only to the people in the audience. If they don't dig it, then it ain't nothing no way.

ETHERIDGE KNIGHT

Thomas Victor

KENNETH KOCH

Kenneth Koch was born in Cincinnati in 1925 and educated at Harvard
and Columbia. He served in the Pacific as a rifleman and later lived in
France and Italy. His books include *Ko: or, A Season on Earth, Thank
You and Other Poems, Sleeping with Women,* and *The Pleasures of
Peace and Other Poems.* He has also written plays, several of which
have been produced off-Broadway, and *Wishes, Lies and Dreams,*
a book about teaching young children how to write poetry. He lives
in New York City.

A POEM OF THE FORTY-EIGHT STATES

1

O Kentucky! my parents were driving
Near blue grass when you became
For me the real contents of a glass
Of water also the first nozzle of a horse
The bakery truck floating down the street
The young baboon woman walking without a brace
Over a fiord

The electric chair steamed lightly, then touched
Me. I drove, upward,
Into the hills of Montana. My pony!
Here you are coming along with your master!
Yet I am your master! You're wearing my sweater.
O pony, my pony!

As in a dream I was waiting to be seventh
To smile at my brothers in the happy state of Idaho
Each and every one of them condemned to the electric
    chair!
What have we done? Is it a crime
To shoe horses? Beside a lemon-yellow stream
There seemed to be compact bassoons,
And I was happy and a crackerjack.

My stovepipe hat! Perhaps you think I am Uncle Sam?
No, I am the State of Pennsylvania. . . .
O hills! I remember writing to a city
So as to be contented with my name
Returning in the mails near the mark "Pennsylvania"!

"Somewhere over that hill is Georgia."
What romance there was for me in the words the old man
    said!
I wanted to go, but was afraid to wander very far.
Then he said, "I will take you in my wagon of hay."
And so we rode together into the Peach State.
I will never forget that day, not so long as I live,
I will never forget the first impressions I had in Georgia!

2

In Zanesville, Ohio, they put a pennant up,
And in Waco, Texas, men stamped in the streets,
And the soldiers were coughing on the streetcar in Min-
    neapolis, Minnesota.
In Minocqua, Wisconsin, the girls kissed each other and
    laughed,
The poison was working in Monroe, Illinois,
And in Stephanie, New Hampshire, burning fragments
    were thrown up.

It was the day of the States, and from Topeka, Kansas,
To Lumberville, New York, trees were being struck
Down so they could put the platforms up. However I lay
    struck
By sunlight on the beach at Waikiki, Hawaii . . .
Why can't Hawaii be one of the United States?
Nothing is being celebrated here; yet the beaches are
    covered with sun . . .

Florida, Vermont, Alabama, Mississippi!
I guess that I will go back to the United States.
Dear friend, let's pack our bags and climb upon the
    steamer!
Do not forget the birds you have bought in the jolly land
    of France,
They are red white orange yellow green and pink and
    they sing so sweetly,
They will make music to us upon the tedious ocean
    voyage.

3

Tedious! How could I have said such a thing?
O sea, you are more beautiful than any state!
You are fuller and bluer and more perfect than the most
    perfect action.
What is a perfect action?
In the streets of Kokomo a cheer goes up,
And the head of the lion is cursed by a thousand
    vicissitudes.

Indiana! it is so beautiful to have tar in it!
How wonderful it is to be back on a trolley car, ding dong
    ding!
I think I will wander into the barbershop and get my hair
    cut!
Just hear the slice of the scissors, look at the comb!
Now to be once more out in the streets of Indiana
With my hair much shorter, with my neck smelling of
    talcum powder!
O lucky streetcar wires to be able to look at me, and
    through whom I can see the sun!

I did not know there was so much sun in North Dakota!
But the old man who is telling me about it nods his head
    and says yes.
I believe him because my skin is peeling. Now I see
    people going to the voting booth.
The voting wagon is red and wooden, it stands on wheels
    where it is anchored to the curb.
I had no idea there were so many old men and old women
    in North Dakota,
But the old man who is explaining things to me says that
    each is above voting age.

4
I cannot remember what all I saw
In northern Florida, all the duck we shot.

You have asked me to recall Illinois,
But all I have is a handful of wrinkles.

Perhaps you would like me to speak of California,
But I hope not, for now I am very close to death.

The children all came down to see the whale in Arkansas,
I remember that its huge body lay attached to the side of
    the river.

5
O Mississippi joys!
I reckon I am about as big and dead as a whale!
I am slowly sinking down into the green ooze
Of the Everglades, that I feared so much when I was a
    child!

I have become about as flat as the dust on a baseball
    diamond
And as empty and clear as the sky when it is just-blue
And you are three, and you stand on the rim of the zone
    of one of the United States
And think about the forty-seven others; then in the
    evening
Air you hear the sound of baseball players, and the splash
    of canoes!
You yourself would like to play baseball and travel, but
    you are too young;
However you look up into the clear flat blue of the
    evening sky
And vow that you will one day be a traveler like myself,
And wander to all the ends of the earth until you are
    completely exhausted,
And then return to Texas or Indiana, whatever state you
    happen to be from.
And have your death celebrated by a lavish funeral
Conducted by starlight, with numerous boys and girls
    reading my poems aloud!

6

O Charleston! why do you always put me in the mood for
    kidding?
I am not dead yet, why do you make me say I am?
But I think I am growing older, my shoes are falling off,
I think it must be that my feet are getting thinner and
    that I am ready to die.
Here comes my pony from Montana, he is a mere skull
    and crossbones,
And here is the old man who told me about North Dakota,
    he is a little baby,
And here is Illinois, and here is Indiana, I guess they are
    my favorite states,
I guess I am dying now in Charleston, South Carolina.
O Charleston, why do you always do this . . . Gasp!
    Goodbye!

7

In Illinois the trees are growing up
Where he planted them; for he has died.

But I am the one who originally intended to read
You the fast movements. Now we will hear the *Branden-
    burg*
Concertos. Now we will go up in an
Airplane. Steady . . . The poet of America, Walt Whitman,
    is dead.
But many other poets have died that are reborn
In their works. He also shall be reborn,
Walt Whitman shall be reborn.

8
I did not understand what you meant by the Hudson
    Tunnel,
But now I understand, New Jersey, I like it fine,
I like the stifling black smoke and the jagged heave-ho of
    the trains,
I like the sunlight too at the end of the tunnel, like my
    rebirth in the poems of Kenneth Koch,
I like the way the rosy sunlight streams down upon the
    silver tracks,
I like the way the travelers awake from their dreams and
    step upon the hard paving stone of the station,
But I reckon what I should like best would be to see
    Indiana again,
Or Texas or Arkansas, or Alabama, the "Cotton State,"
Or Big Rose Pebble Island off the coast of Maine
Where I used to have so much fun during the summer,
    cooking and kidding and having myself a good time,
I like Pennsylvania too, we could have a lot of fun there,
You and I will go there when Kenneth is dead.

YOU WERE WEARING

You were wearing your Edgar Allan Poe printed cotton blouse.
In each divided up square of the blouse was a picture of Edgar Allan
    Poe.
Your hair was blonde and you were cute. You asked me, "Do most
    boys think that most girls are bad?"
I smelled the mould of your seaside resort hotel bedroom on your
    hair held in place by a John Greenleaf Whittier clip.

"No," I said, "it's girls who think that boys are bad." Then we read
    Snowbound together
And ran around in an attic, so that a little of the blue enamel was
    scraped off my George Washington, Father of His Country, shoes.

Mother was walking in the living room, her Strauss Waltzes comb in
    her hair.
We waited for a time and then joined her, only to be served tea in
    cups painted with pictures of Herman Melville
As well as with illustrations from his book *Moby Dick* and from his
    novella, *Benito Cereno*.
Father came in wearing his Dick Tracy necktie: "How about a drink,
    everyone?"
I said, "Let's go outside a while." Then we went onto the porch and
    sat on the Abraham Lincoln swing.
You sat on the eyes, mouth, and beard part, and I sat on the knees.
In the yard across the street we saw a snowman holding a garbage can
    lid smashed into a likeness of the mad English king, George the
    Third.

from THE ART OF LOVE

"What do you know about it?"

1
To win the love of women one should first discover
What sort of thing is likely to move them, what feelings
They are most delighted with their lives to have; then
One should find these things and cause these feelings. Now
A story illustrates: of course the difficulty,
Is how to talk about winning the love
Of women and not also speak of loving—a new
Problem? an old problem? Whatever—it is a something
    secret
To no one who has finally experienced it. Presbyopic. And
    so,
Little parks in Paris, procede, pronounce
On these contributing factors to the "mental psyche
Of an airplane." Renumerate
The forces which gloss our tongues! And then, Betty,

The youngest rabbit, ran, startled, out into the driveway,
Fear that Terry will run over her now calmed. Back
To the Alps, back to the love of women, the sunset
Over "four evenly distributed band lots in
Which you held my hand," mysterious companion
With opal eyes and oval face without whom I
Could never have sustained the Frogonian evening
Wait a minute! if this is to be a manual of love, isn't it
Just about time we began—with something more practical
Than mere esthetics? "Mere?" Er, well, yes. Begin.

Tie your girl's hands behind her back and encourage her
To attempt to get loose. This will make her breasts look
Especially pretty, like the Parthenon at night. Sometimes
    those illuminations
Are very beautiful, though sometimes the words
Are too expected, too French, too banal. Ain't youse a
    cracker,
Though? And other poems. Or Freemasonry Revisited.
    Anyway,
Tie her up. In this fashion, she will be like Minnie Mouse,
    will look
Like starlight over the sensuous Aegean. She will be the
    greatest thing you ever saw.
However, a word of advice, for cold September evenings,
And in spring, summer, winter too, and later in the fall:
Be sure she likes it. Or only at first dislikes it a little bit.
    Otherwise
You are liable to lose your chances for other kinds of
    experiments,
Like the Theseion, for example. Or the two-part song.
    Yes! this
Is Athens, king of the cities, and land of the
Countries of the Fall. Where atoma means person, and
    where was
A lovely epoch once though we however must go on
With contemporary problems in ecstasy. Let's see. Your
Girl's now a little tied up. Her hands stretched behind her
    at
An angle of about 40 degrees to her back, no, say, seventeen
And Z . . . . . . sending his first roses at seventeen (roses
    also work

As well as hand tying but in a different less fractured
Framework) and she receiving them writing "I have never
Received roses before from a man. Meet me at the fountain
At nine o'clock and I will do anything you want." He was
Panicky! and didn't know what to do. What had he wanted
That now seemed impossible? he didn't exactly know
How to do it. So he wrote to her that night amid the
    capitals
Of an arboring civilization, "Fanny I can't come. The maid
    is shocked. The
Butter factory is in an endzone of private feelings. So
The chocolate wasp stands on the Venetian steps. So
The cloudbursts are weeping, full of feeling
And stones, so the flying boats are loving and the tea
Is full of quotients. So—" That's enough cries Fanny she
    tears
It up then she reads it again. One breast may be somewhat
    higher
Than another with the hands tied behind. As Saint Ursula
    and her Virgins
Had the right attitude but were in the wrong field of fancy,
Not the sexual field, so these erogenous zones come
Forward when we need them if we are lucky and now I will
    speak
Of the various different virtues of rope, string, and chicken-
    wire—
If you want her to break loose suddenly in the middle
Of the lovemaking episode when you are inside her and
    cry yes
Yes throwing her arms and hands around you, then try
    string. Otherwise rope is most practical. As at Ravenna
The mosaics that start from the wall stay on the wall, in
The wall and they are the wall, in a sense, like the tracks in
    Ohio,
Pennsylvania, and Illinois. Rounding the bend you will see
    them.
They are hard to tell from the earth. She will kiss you then.

Thank you, parents of loving and passive girls, even a
    little bit masochistic ones
Who like the things this book is recommending. It is to
    you,

Although they do not know you often and
Even if they did might not consider this, men owe these
    joys.

To lack a woman, to not have one, and to be longing for
    one
As the grass grows around the Perrier family home
That is the worst thing in life, but nowhere near the best
    is to have one
And not know what to do. So we continue these instruc-
    tions.

The woman's feet may be tied as well as her hands. I'd
    suggest tying them
Or really the ankles, that's easier, to the legs at the foot of
    the bed
Or of the pool table if that is what you are making love
    upon. I
Remember a day in Paris when a man had a dancing bear
And I walked home to Freesia thinking about ape-mon-
    gering and death—Hold on a minute, there are
White blocks or cubes on the jetty of French poetic-
    political involvement
Which "Love does not Need a Home" will cannily play for
    you on the phonograph
If you are not AC/DC ruining a certain part of the equip-
    ment. Her smile
Will be glorious, a sunrise, her feet tied to the legs of the
    bed.
If her hands are free she can move up and down readily
    (the
Sit up/lie down movement, near the Boulevard Raspail
And in irregular patterns—for some reason certain details
Keep coming back to undermine their candidacies). What
    good this will be to you
I don't know, but her sitting up and then lying down will
    (again)
Make her breasts look pretty (Fountainebleau you are my
    ark,
And Issy you are my loom!) and give tensity to the throat
Muscles and the stomach muscles too! You can simply
    enjoy that

(The tensing in the abdomen) by putting, lightly, your
    fingers on it (the
Abdomen) as one voyages on a Sunday to the Flea Market
Not in the hope of really finding anything but of sensing a
    new light panorama of one's needs,
So much for the pleasure in tensing stomach muscles. Of
    course with the girl tied this way
You can hit her up and down if you like to do that
And she will never be able to get up and walk away
Since she can't walk without her feet, and they are tied to
    the bed.

If you combine tying her hands to the bed and her feet
You can jump on her! She will be all flattened and splayed
    out.
What a fine way to spend an autumn afternoon, or an
    April one!
So delicious, you jumping up and down, she lying there,
    helpless, enjoying your every gasp!
You may enter her body at this point of course as well
As the Postal Museum stands only a few meterage yards
    away.
They have a new stamp there now, of a king with his
    crown
On backwards, dark red, it is a mistake, and worth five
    million pounds!
You can come out and go there, away! Dear, stay with me!!
And she pleads with you there as she lies on the bed,
    attached to the bed
By the cords you have tied with your hands, and attached
    to you by her love
As well, since you are the man who attached her there,
Since you are the knowing lover using information
    gleaned from this volume.

Tying up, bouquets, bouqueting bunch-of-flowers effects.
    Tie her hands and legs
Together, I mean her hands and feet, I mean ankles. There
    are different processes.
Tie the left hand to the left ankle, right hand to right
    ankle.

Spread out in any position and make love. She will be
    capable of fewer movements
But may bring you a deep-sea joy. Crabs and lobsters
    must love like that
And they don't stay down at the bottom of the ocean for
    nothing—
It must be wonderful! In any case you can try it in your
    mistress's bed
Or in your own of course. You can tie left hand to right
    ankle
And so on. This gives a criss-cross effect
And is good after a quarrel. The breasts in all these cases
    look
Exceptionally beautiful. If you do not like liking
These breasts so much you may hit them
If she likes that, and ask her to ask you to hit them, which
Should increase your pleasure in mastery particularly if
    she is all tied up.
"Hit My Tits" could be a motto on the sailboat of your
    happiness. If you don't think
You have gotten your money's worth already
From this book you deserve to turn in an early grave
Surrounded by worm women who assail and hit you
Until there is nothing left of you so hard that they can't
    eat.
But I am sure this is not your feeling. So, having agreed,
Let us go on. You should buy another book
And give it to your best friend, however, if at this point
    you do agree with me.
I will wait, meanwhile we can both stare at your mistress,
    where she is all tied up.

Well, you can roll her like a wheel, though I doubt she'll
    approve of it,
Women rarely do, I knew one once, though, who did. For
This of course you use the right hand right ankle left
Hand left ankle arrangement, using splints on both sides of
    each
Knot so that the limbs will stay in wheel-position. Now
    that she
Looks like that which makes a chariot roll, roll her! If this
    hurts her,

Soothe her a little by kissing her all around, saying
"Ah, my lovely wheel, went over a bump, did it?" and so
    on,
Until she finally is resigned to being your wheel, your
    dear beloved one
And is eager to be rolled about by you. Small objects
    placed on the floor
Will give you brief twinges of sadistic energy and speed
    up your wheeling.
I suggest ending by wheeling her out an opened door
Which you then close and stab yourself to death. This
    procedure, however, is rare.
I was carried away. Forgive me. The next chapters will be
    much more sane.

Nailing a woman to the wall causes too much damage
(Not to the wall but to the woman—you after all want to
    enjoy her
And love her again and again). You can, however, wrap
    tape around her arms, waist, ankles, and knees
And nail this to the wall. You'll enjoy the pleasure of
    nailing
And the very thought of it should make her scream. You
    can fit this tape
On her like tabs, so your girl will be like a paper doll.
And you can try things on her once she is nailed up. You
    can also
Throw things at her, which is something I very much like
    to do—
Small rakes, postal scales, aluminum belt buckles, Venetian
    glass clowns—
As soon as you start to hurt her, you should stop
And kiss her bruises, make much of them, draw a circle
    around each hit
With a bold felt pen. In this way you can try to hit the
    same spots over and over again
As the little park grows larger the more you look at it
But the flowers are in another story, a lemon-covered
    volume, stop! The knees
Of this girl are now looking very pretty, so go and kiss
    them

And slip your hands around the back of them and feel
what is called
The inside of the knee and tell her you love her.
If she is able to talk she will probably ask you to take her
down,
Which you then can do. However, if she wants to stay up
there
As blue day changes to night, and is black in the hemi-
spheres, and boats go past
And you are still feeling wonderful because of her beautiful
eyes
And breasts and legs, leave her there and run up against her
As hard as you can, until the very force of your bumping
Breaks tape from nail or girl from tape or breaks great
chunks of wall
So you and she lie tumbled there together
Bruises on her body, plaster on your shoulders, she bloody,
she hysterical, but joy in both your hearts.
Then pull off the tape if it hasn't come off
And bite her to the bone. If she bites you back, appoint her
"Lover" for a while and let her do all this to you. That is,
If you'd like it. You'll suffer, of course, from being less
beautiful than she
And less soft, less inviting to cause pain to. To be a great
lover,
However, you must be a great actor, so try, at least once.

Oh the animals moving in the stockyards have no idea of
these joys
Nor do the birds flying high in the clouds. Think: tender-
ness cannot be all
Although everyone loves tenderness. Nor violence, which
gives the sense of life
With its dramas and its actions as it is. Making love must
be everything—
A city, not a street; a country, not a city; the universe, the
world—
Make yours so, make it even a galaxy, and be conscious
and unconscious of it all. That is the art of love.

FRESH AIR

1

At the Poem Society a black-haired man stands up to say
"You make me sick with all your talk about restraint and mature talent!
Haven't you ever looked out the window at a painting by Matisse,
Or did you always stay in hotels where there were too many spiders
    crawling on your visages?
Did you ever glance inside a bottle of sparkling pop,
Or see a citizen split in two by the lightning?
I am afraid you have never smiled at the hibernation
Of bear cubs except that you saw in it some deep relation
To human suffering and wishes, oh what a bunch of crackpots!"
The black-haired man sits down, and the others shoot arrows at him.
A blond man stands up and says,
"He is right! Why should we be organized to defend the kingdom
Of dullness? There are so many slimy people connected with poetry,
Too, and people who know nothing about it!
I am not recommending that poets like each other and organize to
    fight them,
But simply that lightning should strike them."
Then the assembled mediocrities shot arrows at the blond-haired man.
The chairman stood up on the platform, oh he was physically ugly!
He was small-limbed and -boned and thought he was quite seductive,
But he was bald with certain hideous black hairs,
And his voice had the sound of water leaving a vaseline bathtub,
And he said, "The subject for this evening's discussion is poetry
On the subject of love between swans." And everyone threw candy
    hearts
At the disgusting man, and they stuck to his bib and tucker,
And he danced up and down on the platform in terrific glee
And recited the poetry of his little friends—but the blond man stuck
    his head
Out of a cloud and recited poems about the east and thunder,
And the black-haired man moved through the stratosphere chanting
Poems of the relationships between terrific prehistoric charcoal whales,
And the slimy man with candy hearts sticking all over him
Wilted away like a cigarette paper on which the bumblebees have
    urinated,
And all the professors left the room to go back to their duty,
And all that were left in the room were five or six poets

And together they sang the new poem of the twentieth century
Which, though influenced by Mallarmé, Shelley, Byron, and Whitman,
Plus a million other poets, is still entirely original
And is so exciting that it cannot be here repeated.
You must go to the Poem Society and wait for it to happen.
Once you have heard this poem you will not love any other,
Once you have dreamed this dream you will be inconsolable,
Once you have loved this dream you will be as one dead,
Once you have visited the passages of this time's great art!

2
"Oh to be seventeen years old
Once again," sang the red-haired man, "and not know that poetry
Is ruled with the sceptre of the dumb, the deaf, and the creepy!"
And the shouting persons battered his immortal body with stones
And threw his primitive comedy into the sea
From which it sang forth poems irrevocably blue.

Who are the great poets of our time, and what are their names?
Yeats of the baleful influence, Auden of the baleful influence, Eliot of
    the baleful influence
(Is Eliot a great poet? no one knows), Hardy, Stevens, Williams
    (is Hardy of our time?),
Hopkins (is Hopkins of our time?), Rilke (is Rilke of our time?), Lorca
    (is Lorca of our time?), who is still of our time?
Mallarmé, Valéry, Apollinaire, Eluard, Reverdy, French poets are
    still of our time,
Pasternak and Mayakovsky, is Jouve of our time?

Where are young poets in America, they are trembling in publishing
    houses and universities,
Above all they are trembling in universities, they are bathing the
    library steps with their spit,
They are gargling out innocuous (to whom?) poems about maple trees
    and their children,
Sometimes they brave a subject like the Villa d'Este or a lighthouse in
    Rhode Island,
Oh what worms they are! they wish to perfect their form.

Yet could not these young men, put in another profession,
Succeed admirably, say at sailing a ship? I do not doubt it, Sir, and
    I wish we could try them.

(A plane flies over the ship holding a bomb but perhaps it will not
    drop the bomb,
The young poets from the universities are staring anxiously at the skies,
Oh they are remembering their days on the campus when they looked
    up to watch birds excrete,
They are remembering the days they spent making their elegant
    poems.)

Is there no voice to cry out from the wind and say what it is like to be
    the wind,
To be roughed up by the trees and to bring music from the scattered
    houses
And the stones, and to be in such intimate relationship with the sea
That you cannot understand it? It there no one who feels like a pair
    of pants?

3
Summer in the trees! "It is time to strangle several bad poets."
The yellow hobbyhorse rocks to and fro, and from the chimney
Drops the Strangler! The white and pink roses are slightly agitated
    by the struggle,
But afterwards beside the dead "poet" they cuddle up comfortingly
    against their vase. They are safer now, no one will compare them to
    the sea.

Here on the railroad train, one more time, is the Strangler.
He is going to get that one there, who is on his way to a poetry reading.
Agh! Biff! A body falls to the moving floor.

In the football stadium I also see him,
He leaps through the frosty air at the maker of comparisons
Between football and life and silently, silently strangles him!

Here is the Strangler dressed in a cowboy suit
Leaping from his horse to annihilate the students of myth!

The Strangler's ear is alert for the names of Orpheus,
Cuchulain, Gawain, and Odysseus,
And for poems addressed to Jane Austen, F. Scott Fitzgerald,
To Ezra Pound, and to personages no longer living
Even in anyone's thoughts—O Strangler the Strangler!

He lies on his back in the waves of the Pacific Ocean.

4
Supposing that one walks out into the air
On a fresh spring day and has the misfortune
To encounter an article on modern poetry
In *New World Writing,* or has the misfortune
To see some examples of some of the poetry
Written by the men with their eyes on the myth
And the Missus and the midterms, in the *Hudson Review,*
Or, if one is abroad, in *Botteghe Oscure,*
Or indeed in *Encounter,* what is one to do
With the rest of one's day that lies blasted to ruins
All bluely about one, what is one to do?
O surely one cannot complain to the President,
Nor even to the deans of Columbia College,
Nor to T. S. Eliot, nor to Ezra Pound,
And supposing one writes to the Princess Caetani,
"Your poets are awful!" what good would it do?
And supposing one goes to the *Hudson Review*
With a package of matches and sets fire to the building?
One ends up in prison with trial subscriptions
To the *Partisan, Sewanee,* and *Kenyon Review!*

5
Sun out! perhaps there is a reason for the lack of poetry
In these ill-contented souls, perhaps they need air!

Blue air, fresh air, come in, I welcome you, you are an art student,
Take off your cap and gown and sit down on the chair.
Together we shall paint the poets—but no, air! perhaps you should
    go to them, quickly,
Give them a little inspiration, they need it, perhaps they are out of
    breath,
Give them a little inhuman company before they freeze the English
    language to death!
(And rust their typewriters a little, be sea air! be noxious! kill them,
    if you must, but stop their poetry!
I remember I saw you dancing on the surf on the Côte d'Azur,
And I stopped, taking my hat off, but you did not remember me,
Then afterwards you came to my room bearing a handful of orange
    flowers
And we were together all through the summer night!)

That we might go away together, it is so beautiful on the sea, there
  are a few white clouds in the sky!

But no, air! you must go . . . Ah, stay!

But she has departed and . . . Ugh! what poisonous fumes and clouds!
  what a suffocating atmosphere!
Cough! whose are these hideous faces I see, what is this rigor
Infecting the mind? where are the green Azores,
Fond memories of childhood, and the pleasant orange trolleys,
A girl's face, red-white, and her breasts and calves, blue eyes, brown
  eyes, green eyes, fahrenheit
Temperatures, dandelions, and trains, O blue?!
Wind, wind, what is happening? Wind! I can't see any bird but the
  gull, and I feel it should symbolize . . .
Oh, pardon me, there's a swan, one two three swans, a great white
  swan, hahaha how pretty they are! Smack!
Oh! stop! help! yes, I see—disrespect of my superiors—forgive me,
  dear Zeus, nice Zeus, parabolic bird, O feathered excellence! white!
There is Achilles too, and there's Ulysses, I've always wanted to see
  them, hahaha!
And there is Helen of Troy, I suppose she is Zeus too, she's so terribly
  pretty—hello, Zeus, my you are beautiful, Bang!
One more mistake and I get thrown out of the Modern Poetry Associ-
  ation, help! Why aren't there any adjectives around?
Oh there are, there's practically nothing else—look, here's *grey, utter,*
  agonized, total, phenomenal, gracile, invidious, sundered, and
  fused,
Elegant, absolute, pyramidal, and . . . Scream! but what can I describe
  with these words? States!
States symbolized and divided by two, complex states, magic states,
  states of consciousness governed by an aroused sincerity, cocka-
  doodle doo!
Another bird! is it morning? Help! where am I? am I in the barn-
  yard? oink oink, scratch, moo! Splash!
My first lesson. "Look around you. What do you think and feel?"
  Uhhh . . . "Quickly!" *This Connecticut landscape would have pleased*
  Vermeer. Wham! A-Plus. "Congratulations!" I am promoted.
OOOhhhhh I wish I were dead, what a headache! My second lesson:
  "Rewrite your first lesson line six hundred times. Try to make it
  into a magnetic field." I can do it too. But my poor line! What a
  nightmare! Here comes a tremendous horse,

Trojan, I presume. No, it's my third lesson. "Look, look! Watch him,
see what he's doing? That's what we want you to do. Of course it
won't be the same as his at first, but . . ." I demur. Is there no other
way to fertilize minds?

Bang! I give in . . . Already I see my name in two or three anthologies,
a serving girl comes into the barn bringing me the anthologies,

She is very pretty and I smile at her a little sadly, perhaps it is my last
smile! Perhaps she will hit me! But no, she smiles in return, and
she takes my hand.

My hand, my hand! what is this strange thing I feel in my hand, on
my arm, on my chest, my face—can it be . . . ? it is! AIR!

Air, air, you've come back! Did you have any success? "What do
you think?" I don't know, air. You are so strong, air.

And she breaks my chains of straw, and we walk down the road,
behind us the hideous fumes!

Soon we reach the seaside, she is a young art student who places her
head on my shoulder,

I kiss her warm red lips, and here is the Strangler, reading the *Kenyon
Review!* Good luck to you, Strangler!

Goodbye, Helen! goodbye, fumes! goodbye, abstracted dried-up
boys! goodbye, dead trees! goodbye, skunks!

Goodbye, manure! goodbye, critical manicure! goodbye, you big fat
men standing on the east coast as well as the west giving poems the
test! farewell, Valéry's stern dictum!

Until tomorrow, then, scum floating on the surface of poetry!
goodbye for a moment, refuse that happens to land in poetry's
boundaries! adieu, stale eggs teaching imbeciles poetry to bolster
up your egos! adios, boring anomalies of these same stale eggs!

Ah, but the scum is deep! Come, let me help you! and soon we pass
into the clear blue water. Oh GOODBYE, castrati of poetry,
farewell, stale pale skunky pentameters (the only honest English
meter, gloop gloop!) until tomorrow, horrors! oh, farewell!

Hello, sea! good morning, sea! hello, clarity and excitement, you
great expanse of green—

O green, beneath which all of them shall drown!

KENNETH KOCH

DENISE LEVERTOV

Thomas Victor

Denise Levertov was born in 1923 in Ilford, Essex, England and edu-
cated at home. She has published many books of poetry, including
*With Eyes at the Back of Our Heads, O Taste and See, The Jacob's
Ladder, The Sorrow Dance, Footprints, Relearning the Alphabet,* and
To Stay Alive, as well as a book of essays on poetry, *The Poet in the
World.* She has taught at many American universities and is married
to the novelist Mitchell Goodman.

OLGA POEMS

Olga Levertoff, 1914–1964

I

By the gas-fire, kneeling
to undress,
scorching luxuriously, raking
her nails over olive sides, the red
waistband ring—

(And the little sister
beady-eyed in the bed—
or drowsy, was I? My head
a camera—)

Sixteen. Her breasts
round, round, and
dark-nippled—

who now these two months long
is bones and tatters of flesh in earth.

II

The high pitch of
nagging insistence, lines
creased into raised brows—

Ridden, ridden—
the skin around the nails
nibbled sore—

You wanted
to shout the world to its senses,
did you?—to browbeat

the poor into joy's
socialist republic—
What rage

and human shame swept you
when you were nine and saw
the Ley Street houses,

grasping their meaning as *slum*.
Where I, reaching that age,
teased you, admiring

architectural probity, circa
eighteen-fifty, and noted
pride in the whitened doorsteps.

Black one, black one,
there was a white
candle in your heart.

III

   1

Everything flows
           she muttered into my childhood,
pacing the trampled grass where human puppets
rehearsed fates that summer,
stung into alien semblances by the lash of her will—

everything flows—
I looked up from my Littlest Bear's cane armchair
and knew the words came from a book
and felt them alien to me

but linked to words we loved
                  from the hymnbook—*Time
like an ever-rolling stream / bears all its sons away*—

   2

Now as if smoke or sweetness were blown my way
I inhale a sense of her livingness in that instant,
feeling, dreaming, hoping, knowing boredom and zest like anyone
                           else—

a young girl in the garden, the same alchemical square
I grew in, we thought sometimes
too small for our grand destinies—
                              But dread
was in her, a bloodbeat, it was against the rolling dark
oncoming river she raised bulwarks, setting herself
to sift cinders after early Mass all of one winter,

labelling her desk's normal disorder, basing
her verses on Keble's *Christian Year,* picking
those endless arguments, pressing on

to manipulate lives to disaster . . . To change,
to change the course of the river! What rage for order
disordered her pilgrimage—so that for years at a time

she would hide among strangers, waiting
to rearrange all mysteries in a new light.

3

Black one, incubus—
        she appeared
riding anguish as Tartars ride mares

over the stubble of bad years.

In one of the years
        when I didn't know if she were dead or alive
I saw her in dream

haggard and rouged
        lit by the flare
from an eel- or cockle-stand on a slum street—

was it a dream? I had lost

all sense, almost, of
        who she was, what—inside of her skin,
under her black hair
                        dyed blonde—

it might feel like to be, in the wax and wane of the moon,
in the life I feel as unfolding, not flowing, the pilgrim years—

IV

On your hospital bed you lay
in love, the hatreds
that had followed you, a
comet's tail, burned out

as your disasters bred of love
burned out,
while pain and drugs
quarreled like sisters in you—

lay afloat on a sea
of love and pain—how you always
loved that cadence, 'Underneath
are the everlasting arms'—

all history
burned out, down
to the sick bone, save for

that kind candle.

V

   1

In a garden grene whenas I lay—

you set the words to a tune so plaintive
it plucks its way through my life as through a wood.

As through a wood, shadow and light between birches,
gliding a moment in open glades, hidden by thickets of holly

your life winds in me.   In Valentines
a root protrudes from the greensward several yards from its tree

we might raise like a trapdoor's handle, you said,
and descend long steps to another country

where we would live without father or mother
and without longing for the upper world. *The birds
sang sweet, O song, in the midst of the daye,*

and we entered silent mid-Essex churches on hot afternoons
and communed with the effigies of knights and their ladies

and their slender dogs asleep at their feet,
the stone so cold—   *In youth*

is pleasure, in youth is pleasure.

   2
Under autumn clouds, under white
wideness of winter skies you went walking
the year you were most alone

returning to the old roads, seeing again
the signposts pointing to Theydon Garnon
or Stapleford Abbots or Greensted,

crossing the ploughlands (whose color I named *murple,*
a shade between brown and mauve that we loved
when I was a child and you

not much more than a child) finding new lanes
near White Roding or Abbess Roding; or lost in Romford's
new streets where there were footpaths then—

frowning as you ground out your thoughts, breathing deep
of the damp still air, taking
the frost into your mind unflinching.

How cold it was in your thin coat, your down-at-heel shoes—
tearless Niobe, your children were lost to you
and the stage lights had gone out, even the empty theater

was locked to you, cavern of transformation where all
had almost been possible.
                    How many books
you read in your silent lodgings that winter,
how the plovers transpierced your solitude out of doors with their
                                        strange cries

I had flung open my arms to in longing, once, by your side
stumbling over the furrows—

Oh, in your torn stockings, with unwaved hair,
you were trudging after your anguish
over the bare fields, soberly, soberly.

VI

Your eyes were the brown gold of pebbles under water.
I never crossed the bridge over the Roding, dividing
the open field of the present from the mysteries,
the wraiths and shifts of time-sense Wanstead Park held suspended,
without remembering your eyes. Even when we were estranged
and my own eyes smarted in pain and anger at the thought of you.
And by other streams in other countries; anywhere where the light
reaches down through shallows to gold gravel. Olga's
brown eyes. One rainy summer, down in the New Forest,
when we could hardly breathe for ennui and the low sky,
you turned savagely to the piano and sightread
straight through all the Beethoven sonatas, day after day—
weeks, it seemed to me. I would turn the pages some of the time,
go out to ride my bike, return—you were enduring in the
falls and rapids of the music, the arpeggios rang out, the rectory
trembled, our parents seemed effaced.
I think of your eyes in that photo, six years before I was born,
the fear in them. What did you do with your fear,
later? Through the years of humiliation,
of paranoia and blackmail and near-starvation, losing
the love of those you loved, one after another,
parents, lovers, children, idolized friends, what kept
compassion's candle alight in you, that lit you
clear into another chapter (but the same book) 'a clearing
in the selva oscura,
a house whose door
swings open, a hand beckons
in welcome'?
              I cross
so many brooks in the world, there is so much light
dancing on so many stones, so many questions my eyes
smart to ask of your eyes, gold brown eyes,
the lashes short but the lids

arched as if carved out of olivewood, eyes with some vision
of festive goodness in back of their hard, or veiled, or shining,
unknowable gaze. . . .

May–August, 1964

DESPAIR

While we were visiting David's grave
I saw at a little distance

a woman hurrying towards another grave
hands outstretched, stumbling

in her haste; who then
fell at the stone she made for

and lay sprawled upon it, sobbing,
sobbing and crying out to it.

She was neatly dressed in a pale coat
and seemed neither old nor young.

I couldn't see her face, and my friends
seemed not to know she was there.

Not to distress them, I said nothing.
But she was not an apparition.

And when we walked
back to the car in silence

I looked stealthily back and saw she rose
and quieted herself and began slowly

to back away from the grave.
Unlike David, who lives

in our lives, it seemed
whoever she mourned dwelt
there, in the field, under stone.
It seemed the woman

believed whom she loved heard her,
heard her wailing, observed

the nakedness of her anguish,
and would not speak.

ADAM'S COMPLAINT

Some people,
no matter what you give them,
still want the moon.

The bread,
the salt,
white meat and dark,
still hungry.

The marriage bed
and the cradle,
still empty arms.

You give them land,
their own earth under their feet,
still they take to the roads.

And water: dig them the deepest well,
still it's not deep enough
to drink the moon from.

THE MALICE OF INNOCENCE

A glimpsed world, halfway through the film,
one slow shot of a ward at night

holds me when the rest is quickly
losing illusion. Strange hold,

as of romance, of glamor: not because
even when I lived in it I had

illusions about that world: simply because
I did live there and it was

a world. Greenshaded lamp glowing
on the charge desk, clipboards
stacked on the desk for the night,

sighs and waiting, waiting-for-morning stirrings
in the dim long room, warm, orderly,
and full of breathings as a cowbarn.

Death and pain dominate this world, for though
many are cured, they leave still weak,

still tremulous, still knowing mortality
has whispered to them; have seen in the folding
of white bedspreads according to rule

the starched pleats of a shroud.
                              It's against that frozen
counterpane, and the knowledge too
how black an old mouth gaping at death can look

that the night routine has in itself—
without illusions—glamor, perhaps. It had

a rhythm, a choreographic decorum:
when all the evening chores had been done

and a multiple restless quiet listened
to the wall-clock's pulse, and turn by turn

the two of us made our rounds
on tiptoe, bed to bed,

counting by flashlight how many pairs
of open eyes were turned to us,

noting all we were trained to note,
we were gravely dancing—starched

in our caps, our trained replies,
our whispering aprons—the well-rehearsed

pavanne of power. Yes, wasn't it power,
and not compassion,
                                    gave our young hearts
their hard fervor? I hated

to scrub out lockers, to hand out trays of
unappetizing food, and by day, or the tail-end of night

(daybreak dull on gray faces—ours and theirs)
the anxious hurry, the scolding old-maid bosses.
But I loved the power
of our ordered nights,

        gleaming surfaces I'd helped to polish
making patterns in the shipshape
halfdark—
                    loved
the knowing what to do, and doing it,
list of tasks getting shorter

hour by hour. And knowing
all the while that Emergency
might ring with a case to admit, anytime,

if a bed were empty. Poised,
ready for that.
                    The camera
never returned to the hospital ward,

the story moved on into the streets,
into the rooms where people lived.

But I got lost in the death rooms a while,
remembering being (crudely, cruelly,

just as a soldier or one of the guards
from Dachau might be) in love with order,

an angel like the *chercheuses de poux,* floating
noiseless from bed to bed,

smoothing pillows, tipping
water to parched lips, writing

details of agony carefully into the Night Report.

ADVENT 1966

Because in Vietnam the vision of a Burning Babe
is multiplied, multiplied,
                           the flesh on fire
not Christ's, as Southwell saw it, prefiguring
the Passion upon the Eve of Christmas,

but wholly human and repeated, repeated,
infant after infant, their names forgotten,
their sex unknown in the ashes,
set alight, flaming but not vanishing,
not vanishing as his vision but lingering,

cinders upon the earth or living on
moaning and stinking in hospitals three abed;

because of this my strong sight,
my clear caressive sight, my poet's sight I was given
that it might stir me to song,
it blurred.

There is a cataract filming over
my inner eyes. Or else a monstrous insect
has entered my head, and looks out
from my sockets with multiple vision,

seeing not the unique Holy Infant
burning sublimely, an imagination of redemption,
furnace in which souls are wrought into new life,
but, as off a beltline, more, more senseless figures aflame.

And this insect (who is not there—
it is my own eyes do my seeing, the insect
is not there, what I see is there)
will not permit me to look elsewhere,

or if I look, to see except dulled and unfocused
the delicate, firm, whole flesh of the still unburned.

THE GULF

(*During the Detroit Riots, 1967*)

Far from our garden at the edge of a gulf,
where we calm our nerves in the rain,

(scrabbling a little in earth to pull weeds
and make room for transplants—

dirt under the nails, it
hurts, almost, and yet feels good)

far from our world the heat's on.
Among the looters a boy of eleven

grabs from a florist's showcase (the *Times* says)
armfuls of gladioli, all he can carry,

and runs with them. What happens?
I see him

dart into a dark entry where there's no one
(the shots, the shouting, the glass smashing

heard dully as traffic is heard).
Breathless he halts to examine

the flesh of dream: he squeezes
the strong cold juicy stems, long as his legs,

tries the mild leafblades—they don't cut.
He presses his sweating face

into flower faces, scarlet and pink and purple,
white and blood red, smooth, cool—his heart is pounding.

But all at once an absence
makes itself known to him—it's like

a hole in the lungs,
life running out. They are without

perfume!
   Cheated, he drops them.
White men's flowers.

They rustle in falling,
lonely he stands there, the sheaves

cover his sneakered feet . . .
     There's no place to go
with or without his prize.

Far away, in our garden he cannot imagine,
I'm watching to see if he picks up the flowers

at last or goes,
leaving them lie.

But nothing happens.
He stands there.

He goes on standing there,
useless knowledge in my mind's eye.

Nothing will move him.
We'll live out our lives

in our garden on the edge of a gulf,
and he in the hundred years' war ten heartbeats long

unchanging among the dead flowers,
no place to go.

THE GOOD DREAM

Rejoicing
because we had met again
we rolled laughing
over and over upon the big bed.

The joy was
not in a narrow sense
erotic—not
narrow in any sense.
It was

that all impediments,
every barrier, of history,
of learn'd anxiety,
wrong place and wrong time,

had gone down,
vanished.
It was the joy

of two rivers
meeting in depths of the sea.

BY RAIL THROUGH THE EARTHLY PARADISE, PERHAPS BEDFORDSHIRE

The fishermen among the fireweed.

Towpath and humpbacked bridge. Cows
in one field, slabs of hay
ranged in another.

Common day
precious to me.
There's nothing else
to grasp.

The train
moves me past it too fast, not much,
just a little, I don't want
to stay for ever.
                    Horses,
three of them, flowing across a paddock
as wind flows over barley.

Oaks in parkland, distinct,
growing their shadows.
A man from Cairo across from me
reading *A Synopsis of Eye Physiology*.
The brickworks,
fantastical slender chimneys.

I'm not hungry,
not lonely. It seems
at times I want nothing,
no human giving and taking.
Nothing I see
fails to give pleasure,

no thirst for righteousness
dries my throat, I am silent
and happy, and troubled only
by my own happiness. Looking,

looking and naming. I wish the train now
would halt for me at a station in the fields,
(the name goes by
unread).
           In the deep aftermath
of its faded rhythm, I could become

a carved stone
set in the gates of the earthly paradise,

an angler's fly
lost in the sedge to watch the centuries.

In an interview with me in 1964, Walter Sutton asked me to talk at
some length about a short poem of mine. I chose "The Tulips" from
The Jacob's Ladder:

> Red tulips
> living into their death
> flushed with a wild blue
>
> tulips
> becoming wings
> ears of the wind
> jackrabbits rolling their eyes
>
> west wind
> shaking the loose pane
>
> some petals fall
> with that sound one
> listens for

First, there was the given fact of having received a bunch of red
tulips, which I put in a vase on the window sill. In general I tend to
throw out flowers when they begin to wither, because their beauty is
partly in their *short* life, and I don't like to cling to them. I thought of
that sentence of Rilke's about the unlived life of which one can die;
and, looking at these tulips, I thought of how they were continuing
to be fully alive, right on into their last moments. They hadn't given
up before the end. As red tulips die, some chemical change takes
place which makes them turn blue, and this blue seems like the flush
on the cheeks of someone with fever. I said "wild blue" because, as
I looked at it, it seemed to be a shade of blue that suggested to me
perhaps far-off parts of sky at sunset that seemed untamed, wild.
There seem to be blues that are tame and blues that are daring. Well,
these three lines constitute the first stanza . . . Then came a pause. A
silence within myself when I didn't see or feel more, but was simply
resting on this sequence that had already taken place. Then, as I
looked, this process continued. You can think of it as going on
throughout a day; but when cut flowers are in that state, things
happen quite fast; you can almost see them move. The petals begin
to turn back. As they turn back, they seem to me to be winglike. The
flowers are almost going to take off on their winglike petals. Then
"ears of the wind." They seem also like long ears, like jack rabbits'

ears turned back and flowing in the wind, but also as if they were the wind's own ears listening to itself. The idea of their being jack rabbits' ears led me to the next line, which is the last line of this stanza, "jackrabbits rolling their eyes," because as they turn still further back they suggest, perhaps, ecstasy. Well, this was the second unit. Then another pause. The next stanza, "west wind / shaking the loose pane," is a sequence which is pure observation without all that complex of associations that entered into the others. The flowers were on the window sill, and the pane of glass was loose, and the wind blew and rattled the pane. This is background.

Is it part of the sound that comes in, as you mentioned earlier?

Yes, although it doesn't really get into the poem quite as sound. Then again a short pause, and then, "some petals fall / with that sound one / listens for." Now, the petals fall, not only because the flowers are dying and the petals have loosened themselves, in death, but also because perhaps that death was hastened by the blowing of the west wind, by external circumstances. And there is a little sound when a petal falls. Now why does the line end on "one"? Why isn't the next line "one listens for"? That is because into the sequence of events entered a pause in which was an unspoken question, "with that sound one," and suddenly I was stopped: "one what?" Oh, "one listens for." It's a sound like the breath of a human being who is dying; it stops, and one has been sitting by the bedside, and one didn't even know it, but one was in fact waiting for just that sound, and the sound is the equivalent of that silence. And one doesn't discover that one was waiting for it, was listening for it, until one comes to it. I think that's all.

I think the line also turns back with the "one." There is a kind of reflexive movement for me, as you read it, emphasizing the solitary nature of the sound. Now in your comments on this poem you have talked mostly about the meanings, the associations of the experience, and their relation to images.

Also, though, about their relation to rhythm, about where the lines are broken and where the silence is, about the rests.

Where the silences fall. Now, "variable foot" is a difficult term. Williams said that it involves not just the words or the phrases but also the spaces between them. Is that your meaning also? That a pause complementing a verbal unit is a part of the sequence of events?

Yes, and the line-end pause is a very important one; I regard it as equal to half a comma, but the pauses between stanzas come into it too, and they are much harder to evaluate, to measure. I think that what the idea of the variable foot, which is so difficult to understand, really depends on is a sense of a pulse, a pulse in behind the words, a pulse that is actually sort of tapped out by a drum in the poem. Yes, there's an implied beat, as in music; there is such a beat, and you can have in one bar just two notes, and in another bar ten notes, and yet the bar length is the same. I suppose that is what Williams was talking about, that you don't measure a foot in the old way by its syllables but by its beat.

Though not by what Pound called the rhythm of the metronome?

Well, there is a metronome in back, too.

Is it like the mechanical beat of the metronome or the necessarily variable beat of a pulse? Is it a constant beat? Or is it a beat that accelerates and slows?

Oh, it accelerates and slows, but it has a regularity, I would say. I'm thinking of *The Clock* symphony of Haydn. Well, there's where the pulse behind the bars is actually heard—p*um*-pum, p*um*-pum, and so on. But then, winding around that pum-pum, it's going *dee*-dee-*dee*-dum, and so forth. Well, I think perhaps in a poem you've got that melody, and not the metronomic pum-pum; but the pum-pum, pum-pum is implied.

When you think of the variable foot, then, you think of beats rather than of the spacing of phrases or of breath-spaced units of expression?

I've never fully gone along with Charles Olson's idea of the use of the breath. It sees to me that it doesn't work out in practice.

Of course, he thinks of this as one of the achievements of the modernist revolution—that Pound and Williams inaugurated the use of breath-spaced lines.

But I don't think they really are breath-spaced. There are a lot of poems where you actually have to draw a big breath to read the phrase as it's written. But so what? Why shouldn't one, if one is capable of drawing a deep breath? It's too easy to take this breath idea to mean literally that a poet's poems *ought* by some moral law to sound very much like what he sounds like when he's talking. But I think this is unfair and untrue, because in fact they may reflect his *inner* voice, and he may just not be a person able to express his inner voice in actual speech.

You think, then, that the rhythm of the inner voice controls the rhythm of the poem?

Absolutely, the rhythm of the inner voice. And I think that the breath idea is taken by a lot of young poets to mean the rhythm of the outer voice. They take that in conjunction with Williams's insistence upon the American idiom, and they produce poems which are purely documentary.

What do you mean by the inner voice?

What it means to me is that a poet, a verbal kind of person, is constantly talking to himself, inside of himself, constantly approximating and evaluating and trying to grasp his experience in words. And the "sound," inside his head, of that voice is not necessarily identical with his literal speaking voice, nor is his inner vocabulary identical with that which he uses in conversation. At their best sound and words are song, not speech. The written poem is then a record of that inner song.

DENISE LEVERTOV

PHILIP LEVINE

Philip Levine was born in Detroit in 1928. Educated at Wayne State, Iowa, and Stanford, he has taught for many years at the California State University in Fresno. Among the many young poets who have been his students are Larry Levis, Omar Salinas, Herb Scott, Glover Davis, and Michael Harper. Except for two years in Spain, he has lived in Fresno with his wife and sons since 1958. His books include *On the Edge, Not This Pig, They Feed They Lion, Red Dust,* and *1933.* In 1974, he was awarded a Guggenheim Fellowship and served as a judge for the National Book Award.

Cathleen McGuigan

SALAMI

Stomach of goat, crushed
sheep balls, soft full
pearls of pig eyes,
snout gristle, fresh earth,
worn iron of trotter, slate
of Zaragoza, dried cat heart,
cock claws. She grinds
them with one hand and
with the other fists
mountain thyme, basil,
paprika, and knobs of garlic.
And if a tooth of stink thistle
pulls blood from the round
blue marbled hand
all the better for
this ruby of Pamplona,
this bright jewel of Vich,
this stained crown
of Solsona, this
salami.
        The daughter
of mismatched eyes,
36 year old infant smelling
of milk. Mama, she cries, mama,
but mama is gone,
and the old stone cutter
must wipe the drool
from her jumper. His puffed fingers
unbutton and point her
to toilet. Ten, twelve hours
a day, as long as the winter sun
holds up he rebuilds
the unvisited church
of San Martin. Cheep cheep
of the hammer high above
the town, sparrow cries
lost in the wind or lost
in the mind. At dusk he leans
to the coal dull wooden Virgin

and asks for blessings on
the slow one and peace
on his grizzled head, asks
finally and each night
for the forbidden, for
the knowledge of every
mysterious stone, and
the words go out on
the overwhelming incense
of salami.

          A single crow
passed high over the house,
I wakened out of nightmare.
The winds had changed,
the Tremontana was tearing
out of the Holy Mountains
to meet the sea winds
in my yard, burning and
scaring the young pines.
The single poplar wailed
in terror. With salt,
with guilt, with the need
to die, the vestments
of my life flared, I
was on fire, a stranger
staggering through my house
butting walls and falling
over furniture, looking
for a way out. In the last room
where moonlight slanted
through a broken shutter
I found my smallest son
asleep or dead, floating
on a bed of colorless light.
When I leaned closer
I could smell the small breaths
going and coming, and each
bore its prayer for me,
the true and earthy prayer
of salami.

AUTUMN

Out of gas south
of Ecorse. In the dark
I can smell the dogs
circling behind the
wrecked cars.
           On a sidestreet,
unlighted, we find a
new Chevy. I suck
the tube until
my mouth fills
and cools with new
American wine.

_____

Old man says,
Elephant moves slow, tortoise
don't hardly move at all and they
has no trouble to be
a hundrid.
           The small
ladders of hair dangle
from his nostrils, hands
peppered like old eggs.

_____

I left you in Washington,
honey, and went to Philly. All the
way beside the tracks, empires
of metal shops, brickflats, storage tanks,
robbing the air.
           Later, behind
barbed wire, I found small arms
swaddled in cosmoline, tanks, landing
craft, half tracks smiling
through lidded eyes,
grenades blooming in
their beds.
           April,
1954, we've got each other
in a borrowed room.

_____

Who comes before dawn through
the drifts of dried leaves
to my door? The clawed gopher,
the egret lost on his way, the inland
toad, the great
Pacific tortoise?
                        I rise
from a warm bed and go and
find nothing, not a neighbor
armed and ready, not a cop
not even my own son
deserting.
                I stand
in a circle of light, my heart
pounding and pounding at the door
of its own wilderness.

————————

Snow steaming on the still
warm body of the jackrabbit
shot and left, snow
on the black streets
melting, snow falling endlessly
on the great runways that
never fill.
                        The twentieth autumn
of our war, the dead heart
and the living clogged
in snow.
                A small clearing
in the pines, the wind
talking through the high trees,
we have water, we
have air, we have bread, we have
a rough shack whitening,
we have snow on your eyelids,
on your hair.

RED DUST

This harpie with dry red curls
talked openly of her husband,
his impotence, his death, the death
of her lover, the birth and death
of her own beauty. She stared
into the mirror next to
our table littered with the wreck
of her appetite and groaned:
Look what you've done to me!
as though only that moment
she'd discovered her own face.
Look, and she shoved the burden
of her ruin on the waiter.

I do not believe in sorrow;
it is not American.
At 8,000 feet the towns
of this blond valley smoke
like the thin pipes of the Chinese,
and I go higher where the air
is clean, thin, and the underside
of light is clearer than the light.
Above the treeline the pines
crowd below like moments of the past
and on above the snow line
the cold underside of my arm,
the half in shadow, sweats with fear
as though it lay along the edge
of revelation.

And so my mind closes around
a square oil can crushed on the road
one morning, startled it was not
the usual cat. If a crow
had come out of the air to choose
its entrails could I have laughed?
If eagles formed now in the
shocked vegetation of my sight
would they be friendly? I can hear
their wings lifting them down, the feathers

tipped with red dust, that dust which
even here I taste, having eaten it
all these years.

HOW MUCH EARTH

Torn into light, you woke wriggling
on a woman's palm. Halved, quartered,
shredded to the wind, you were the life
that thrilled along the underbelly
of a stone. Stilled in the frozen pond
you rinsed heaven with a sigh.

How much earth is a man.
A wall lies down and roses
rush from its teeth; in the fists
of the hungry, cucumbers sleep
their lives away, under your nails
the ocean moans in its bed.

How much earth.
The great ice fields slip
and the broken veins of an eye
startle under light, a hand is planted
and the grave blooms upward
in sunlight and walks the roads.

IN THE NEW SUN

Filaments of light
slant like windswept rain.
The orange seller hawks
into the sky, a man with a hat
stops below my window
and shakes his tassels.
                              Awake

in Tetuan, the room filling
with the first colors, and water running
in a tub.

*

A row of sparkling carp
iced in the new sun, odor
of first love, of childhood,
the fingers held to the nose
for hours while the clock hummed.

The fat woman in the orange smock
places tiny greens at mouth
and tail as though she remembered
or yearned instead for forests, deep floors
of needles, and the hushed breath.

*

Blue nosed cannisters
as fat as barrels silently
slipping by. "Nitro," he says.
On the roof he shows me
where Reuban lay down
to fuck-off and never woke.
"We're takin little wiffs
all the time."
                    Slivers
of glass work their way
through the canvas gloves
and burn. Lifting my black glasses
in the chemical light, I stop
to squeeze one out and the asbestos
glows like a hand in moonlight
or a face in dreams.

*

Pinpoints of blue
along the arms, light rushing
down across the breasts
missing the dry shadows
under them.

        She stretches
and rises on her knees

and smiles and far down
to the sudden embroidery of curls
the belly smiles
that three times stretched slowly moonward
in a hill of child.

        *

Sun through the cracked glass,
bartender at the cave end
peeling a hard-boiled egg. Four
in the afternoon,
the dogs asleep, the river
must bridge seven parched flats
to Cordoba by nightfall.
It will never make it.
                I will
never make it. Like the old man
in gray corduroy asleep
under the stilled fan, I have
no more moves,
stranded on an empty board.

        *

From the high hill
behind Ford Rouge, we could see
the ore boats pulling
down river, the rail yards,
and the smoking mountain.
East, the city spreading
toward St. Clair, miles of houses,
factories, shops burning
in the still white snow.

"Share this with your brother,"
he said, and it was always winter
and a dark snow.

AT THE FILLMORE

The music was going on.
The soldier paced outside
his shoes slowly filling

with rain. Morning
would walk early
over the wards of the wounded,

row after row
of small white faces
dragged back.

She dozed in the Ladies
wondering should she
return. This warmth

like the flush of juice
up the pale stem
of the flower, she'd known

before, and its aftermath—
seeing the Sisters
and the promises again.

The music was going on,
a distant pulsing only
from the wilderness of strobes.

He climbed back up
the crowded stairs cloaked
in a halo of rain, and no one

noticed or called.
Nor were those the waters
of the heart she heard

rushing in the booth
beside her. She stubbed
her cigarette and rose.

The music was going on
gathering under
the turning lights, mounting

in the emptying hall
toward the end. They stood
blinded a moment,

and then she offered herself
to his arms and opened
her arms to him, both

of them smiling as they
claimed the other
and whatever else was theirs.

THE POEM CIRCLING HAMTRAMCK, MICHIGAN ALL NIGHT IN SEARCH OF YOU

He hasn't gone to work,
he'll never go back to work.
The wife has gone home, mad,
with the baby on one arm.
Swaying on his good leg,
he calls out to the bare bulb
a name and opens his arms.
The old woman,
the beer gone from her glass,
turns back to the bar.
She's seen them before
with hard, knotted bellies,
with the bare white breasts of boys.
How many times has she stared
into those eyes glistening
with love or pain
and seen nothing
but love or pain.
Deep at night, when she
was coldest, he would always

rise and dress so as not
to miss the first streetcar
burning homeward, and she
would rock alone toward dawn.

If someone would enter now
and take these lovers—for they
are lovers—in his arms
and rock them together
like a mother with a child
in each arm, this man
with so much desire, this woman
with none, then it would not be
Hamtramck, it would not be
this night. They know it
and wait, he staring
into the light, she into
the empty glass. In the darkness
of this world men
pull on heavy canvas gloves,
dip into rubber coats
and enter the fires. The rats
frozen under the conveyors
turn to let their eyes
fill with dawn. A strange star
is born one more time.

ZAYDEE

Why does the sea burn? Why do the hills cry?
My grandfather opens a fresh box
of English Ovals, lights up, and lets the smoke
drift like clouds from his lips.

Where did my father go in my fifth autumn?
In the blind night of Detroit
on the front porch, Grandfather points up
at a constellation shaped like a cock and balls.

A tiny man, at 13 I outgrew his shirts.
I then beheld a closet of stolen suits,
a hive of elevator shoes, crisp hankies,
new bills in the cupboard, old in the wash.

I held the spotted hands that passed over
the breasts of airline stewardesses,
that moved in the fields like a wind
stirring the long hairs of grain.

Where is the ocean? the flying fish?
the God who speaks from a cloud?
He carries a cardtable out under the moon
and plays gin rummy and cheats.

He took me up in his arms
when I couldn't walk and carried me
into the grove where the bees sang
and the stream paused forever.

He laughs in the movies, cries in the streets,
the judges in their gowns are monkeys,
the lawyers mice, a cop is a fat hand.
He holds up a strawberry and bites it.

He sings a song of freestone peaches
all in a box,
in the street he sings out Idaho potatoes
California, California oranges.

He sings the months in prison,
sings salt pouring down the sunlight,
shovelling all night in the stove factory
he sings the oven breathing fire.

Where did he go when his autumn came?
He sat before the steering wheel
of the black Packard, he turned the key,
pressed the starter, and he went.

The maples blazed golden and red
a moment and then were still,
the long streets were still and the snow
swirled where I lay down to rest.

UNCLE

I remember the forehead born
before Abraham
and flecked with white paint,
the two hands kneading
each other at the sink.
In the basement on Grand
he showed me
his radio,
Manila, Atlantis,
the cities of the burning plains,
the coupons
in comic books, the ads of the air.
Prophet of burned cars
and broken fans, he taught
the toilet the eternal,
argued the Talmud
under his nails. The long boats
with the names of winds
set sail
in the sea of his blind eye.

How could he come
humpbacked
in his crisp undershirt
on the front porch in black Detroit
bringing in the milk,
the newspaper, the bills
long past noon? His truck howls
all night to Benton Harbor, Saginaw,
Dog of the Prairie.
In the high work camps
the men break toward dawn.

He sleeps under a mountain.
Uncle, I call you again Uncle,
I come too late
with a bottle of milk
and a chipped cup of Schnapps
to loosen your fever, undo
your arms and legs
so you can rise
above Belle Isle and the Straits,
your clear eye
rid of our rooms forever,
the glass of fat, the blue flame.

TO MY GOD IN HIS SICKNESS

1

A boy is as old as the stars
that will not answer
as old as the last snows
that blacken his hands
though he wakes at 3
and goes to the window
where the crooked fence is blessed
and the long Packard
and the bicycle wheel
though he walks the streets
warm in the halo of his breath
and is blessed over and over
he will waken in the slow dawn
he will call his uncles out
from the sad bars of Irish statesmen
all the old secret reds
who pledge in the park
and raise drinks
and remember Spain

Though he honor the tree
the sierra of snow
the stream that died years ago
though he honor his breakfast

the water in his glass
the bear in his belly
though he honor all crawling
and winged things
the man in his glory
the woman in her salt
though he savor the cup of filth
though he savor Lake Erie
savor the rain burning down
on Gary, Detroit, Wheeling
though my grandmother argues
the first cause of night
and the kitchen cantor mumbles his names
still the grave will sleep

I came this way before
my road ran by your house
crowded with elbows of mist
and pots banging to be filled
my coat was the color of rain
and six gray sparrows sang
on the branches of my grave

2
A rabbit snared in a fence of pain
screams and screams
I waken, a child again
and answer
I answer my father
hauling his stone up the last few breaths
I answer Moses bumbling before you
the cat circling three times
before she stretches out and yawns
the mole gagged on fresh leaves

In Folsom, Jaroubi, alone before dawn
remembers the long legs of a boy
his own once and now his son's
Billy Ray holds my hand to his heart
in the black and white still photograph
of the exercise yard
In the long shadows of the rifle towers

we say goodbye forever
Later, at dusk the hills
across the dry river bed
hold the last light
long after it's gone
and glow like breath

I wake
and it's not a dream
I see the long coast of the continent
writhing in sleep
this America we thought we dreamed
falling away flake by flake
into the sea
and the sea blackening and burning

I see a man curled up, the size of an egg
I see a woman hidden in a carburetor
a child reduced to one word
crushed under an airmail stamp
or a cigarette

Can the hands rebuild the rocks
can the tongue make air or water
can the blood flow back
into the twigs of the child
can the clouds take back their deaths

3
First light of morning
it is the world again
the domed hills across the gorge
take the air slowly
the day will be hot and long
Billy Ray, Gordon, Jaroubi
all the prisoners have been awake
for hours remembering
I walk through the dense brush
down to the river
that descended all night from snow
small stones worn away
old words, lost truths
ground to their essential nonsense

I lift you in my hand
and inhale, the odor of light
out of darkness, substance out of air
of blood before it reddens and runs

When I first knew you
I was a friend to the ox and walked
with Absalom and raised my hand
against my hand
and died for want of you
and turned to stone and air and water
the answer to my father's tears

NEW SEASON

My son and I go walking in the garden.
It is April 12, Friday, 1974.
Teddy points to the slender trunk
of the plum and recalls the digging
last fall through three feet
of solid hard pan and opens his palms
in the brute light of noon, the heels
glazed with callus, the long fingers
thicker than mine and studded with
silver rings. My mother is 70 today.
He flicks two snails off a leaf
and smashes them underfoot
on the red brick path. Saturday,
my wife stood here, her cheek cut
by a scar of dirt, dirt on her bare
shoulders, on the brown belly,
damp and sour in the creases
of her elbows. She held up a parsnip
squat, misshapen, a tooth pulled
from the earth, and laughed
her great white laugh. Teddy talks
of the wars of the young, Larry V
and Ricky's brother in the movies,
on Belmont, at MacDonald's,

ready to fight for nothing, hard,
redded or on air, "low riders,
grease, what'd you say about my mama."
Home late, one in the back seat,
his fingers broken, eyes welling
with pain, the eyes and jawbones
swollen and rough. 70 today, the woman
who took my hand and walked me
past the corridor of willows
to the dark pond where the one swan
drifted. I start to tell him
and stop, the story of my 15th spring.
That a sailor had thrown a black baby
off the Belle Isle bridge was
the first lie we heard, and the city
was at war for real. We would waken
the next morning to find Sherman tanks
at the curb and soldiers camped
on the lawns. Damato said he was
"goin downtown bury a hatchet
in a nigger's head." Women
took coffee and milk to the soldiers
and it was one long block party
till the trucks and tanks loaded up
and stumbled off. No one saw
Damato for a week, and when I did
he was slow, head down, his right arm
blooming in a great white bandage.
He said nothing. On mornings I rise
early, I watch my son in the bathroom,
shirtless, thick-armed and hard,
working with brush and comb
at his full blond head that suddenly
curled like mine and won't
come straight. 7 years passed
before Della Daubien told me
how three white girls from the shop
sat on her on the Woodward Streetcar
so the gangs couldn't find her
and pull her off like they did
the black janitor and beat
an eye blind. She would never

forget, she said, and her old face
glows before me in shame
and terror. Tonight, after dinner,
after the long, halting call
to my mother, I'll come out here
to the yard rinsed in moonlight
that blurs it all. She will not
become the small openings
in my brain again through which the wind
rages, though she was the ocean
that ebbed in my blood, the storm clouds
that battered my lungs, though I hide
in the crotch of the orange tree
and weep where the future grows
like a scar, she will not come again
in the brilliant day. My cat Nellie,
15 now, follows me, safe
in the dark from mockingbird
and jay, her fur frost tipped
in the pure air, and together we hear
the wounding of the rose, the willow
on fire—to the dark pond
where the one swan drifted, the woman
is 70 now—the willow is burning,
the rhododendrons shrivel
like paper under water, all
the small secret mouths are feeding
on the green heart of the plum.

STANDING ON THE CORNER

until Tatum passed
blind as the sea,
heavy, tottering
on the arm of the young
bass player, and they
both talking
Jackie Robinson.
It was cold, late,

and the Flame Show Bar
was crashing
for the night, even
Johnny Ray
calling it quits.
Tatum said, Can't
believe how fast
he is to first. Wait'll
you see Mays
the bass player said.
Women in white furs
spilled out of the bars
and trickled toward
the parking lot. Now
it could rain, coming
straight down. The man
in the brown hat
never turned his head up.
The gutters swirled
their heavy waters,
the streets reflected
the sky, which was
nothing. Tatum
stamped on toward
the Bland Hotel, a wet
newspaper stuck
to his shoe, his mouth
open, his vest
drawn and darkening.
I can't hardly wait, he said.

THEY FEED THEY LION

Out of burlap sacks, out of bearing butter,
Out of black bean and wet slate bread,
Out of the acids of rage, the candor of tar,
Out of creosote, gasoline, drive shafts, wooden dollies,
They Lion grow.

                    Out of the gray hills
Of industrial barns, out of rain, out of bus ride,
West Virginia to Kiss My Ass, out of buried aunties,
Mothers hardening like pounded stumps, out of stumps,
Out of the bones' need to sharpen and the muscles' to stretch,
They Lion grow.
                    Earth is eating trees, fence posts,
Gutted cars, earth is calling in her little ones,
"Come home, Come home!" From pig balls,
From the ferocity of pig driven to holiness,
From the furred ear and the full jowl come
The repose of the hung belly, from the purpose
They Lion grow.
                    From the sweet glues of the trotters
Come the sweet kinks of the fist, from the full flower
Of the hams the thorax of caves,
From "Bow Down" come "Rise Up,"
Come they Lion from the reeds of shovels,
The grained arm that pulls the hands,
They Lion grow.
                    From my five arms and all my hands,
From all my white sins forgiven, they feed,
From my car passing under the stars,
They Lion, from my children inherit,
From the oak turned to a wall, they Lion,
From they sack and they belly opened
And all that was hidden burning on the oil-stained earth
They feed they Lion and he comes.

FIXING THE FOOT: ON RHYTHM

for Lejan

Yesterday I heard a Dutch doctor talking to a small girl who had cut her foot, not seriously, and was very frightened by the sight of her own blood. "Nay! Nay!" he said over and over. I could hear him quite distinctly through the wall that separated us, and his voice was strong and calm, he spoke very slowly and seemed never to stop speaking, almost as though he were chanting, never too loud or too soft. Her voice, which had been explosive and shrill at first, gradually softened until I could no longer make it out as he went on talking and, I supposed, working. Then a silence, and he said, "Ah" and some words I could not understand. I imagined him stepping spryly back to survey his work. And then another voice, silent before, the girl's father, thanking him, and then the girl thanking him, now in a child's voice. A door opening and closing. And it was over.

PHILIP LEVINE
Amsterdam
June 1974

JOHN LOGAN

John Logan was born in Red Oak, Iowa, in 1923. He holds degrees in biology and has done advanced work in philosophy. He has been poetry editor of *The Nation* and *Choice*. Among his books of poems are *Spring of the Thief, Ghosts of the Heart, The Zig Zag Walk,* and *The Anonymous Lover.* He has also written criticism and fiction, has taught at San Francisco State and Notre Dame, and is presently a professor of English at the State University of New York at Buffalo.

A TRIP TO FOUR OR FIVE TOWNS

to James Wright

1

The gold-colored skin of my Lebanese friends.
Their deep, lightless eyes.
The serene, inner, careful
balance they share. The conjugal
smile of either for either.

2

This bellychilling, shoe soaking, factory-
dug-up-hill smothering Pittsburgh weather!
I wait for a cab in the smart mahogany
lobby of the seminary.
The marble *Pietà* is flanked around
with fake fern. She cherishes her dead son
stretched along her womb he triple crossed.
A small, slippered priest
pads up. Whom do you seek, my son?
Father, I've come in out of the rain.
I seek refuge from the elemental tears,
for my heavy, earthen body runs to grief
and I am apt to drown
in this small and underhanded rain
that drops its dross so delicately
on the hairs of the flowers, my father,
and follows down the veins of leaves
weeping quiet in the wood.

My yellow cab never came,
but I did not confess
beneath the painted Jesus Christ. I left
and never saved myself at all
that night in that late, winter rain.

3

In Washington, was it spring?
I took the plane.
I heard, on either side,
the soft executives, manicured and
fat, fucking this and fucking that.

My heavy second breakfast
lay across my lap.
At port, in the great concourse,
I could not walk to city bus
or cab? or limousine?
I sweat with shock, with havoc
Of the hundred kinds of time,
trembling like a man away from home.

At the National Stripshow
where the girls wriggle right
and slow, I find I want to see in
under the sequin stepin.
And in my later dream of the negro girl's room
strong with ancient sweat and with her thick
aroma, I seem to play a melodrama
as her great, red dog barks twice
and I stab it with my pocket knife.

4
In Richmond the azalea banks
burst in rose and purple gullies by the car,
muted in the soft, wet
April twilight. The old estates
were pruned and rolled fresh   •
with spring, with splendor, touch-
ing the graceful stride of the boy who brings the paper.

5
My friend has a red-headed mother
capable of love in any kind
of weather. I am not sure
what she passes to her daughters
but from her brown eye and from her breast
she passes wit and spunk to her big sons.
And she is small and pleased when they put
their arms around her, having caught her.
They cut the grass naked to the waist.
They cure the handsome skins of chipmunks and of snakes.
And when they wake in their attic room
they climb down the ladder, half
asleep, feeling the rungs' pressure

on their bare feet, shirt tails out,
brown eyes shut. They eat
what she cooks. One shot a gorgeous colored hawk
and posed with it, proud, arms and full wings
spread. And one, at the beach,
balanced on his hands, posed
stripped, in the void of sand,
limbs a rudder in the wind,
amid the lonely, blasted wood.
And two sons run swift roans in the high, summer grass.
Now I would guess
her daughters had at least this same
grace and beauty as their mother,
though I have only seen their picture.
I know she is happy with her three
strong sons about her, for they are not clumsy
(one, calmed, so calmly,
bends a good ear to his guitar)
and they are not dull:
one built a small electric shaft topped with a glowing ball.

6
In New York I got drunk, to tell the truth,
and almost got locked up when a beat
friend with me took a leak in a telephone booth.
(e. e. cummings on the Paris lawn.
"Reprieve pisseur Américain!")
At two o'clock he got knocked out
horning in with the girl in the room over him.
Her boy friend was still sober,
and too thin. I saw the blood of a poet
flow on the sidewalk. Oh, if I mock,
it is without heart. I thought
of the torn limbs of Orpheus
scattered in the grass on the hills of Thrace.
Do poets have to have such trouble with the female race?
I do not know. But if they bleed
I lose heart also.
When he reads, ah, when he reads, small but deep voiced,
he reads well: now weeps, now is cynical,
his large, horned eyes very black and tearful.

And when we visited a poet father
we rode to Jersey on a motor scooter.
My tie and tweeds looped in the winds.
I choked in the wake
of the Holland Pipe, and cops,
under glass like carps, eyed us.
That old father was so mellow and generous—
easy to pain,
white, open and at peace, and of good taste,
Like his Rutherford house.
And he read, very loud and regal,
sixteen new poems based on paintings by Breughel!

7
The last night out,
before I climbed on the formal
Capital Viscount and was shot home
high, pure and clear,
seemed like the right time
to disappear.

SPRING OF THE THIEF

But if I look the ice is gone from the lake
and the altered air
no longer fills with the small
terrible bodies of the snow.
Only once these late winter weeks
the dying flakes
fell instead as manna or as wedding rice
blooming in the light
about the bronze Christ
and the thieves. There these three
still hang, more than man-
sized and heavier than life
on a hill over the lake
where I walk
this Third Sunday of Lent.
I come from Mass

melancholy at its ancient story
of the unclean ghost
a man thought he'd lost.
It came back into his well-swept house
and at the final state that man
was worse than he began.
Yet again today
there is the faintest edge of green
to trees about St. Joseph's Lake.
Ah God if our confessions show contempt
because we let them free us of our guilt
to sin again
forgive us still . . . before the leaves . . .
before the leaves have formed
you can glimpse the Christ and Thieves
on top of the hill. One of them was saved.
That day the snow had seemed to drop like grace
upon the four of us,
or like the peace of intercourse,
suddenly I wanted to confess—
or simply talk.
I paid a visit to the mammoth Sacred Heart
Church, and found it shut.
Who locked him out or in?
Is the name of God changing in our time?
What is his winter name?
Where was his winter home.
Oh I've kept my love to myself before.
Even those ducks weave down the shore
together, drunk with hope
for the April water. One spring festival
near here I stripped and strolled
through a rain filled field.
Spread eagled on the soaking earth
I let the rain
move its audible little hands
gently on my skin . . . let the dark rain
raise up my love.
But why? I was alone
and no one saw how ardent I grew.
And when I rolled naked in the snow one night
as St. Francis with his Brother Ass

or a hard bodied Finn
I was alone. Underneath
the howling January moon
I knelt and dug my fist
full of the cold winter sand
and rubbed and
hid my manhood under it.
Washed up at some ancient or half-heroic shore
I was ashamed that I was naked there.
Before Nausicaä and the saints. Before myself.
But who took off my coat? Who put it on?
Who drove me home?
Blessed be sin if it teaches men shame.
Yet because of it we cannot talk
and I am separated from myself.
So what is all this reveling in snow and rain?
Or in the summer sun when the heavy gold
body weeps with joy or grief or love?
When we speak of God, is it God we speak of?
Perhaps his winter home
is in that field where I rolled or ran . . .
this hill where once the snow
fell serene as rain.
Oh I have walked around the lake
when I was not alone—
sometimes with my wife have seen these swans
dip down their necks
graceful as a girl, showering white and wet!
I've seen their heads delicately turn.
Have gone sailing with my quiet, older son.
And once on a morning walk
a student who had just come back
in fall found a perfect hickory shell
among the bronze and red
leaves and purple flowers of the time
and put its white bread into my hand.
Ekelöf said there is a freshness
nothing can destroy in us—
not even we ourselves.
Perhaps that
Freshness is the changed name of God.
Where all the monsters also hide

I bear him in the ocean of my blood
and in the pulp of my enormous head.
He lives beneath the unkempt potter's grass
of my belly and chest.
I feel his terrible, aged heart
moving under mine . . . can see the shadows
of the gorgeous light
that plays at the edges of his giant eye . . .
or tell the faint press and hum
of his eternal pool of sperm.
Like sandalwood! *Like sandalwood*
the righteous man
perfumes the axe that falls on him.
The cords of elm, of cedar oak and pine
will pile again in fall.
The ribs and pockets of the barns will swell.
Winds and fires in the field rage
and again burn out each
of the ancient roots.
Again at last the late November snow
will fill those fields, change this hill,
throw these figures in relief
and raining on them
will transform
the bronze Christ's brow and cheek,
the white face and thigh of the thief.

A CENTURY PIECE FOR POOR HEINE (1800–1856)

to Paul Carroll

Give up these everlasting complaints about love; show
these poets how to use a whip.
                                        Marx

My forefathers were not the hunters. They were the hunted.
                                        Heine

1
Heine's mother was a monster
Who had him trained
In business, war and law;

In the first she failed the best:
At work in his uncle's office
He turned a book of Ovid's
Into Yiddish. And Harry's memories
Don't even mention the family's
Chill and scare at the chance
Of a fortune from a millionaire. But a grown
Heine fainted and wept
If an uncle failed to provide;
And there was no money in the house when he died:

2
Except what he got from mother.
Syphilis brought
Its slow and fictional death—
Still he never would tell
His folks how sick he was of sex.
He wrote her frequently
To give no cause for alarm
Dictating because of a paralyzed
Arm, into the willing
And ready ear of some
Lady fair, reporting
For today, criticizing his wife
And telling the details of nearly-married life.

3
He called his mother a dear old
"Pussy cat";
His wife was a "wild cat";
She was the stupid Cath-
Olic opposite of the Jewish
Other—and cared even less
For his verse, being unable
To read and listening little,
Which is worse. Their need for love
So shocked him, he ran away
To a princess friend—like his sister
A rather crystalline dolly
Charitable toward sexual folly.

4

Two weeks after his mother
I mean his wife
And he were married, having harried
Each other for a number of years,
He put himself in a fight
With a man he got a cuckold;
He chose the absolute pistol,
But found he was only shot
In the thigh—and his own weapon
Of course went high.
So he went to visit his mom
After years of exile from home
Because of politics he put in a pome.

5

He left his mother I mean
His other at home
With her nervous bird and her
Shrieking tantrums—or else
He left the bird with the wife,
Et cetera—he wrote her a letter a
Day like a scolding parent
Afraid she'd become a Paris
Whore as he hoped she would
(And as he was) but she stayed
Till death, tho she shattered a glass
In her teeth, and all the rest—
Such as throwing a fish in the face of a guest.

6

As soon as he left himself
To the needs of a wife
He was shook to find in the face
In the mirror the eyes of his father
When his flesh had started to fade:
He began to be blind, and gave in
To a kind of paralysis that made him
Lift the lid of his eye
By hand to see his wife.
At the end, cones of opium,
Burned on his spine, helped him

To dream of a younger father
Doing his hair in a snow of powder;

7
He tried to kiss his father's
Hand but his pink
Finger was stiff as sticks
And suddenly all of him shifts—
A glorious tree of frost!
Unburdened of the sullied flesh.
His father died before him
Leaving him free to be
The Jew—he had fled their flight
To that of the protestant fake
Exacted in Christian states,
But pain had him lucid (or afraid)
Till the ancient covenant with God was made.

8
But his tough old mother stayed on
And he never became
The husband; he took to his marriage
Couch interesting women,
Remaining a curious virgin.
In the last years of his life
He wept at the pain of lust
Stirred in his tree-like limbs
Already dry. And he left
Framing with paralyzed lips
One more note to his mother.
Only the ambiguous Dumas cried
At the holy rite they danced when he died.

9
His soft old flesh slipped
Inside its great
Trunk with a sound he held
Too long inside his skull.
God absolve his mother,
His wife and him: after all
As Heine said, thrusting
Again that Freudian wit

He showed to prove to friends
And self his sanity had not
Come to the fate of potency—
"It is God's business to have mercy."

10
There is no need to forgive
His saintly poems
As there is for the work of another,
To whose New York park
The marble Lorelei fled—
Banned with the books of her maker—
To mock and lure at him
And us from a Catholic plot
Like a baptized, voluptuous mother
Powerful over the figure
Of the frantic Harry, and over the
Three mother-fishes:
Melancholy, an idol of the Hebrew Smart,
And one with the mended, broken arm of Art.

After Antonina Valentin
and after a memorial to Heine
in Kilmer Park

SAN FRANCISCO POEM

"A pier," Stephen said. "Yes,
a disappointed bridge."
—James Joyce

1
We moved like fingers
over the curved arms of the rock
pier at Aquatic Park,
saw the black-
haired, half-stripped boy haul back
from the sea the huge, live hand
of a crab. It charmed
and scared a playing kid.
"O-o-o-oh," she said

and jumped
right straight up
in the air,
where she changed
into a low, light-limbed star.

2
And where we walked
in that watery park
the formally
happy families
fished on the pier.
From his one good eye a floored flounder
gazed with long despair,
and the dogfish shark
writhed on the concrete walk—
shucked aside
by the female touch of time.
Half-dissected by a gull
he bleeds his tears of oil.

3
Purple flowers shadowed the island prison
(windows closer than I had ever seen).
The small harbor freight train screamed
along the sand
across
from the curved pier, across
from us.
Its racket shook the ancient circus
sprawling in the sun:
the bursting muscle man,
a lovely, light-haired gamin
of a girl in blue (and little else)
whose breasts were never false
to man;
it nudged a midget growing like a stalk of corn;
an old salt who blends
with the sand, living out of sacks,
purple bats
and mothers inked along his back,
once-bright snakes
dying in the heat blackened

flesh of his aged arms.
(And other oldsters roll
their bocce ball
about the nearby green.)
When they hear the train
stark-naked kids all pause in their paradigms.
The little girls tell the little boys.
Gulls wheel about the dinging buoys.

4
At last we walk
to the far end of the break-
water pier, which turns
so gen-
tly in the sun
of the long, April afternoon.
There is some grotesque, giant thing
still there
left behind by a war
(or a very melancholy sculptor).
At the circular edge
of this stone stage
I can hear the little herds of fish
be still, or stir and shift to graze
on the sea's beautiful grass.
The pied, ambitious ducks dive
and are gone away
(long or shorter as the case may be)
under the mild surface of the bay.
One sleek,
brown-and-black duck
suddenly comes back
with a meal quivering in its beak.
Another dives and appears,
dives and reappears,
still poised but quite pissed
off at the absence of a fish.
The few colorful birds
(absorbed)
dive and dot
the black,
shimmering canvas, alive, abstract.

5

You and I sit on the concrete bench
at pier's end and watch—
each
other and the far folks upon the beach.
They watch you as you take a leak
with no attempt to hide.
We read Roethke's "Words for the Wind,"
smile at the faggot with the fat behind,
admire together
a white, three-masted schooner,
and read the signs that tell us where
we are.
"Ghiradelli Square." "Drink Hamm's Beer."
"Cable Crossing. Do not anchor here."
Because the concrete spot
where I sit
suddenly grows too hard
(and because I am really tired)
I tuck the body of your coat under my head,
curl up on my arm
and fall easily into a dream:
Two people surface and begin to swim.

SATURDAY AFTERNOON AT THE MOVIES

Movies are badder
                 than ever
in San Francisco.
Man, if you wish to go,
then perhaps you should listen
to what a midwestern
buff has to say:
They
      showed nude girls before
(crotch shots looming up near)
and, usually on alternate days,
they showed nude guys.

Next they let the naked fel-
low pretend to ball
(rather softly)
     the wildly
frenzied, faking girl.
But some of these
      amateurs could
not help taking their scenes
harder than they were told.
So now there's no pretense—
and, hence, this melancholy singing.
Frisco's dirty flicks are really into something!
Fucking, blowing, sixty-nine.
      And, *che sera*
         sera

let whatever comes, come.
Trouble is
   I'm not at all at ease
with the technicolored sur-
      facing of sperm,
sentimental music piped
     behind.
Trouble is
the patterning of pubic hairs
is not
  abstract.
Trouble is inside the cunt
I see more than a hint
of a human face
hooded, primitive, unfinished.
And there's a face in the head
of the erect
cock. A changing face rolls
in the balls
    as they make a further thrust.
Also a face at the breast
that will
   gather
round the eye or
the little
tough nose of the nipple.

There's another, more hairy face
in the man's chest.
Or in the back of the cares-
sing hand,
                the hollows of the thighs.
And
        always there is this
face
        in the *face*.
For our conscience views itself
in the mirror of the flesh.
Satur-
        day after-
                        noon at the
movies. A far cry from the
Grande Theatre in Red Oak, Iowa.
Shit. With the porn
there's not even any popcorn.
So what should a boy from the Iowa farm
do when
                he finds himself in San
Francisco at a pornographic film?
Well, I guess
                he should just face the facts
and get his ass home.

Poets and poetry today. Yes, but where is poetry itself? Or as
Cummings might ask, "Who is poetry, anyway?" Poetry is existentially
first among the great genres because, thinking of poetry as lyric
contrasted to tragic or epic and agreeing with Yeats that out of our
quarrels with ourselves we make poetry, we can say that this thing,
poetry, is the expression in literature of the narrowest or first circle of
encounter, the circle of one's self, whereas tragedy is the expression
of encounter with the immediate community, the community of family,
and epic the expression of encounter with the larger community of the
nation or the race. Under this view the novel is a mixed form of
poetry which may be primarily lyric as in Proust, primarily tragic as in
Dostoevsky and Faulkner or primarily epic as in Tolstoy. But given this
manner of definition, with its increasingly large circles of encounter
one expects the larger circles to include the smaller, so that one
anticipates in tragedy certain lyric moments as in Claudius's
monologue at prayer in *Hamlet* and one expects in epic both the
lyric moment (as in Achilles' soliloquy by the sea) as well as certain
tragic figurings (as that of Achilles and Patroclus in the *Iliad*).

The question arises rather naturally why lyric poets die so young—
i.e., why they do not survive to surmount tragic encounters and reach
the larger circle of epic involvements (or as we might say political
involvement): Keats, Shelley, Byron, Hart Crane, Dylan Thomas, the
latter remaining a little longer, Rimbaud a little less long, having
abandoned as a teenager any powerful production of words and
surviving only to write domestic or business letters.

I would like to expand my definitions in a different direction to
include comedy in order to say what I think about it: There are two
tragic moments allied to levels of personal maturity or (looked at from
inside the hero) as rites of passage: the tragedy of the young man, of
Hamlet or Oedipus Rex who moves from young manhood to maturity,
and the tragedy of the older man, of Lear or Oedipus at Colonus (or
in a certain reading of Willy Loman) who moves from maturity to
sanctity or *superior* manhood. The first is a movement embracing life
as the fulfillment of youth and the other is a movement embracing
death as a fulfillment of life. Oedipus must leave Thebes in order to
make himself available to other states. Christ must leave us locally, he
says, in order to be really with us. Hamlet died for us.

Between these two tragic moments lies Comedy, which is the
moment of wedding, as in TWELFTH NIGHT, comedy par excellence,

where three couples marry at the close or in ULYSSES which ends with Molly Bloom's powerful yea-saying to the idea of renewed honeymoon. It is at the moment of wedding where the young tragic problem is solved: the encounter with the family is reconciled by one's stepping out of the family he is born into in order to found his own. But this healing action involves love and love must be learned. The source of tragic conflict is ambivalence, and the problem of learning to love is the problem of learning to exorcise the ambivalence in one's relationship with another. Language enters the discussion at this point because we are all stutterers in the face of love; all of us then are country bumpkins who must learn to speak, to utter our love without ambivalence. Thus all of us, as poor lovers, identify with the mute or inarticulate heroes, the Benjys, the jongleurs, the lonely hunters of the heart. "We fog bound people are all stammerers," O'Neill says.

The final moment of inarticulation is the moment of silence, the moment of late tragedy, as the other inarticulation is the moment of young tragedy. In the later inarticulateness one hears this "Be still and know that I am God." It is the silence of Hamlet (who moves so swiftly from the one tragic moment to the other, combining the acceptance of life with the acceptance of death) as opposed to the self-castrating silence of Iago. *Wovon man nicht sprechen kann darüber müss man schweigen.*[1] As distinct from these two moments of inarticulation the very first such moment, of which I shall speak later, is that of infancy. To say a paradox: Man's inarticulations mark the joints in his life.

Now as it is practically impossible to rid ourselves utterly of ambivalence, so at the time of wedding we still stutter and the Comedy is imperfect; thus Tragi-comedy is the most existential dramatic form, the one closest to the truth of the human situation, and Beckett knew acutely what he was about when he used this genre.

"I suppose the easiest part of the production of art is the suffering," I have written elsewhere. "Artists have not minded pain so long as they could keep it from killing them and get their work done: so long as the mad man, the beast and the angel Dylan Thomas found inside himself or the boy, the man and the woman James Joyce found in himself, did not crack the china skull in which they sprouted so dangerously together."

But many poets have chosen death rather than to continue their work, and some poets (I have mentioned Rimbaud) have been able to survive only if they did not write but committed instead the symbolic

---

1 Wittgenstein "Whereof man cannot speak of this he must remain silent."

castration of the murder of the gift, the excision of power in themselves. The trauma of continued life for a poet is I believe allied to the problem of continuing to build what we call "the body of work" a man forms. The word body ("corpus") is important. One of my colleagues at State University of New York has found that Sylvia Plath's work shows a fantasy of building the body of the father, the COLOSSUS of her title—that her poems are fragments of this body and that her suicide coincides with the inability to continue such work. This exactly corroborates for the female poet what I have suggested for the male lyric poet: that he builds in his work the body of his mother—that he wishes to give birth to her as she has done for him. In building the body of the parent of the opposite sex through his work the poet establishes a sexual relationship with his own work and dramatizes at the lyric level (the battle with himself, that is) the tragic battle (the battle with the parent). Thus he plays out within himself the primal scene, one part of himself taking the feminine role another the masculine. It is because of this fact, that one forms a body with his poetry, that we must demand of poetry a surface of sensual beauty.[2] The poet must conjure the vision of the mother and he must make her sing to him (and, in narrative poetry, tell him "a story").

The fact that so many lyric poets die young, or, in Dante's phrase, "midway through life" (Hart Crane was nearly 33) suggests that they cannot duplicate in their work the lower half of the mother's body, the part that *takes* as well as giving with the upper part. A poet who survives may find himself like Yeats writing poetry which is more sexually oriented in his later years. I find it significant here that one's breaking into syntax, an advance which makes poetry possible, comes about rather suddenly as another acquaintance of mine has found, in connection with attempts to deal with the separation from the mother at about the age of 1½. Separated from the breast the poet begins to rebuild that portion of the mother's body with the mouthing of his poetry, having already as a child rebuilt her face in another way into that of his dolls or his toy animals. But oftentimes the poet would rather die than face the sexuality of the mother (and hence, of the parents together), which keeps him separated from her in the tragic fashion. He chooses death over the tragic encounter, remaining a lyric poet, holding onto his melancholy for dear life, as it were, and falling far short of the true comic moment, the moment of wedding free of ambivalence [the wedding which on the other hand is so often also the wake (as in Shakespeare, Joyce and Faulkner)].

2 In my opinion the poets who most show this in my time are James Wright, Galway Kinnell and Robert Bly.

This concern of the poet with the mother's body as I see it helps me to understand why New York School poetry is so unfeeling. Whether Kenneth Koch writes about "The Pleasures of Peace" or whether he writes about "Sleeping with Women" all feeling is leveled, and one is left with brilliant ratiocination and with a bastard comedy which has somehow short-circuited the moment of the truly comic, the moment, I repeat, of wedding. Perhaps we laugh at this poetry for the same reason we laugh at jokes, because we are spared the expenditure of energy necessary to deal with anxieties roused by feelings, and this excess of energy can emerge in the smile. It is easy to see why Koch is such a great teacher of children. There is no body of the mother and no scene of the parents in New York School poetry and so this poetry shows its kinship with abstract painting, which it grew up with. Abstract painting has got rid of the human figure and thus got rid of erotic feeling, for Kenneth Clark has pointed out that there is erotic feeling present at the base of the use of the nude in painting. All figures painted (once undressed in the eyes of the beholder) lead to the nude and hence to the primal scene. The audience as voyeur is spared sexual anxiety in abstract painting. However it is a self-defeating movement for, as Plato pointed out in the *Meno,* where there is color there shape goes also, and wherever there is shape I add there lurks finally (to "rorshock" us) the figure of the parent and its display in the primal scene. The figure finds its way back into pop art and pop poetry only through the elaboration of the child's comic strip (I now see "comic strip" as an unconscious pun) with its curious pointillist composition which visualizes the minute bullets the TV gun shoots us with to form its images. Or again pop art (should I call it mom art also?) elevates into totem status the baked goods and the cans of the kitchen or tubes of the bathroom and so uses figures which hide again the parents and their scene together.

As painting shows erotic concern at its root (a painter paints with the brush of his penis said D. H. Lawrence) so does poetry both at the fantasy level of the body of the work and also at the level of immediate presence, for in poetry there is always breath, the breath of the mouth, and behind it of moist, hidden organs, with their enactment of expulsions. To use an earlier myth one might say that every breathing of a poem is an expulsion from the garden of Eden, which by the poem's content and by its ritual rhythms, its yearnings, tries to dramatize our return to that Garden. Here, however, I am more directly concerned with genital expulsion out of the mouth—I am more concerned with the displacement upwards from that "other mouth" which the man and woman know, and with the expelling itself, which looked at from the masculine point of view, is ejaculation, while looked at from the feminine it is giving birth.[3]

The aggressive poetry of hatred, of warmongering or antiwarmongering, of racism or antiracism tries to hide behind the skirts of the poet's mouth to say that the poet is only masculine (and this whether the mouth speaks feminist content or not). I am not saying there is no place in poetry for militancy, the politically persuasive, the feminist or the masculinist. I am saying that what makes something *poetry* in the first place is its musical quarrel with the self, its lyricism. Without that there *is* no poetry though there may well be something else. David Ray once asked me to write a poem about the Hungarian Revolution and I told him all my poetry was about the Hungarian Revolution. "Out of our quarrels with others we make rhetoric," Yeats said. "And out of our quarrels with ourselves we make Poetry." "The spiritual combat," Rimbaud told us, "is more bloody than any human battle." And he should know for he died a slow death of it. Some poets brandish their swords to make us forget they are using words and that words are of the mouth, of the mother, and to make us forget that poetry is learned first as a way of separating from the mother's breast, as a way of realizing, through the pain of weaning, the radical separateness, the identity indeed, of the self. So Robert Bly in his "Deep Image" School as it is sometimes called writes brilliant, strong poetry of the war (against it to be sure) as in "The Teeth Mother Naked at Last" but reminds us in discussion that the true job of the poet is to lead the masculine, aggressive function back a certain way toward the wings of the feminine function. (I may say here that I am mildly suspicious of how successful Bly's aesthetic is at exorcizing the aggressive element, for in an essay he speaks of "dipping down into the unconscious" when this active procedure can in fact scarcely work. One does not dip down into the unconscious, one finds a method of allowing it to well up into one's poem.)

To return, when I spoke of the poet's leading "The masculine aggressive function back a certain way toward the wings of the feminine function" I was not basically using a theatrical image, but I might do that: The poet comes out on the stage in the masculine light of day, under the sun, sometimes too much "I' the sun," indeed having emerged from the dark belly of Jonah's whale onto the shore or, in my present image, having just emerged from the wings. But he must return there, to the belly or the wings, in order to recoup and nourish himself so that he can nourish us, feed us bread, not stones.

3 While as an image common to male and female it might be seen as displaced anal activity.

Returning from the wings onto the stage the poet may well lead his brothers, the members of his school, and one thinks first here of the school coming out of the shadow of Black Mountain. I may say that this celebration of brothers too is a way of short-circuiting the tragic encounter with the parents, with their primal scene and their judgmental function. One needn't deal with the parents if one keeps in touch primarily with the brothers. In so far as paternal figures are relevant for the Black Mountain group, they indeed seem more maternal or matriarchal than patriarchal even though they be sexually male (Olson and Williams); for there is more concern in this group with its members being of the same earth than with a judgmental hierarchy of first and second sons or daughters. But I am particularly concerned here with the following fact: In showing us what good brothers and sisters they are the Black Mountain poets deny the *fight* with the brothers. Now Melanie Klein in her analysis of youngsters has found that sibling battles dramatize the primal scene. The Black Mountain poets thus deny their involvement in that. I know that fraternity is more important for instance to Duncan than hierarchy for when I wrote him in 1961 or 1962 at the time of the beginning of my poetry magazine CHOICE and asked him for poems (having stated that I did not believe in schools because schools tended to elevate lesser talents in the same swim and to ignore greater talents not in the same swim), Robert replied that he did not agree with the policy of printing the best wherever you could find it and thought it much more important to print members of a group. I also know that fraternity is very important not only to the Black Mountain School as such but to the San Francisco Beat group as well, which constantly talk about one another in their poems and have their pictures taken and published together. The two schools often overlap and give readings or workshops together. I remember a wonderful quotation from Ginsberg who was being interviewed in San Francisco after he, Creeley, Levertov, and Duncan had given a workshop together in Vancouver. "Mr. Ginsberg," asked the interviewer, "I understand you and Miss Levertov and Mr. Duncan taught the craft of verse up at UBC in Vancouver." "No," said Ginsberg, "Denise and Robert and I did not teach the craft of verse. We were all emotionally bankrupt and went around weeping and asking our students for love."

He is right about that. We must love one another or die said Auden, and before him a character in "Brothers Karamazov." Poets say they want everybody to love everybody but they (we) mainly want you the audience to care about us, and so we do what we can to make you feel that we care about you. The poet is an anonymous lover I believe, and his poetry is an anonymous reaching out, which occasionally becomes personal—when there are those present who care to listen. At the personal moment a mysterious thing happens, which reminds us of magic, and hence of the power of Orpheus: the loneliness each of us feels locked inside his own skin, and the anonymous reaching each of us does therefore, becomes a *bond* and hence we are neither alone nor anonymous in the same sense as we were before.

I for my part am a loner, not a member of a school. I want to help others discover their own voices in workshops and I want others upon hearing my work to hear their own voices echoing inside themselves.

Does this allow me to say I have escaped the flight from the primal scene somehow? That I have faced it and stood alone, having earned the right to wear a necklace of "the bad mother's" teeth, having come away from them unbidden and unbitten? Or that I have watched the primal scene untraumatized and been enabled to move on without the support of sisters and brothers? I might wish it did, but in fact it does not, for in some ways I am jealous of the brotherhoods of poets, which do not number me among them. And as a loner reaching out to you the audience with the long penis of my tongue of poems, showering the sperm of my syllables and breathing on you with the passion of my warm breath, I have only recently learned to look at you as you are looking at me. (It is easier for me to imagine that I am an exhibitionist in the spot light than that I am a voyeur, which is probably closer to the truth, wanting to peer into the curtained windows of your inmost heart to see what I may be fertilizing there.) In other words I too displace the battle of the primal scene and in still another way: for it takes place between you and me which is (in my terms) more tragic than lyric, for it is the displacement of relationships from my own parents and siblings, with whom I am not at ease. Why do we so much fear that primal scene? Why do poets go to such great lengths (my phrase) to displace, dramatize and (right word) *embody* it? Perhaps because otherwise we would have to see that we are gods: that we have the power and thus the responsibility to give life or to withhold it, to love or to murder, engender or destroy. Though this be true for poet and nonpoet alike the poet feels it especially: for, unable to account for the gift he possesses, he has already begun to suspect for this other reason that he may be a god. Such anointment, such mixed blessing brings special, powerful guilt. As I have said in another place and still deeply believe and repeat: "It's not the skeleton in the closet we are afraid of, it's the god."

JOHN LOGAN

THOMAS McGRATH

Thomas McGrath was born in North Dakota and educated at the University of North Dakota, Louisiana State, and New College, Oxford, where he was a Rhodes Scholar. He has taught at various schools and worked as a free-lance writer. With his wife, Eugenia, he is the co-founder of the magazine *Crazy Horse*. His books include *Longshot O'Leary's Garland of Practical Poesy*, *A Witness to the Times*, *Figures from a Double World*, *New and Selected Poems*, and *Letter to an Imaginary Friend*, a work of epic proportions and still in progress. He has written several children's books, scripts for documentary films, and is the author of a novel, *The Gates of Ivory, The Gates of Horn*. He teaches at Moorhead State College in Minnesota.

Wayne Gudmundson

from LETTER TO AN IMAGINARY FRIEND, Part One

II

2
And I hear the pad of feet to the union hall—
But that is New York (17th Street): Showboat Quinn
Goes by barefoot: fanfare of baseball bats—
They are whacking the seamen like mamba gourds down Hudson.
And elsewhere old Mister Peets is saying "Eeyah! He's the man!"—
Listening to Morrison blasting dead Huey Long
As the moon spins over Baton Rouge in the freezing Christmas,
And the waterworks crackle.
                              Plumber Peets cocks an eye,
As the pipes burst like shrapnel and the citizens, crazed,
Unshaven, their bladders bursting, bray at the moon.
At the moon and Peets, who sits at the radio, high
As a coon in a tree, near the rasping gas-fire, sucking
His sugar-tit pipe and his politics.
                                    The Phony War
Sings in the streets.
                    Jimmy plays football.
                                        Warren,
Pinched and poor-favored as a parson's luck,
Carrying his future—that North Sea grave—like a mile
Of invisible water, comes by . . .

    Now, down in these flats, the imagined city dreams
    In its fiery cages . . .
            Cacodemons and Agathodemons
                            struggling in the pit,
    And, in the heavens, the endless feuds and follies of the blazing far
                                                            stars:
    Ancestral vendettas.
                    Among whom I was born,
        Among the flat fields, flat stores, and the bombed-flat burning towns
    Under the sign of our degenerate fire . . .

Christ! but it's cold.
My garden bears in its tide the wreckage of summer flowers.
In the south Forty the flax is flat with the rust . . .

THOMAS McGRATH 243

VIII

4

We go out in the stony midnight.
Meridian cold.
The stars,

Pure vitriol, framed in the blank obsidian dark,
Like skaters icy asterisks; smolder; and sing; and flame.
In the flickering light, auroral, of the North lifting its torch,
The stacks of the powerhouse fume and sigh. . .
High up, streaking

The lower dark, the smoke whisks east in the slack of a cranky breeze.
A train mourns. Distant. A broken fifth of its spoor
Crowns the brow of the night with its wild mystique.
And under the hysteria of the time, its blind commitments,
Is the talk and electric whisper of the power
Loud in forgotten counties where the poor
Sharpen their harps and axes in the high shine of the dark.

That was our wintry idyl, our pastorale in the cold.
The train whistle for the journey, the smoking stacks for power,
And in every country the need and the will to change.
O landscape of romance, all iron and sentiment
Under the prose of snow!

Later, crossing the black yards of the campus,
We heard the dead cry out from the long marble of sleep—
The old heads of the past, a-dream in their stony niches,
Above their Latin Wisdom.
Being classical—
In the teeth of the northwest wind.
The old dead, and the dead

Still walking around.

I saw all that as the moon spun down toward the Badlands
In the singing cold that only our blood could warm.
A dream surely. Sentimental with its
Concern for injustice (which no one admits can exist).
And some of them died of it, giving blood to the dream.
And some of them ran away; and are still running.

And it's all there, somewhere.
Under the hornacle mine . . .

In the tertiary deposits . . .
                    —Ten minutes before the invention of money . . .

from LETTER TO AN IMAGINARY FRIEND, Part Two

II

   2
Windless city built on decaying granite, loose ends
Without end or beginning and nothing to tie to, city down hill
From the high mania of our nineteenth century destiny—what's loose
Rolls there, what's square slides, anything not tied down
Flies in. . .
            kind of petrified shitstorm.
                              Retractable
Swimming pools.
            Cancer farms.
                    Whale dung
At the bottom of the American night refugees tourists elastic
Watches. . .

            Vertical city shaped like an inverse hell:
At three feet above tide mark, at hunger line, are the lachrymose
Cities of the plain weeping in the sulphurous smog; Annaheim:
South Gate (smell of decaying dreams in the dead air)
San Pedro Land's End. . .
                    —where the color of labor is dark—
(Though sweat's all one color) around Barrio No Tengo,
Among the Nogotnicks of the Metaphysical Mattress Factory, where the
                              money is made.

And the second level: among the sons of the petty B's—
The first monkey on the back of South Gate, labor—at the ten
Thousand a year line (though still in the smog's sweet stench)
The Johnny Come Earlies of the middling class:
                              morality
                                   fink-size
Automatic rosaries with live Christs on them and cross-shaped
                                        purloined
Two-car swimming pools full of holy water. . .
                    From here God goes
Uphill

Level to level.
                Instant escalation of money—up!
To Cadillac country.

                Here, in the hush of the long green,
The leather priests of the hieratic dollar enclave to bless
The lush-working washing machines of the Protestant Ethic ecumenical
Laundries: to steam the blood from the bills—O see O see how
Labor His Sublime Negation streams in the firmament!
Don't does all here; whatever is mean is clean.

And to sweep their mountain tops clear of coyotes and currency
                                                    climbers
They have karate-smokers and judo-hypes, the junkies of pain,
Cooking up small boys' fantasies of mental muscles, distilling
A magic of gouged eyes, secret holds, charm
Of the high school girls demi-virginity and secret weapon
Of the pudenda pachucas (takes a short hair type
For a long hair joke) power queers; socially-acceptable sadists—
Will tear your arm off for a nickel and sell it back for a dime.
And these but the stammering simulacra of the Rand Corpse wise
                                                    men—
Scientists who have lost the good of the intellect, mechanico-
                                                    humanoids
Antiseptically manufactured by the Faustian humunculus process.
And how they dream in their gelded towers these demi-men!
(Singing of overkill, kriegspiel, singing of blindfold chess—
Sort of ainaleckshul rasslin matches to sharpen their fantasies
Like a scout knife.)
                Necrophiles.
                        Money protectors. . .
—They dream of a future founded on fire, on a planned coincidence
Of time and sulphur. . .
                Heraclitian eschatology. . .

And over it all, god's face,
                        or perhaps a baboon's ass
In the shape of an IBM beams toward another war.
One is to labor, two is to rob, three is to kill.
Executive
        legislative
                judiciary. . .
                        —muggery, buggery, and thuggery

All Los Angeles
America
is divided into three parts.

*   *   *   *   *   *

3

Phase change around midnight. By the light of the underground moon
That wake I ride through this range of loss and these wide loose acres
Of stony total damnation in the white unparalleled lost
City. . .

Many nights, ghosting these shores in the shifting moonshine,
I read the weather-signs of the spirit and the spoor of the sour times:
The citizens wrapped like mummies in their coats of poisoned sleep,
The dreamers, crazed, in their thousands, nailed to a tree of wine,
And written on the bold brow of the filthy unbending sky,
And sung among imperfect strangers, chanted in studio back lots,
Among three-way Annies and gay caballeros at home on all ranges,
Or shouted in top-secret factories where they make inflatable breasts,
Sung by the glove-faced masters of money with the sex of knives,
By the million grandmothers drying like cod, like anti-cod, like blind
Robins in the smoky terraces of Pasadena, rung out
On the gold-plated telephones in bankers graves at Forest Lawn,
In the unbalanced books of sleep where the natives dream on credit—
Sung out in every language, alive in the sky as fire,
Is the Word:
the little word:
the word of their love:
to die.

*   *   *   *   *   *

"Traveller under the street lamp, I am farther from home than you."
Not so, old poet, Dreamy Don Gordon. No farther than I was:
Among the gigantico-necrosaurs, who misread size
For vitality, wheeling dervishes mistaking speed for movement—
These records put down between flash floods and forest fires:
(My duty to keep the tally-book: me: ring-tailed roarer
And blue blazer—I'm wearing my blazer) this sacred page
The burning bush and rune stone emblem of Plague Harbor
Necessary document
laughter out of the dark
this sign

THOMAS McGRATH 247

Of a time when the wood was in love with fire, the fire with water. . .

Not all of it like that either, no place being perfect in death.
Myself there to make a winter count and to mine my bread.
And others like me:
                                    mavericks in lonesome canyons, singing
Into the desert. . .
                         Bone-laced shining silence faced us. . .
—But sang there!
                         "Making a little coffee against the cold"—
(Alvaro showed me.)
                              Inventing again the commune and round
Song gathering the Crazy Horse Resistance and Marsh St. Irregulars,
Building the Ramshackle Socialist Victory Party (RSVP)
And Union of Poets.
                         Bad times.
                                    The Revolution
Decaying as fast as the American Dream—whose isotope lead
Bloomed in the nightsticks of the company cops.
                                             And we offered our bodies:
On the Endless Picket Line of the Last of the Live-O Americans
For the Rosenbergs, murdered by Truman and Ironhead Eisenhower—
For all the lost strikes sold out by the labor fakers
Of Business Unionism Reuther Meany Social Plutocracy;
For Communists jailed or on the run in the violent darkness;
For the Negro sold again and again in slavetrade Washington—
And lent them our bodies there, giving our blood to that other
Dream. . .
              It still lives somewhere. . .
                                        accept these tokens. . .

Lived there.
              And every morning down to the hornacle mine,
To the vast dream foundries and mythical money go-downs
Of the city of death. (And always with Comrades Flotsam and Jetsam!)
Reading the wish to die in translatable shirts of autochthons,
Blacklisted by trade unions we once had suffered to build,
Shot down under a bust of Plato by HUAC and AAUP.

Outlaws
              system beaters
                              we held to the hard road

(While Establishment Poets, like bats, in caves with color T.V.
Slept upside down in clusters: a ripe fruited scrambling of ass holes.)
But it's a hard system to beat: working under the hat
On the half-pay offered to outlaws by the fellow-travellers of money:

And time runs fast on a poor man's watch.
                           Marsh St. eroded.
Dry wells. . .
         But I still remember the flowers and Cisco singing
Alive
     and the flowering names of that commune of laughter and light
Those I have named and the others—flowers of a bitter season—
They'll know who I mean . . .
                 And I worked there.
                       I went to work in the dark.

I made poems out of wreckage, terror, poverty, love.
Survived.
       But times end.
              My wife was looking uphill
Toward the Gadget Tree (was last seen crossing over the smog line
Approaching an outpost of sports cars).
                  We came at last to a house
With more windows than money: and written over the door—
(In fire I think)—NO DREAMS IN THIS HOUSE!
                  But my dream begins
Three dreams to the left. . .

        * * * * * *

            Well—money talks. It's hard
To say "love" loud enough in all that mechanical clamor
And perhaps the commune must fail in the filth of the American
                          night—
Fail for a time. . .
        But all time is redeemed by the single man—
Who remembers and resurrects.
              And I remember.
                  I keep
The winter count.
        And will remember and hold you always although
Fortuna, her heavy wheel, go over these hearts and houses.

Marsh Street. . .
>blowing into the universe. . .
>>winds rising
>>>change.

4

Twice, now, I've gone back there, like a part-time ghost
To the wrecked houses and the blasted courts of the dream
Where the freeway is pushing through.
>Snake country now.
>>Rats-run—

Bearable, bearable—
Winos retreat and the midnight newfound lands—
Bearable, perfectly bearable—
Of hungering rich lovers under the troubling moon
Their condominium;
>bowery close; momentary
>>kingdom—
Wild country of love that exists before the concrete
Is poured:
>squatters there.
>>That's all
O.K. with me.

>*   *   *   *   *   *

First time I went back there—about an age ago come Monday—
I went hunting flowers: flowering bushes, flowering shrubs, flowering
Years-grown-over gardens: what was transportable.
What was transportable had been taken long away.
Among the detritus, rock-slides, confessions, emotional morrains—
Along the dream plazas and the alleys of the gone moon—
Some stragglers and wildlings: poppy, sorrel, nightblooming
Nothing.
>And found finally my own garden—where it had been—
A pissed-upon landscape now, full of joy-riding
Beer cans and condoms all love's used up these days
Empty wine bottles wrappers for synthetic bread

>*   *   *   *   *   *

Larkspur, lupin, lavender, lantana, linaria, lovage.
And the foxglove's furry thimble and the tiny chime of fuchsia
All gone.
>The children's rooms have a roof of Nothing

And walls of the four wild winds.
                              And, in the rooms of the night,
The true foundation and threshing floor of love,
Are the scars of the rocking bed, and, on certain nights, the moon.
Unending landscape. . .
                    dry. . .
                              blind robins. . .

                    *   *   *   *   *   *

Blind Robins, Blind Robins—Fisherman, do you take Blind Robins
In the stony trough of the dry Los Angeles river?
No charmed run of alewives or swarming of holy mackerel
From the pentecostal cloud chambers of the sex-charged sea, no
Leaping salmon on the light-embroidered ladders of eternal
                                             redemption?
Damnation of blind robins. . .
                         bacalao. . .
                              dried cod, is that,
Is that all you take on your dead-rod green-fishing Jonah,
Poor boy, mad clean crazy lad I pulled once from this river in spate it
                                             is not

Bearable.

                    *   *   *   *   *   *

    5
____All funeral wreaths must wilt around my neck
In time.
        From that place they ship all bodies east.
And eastward I went
                    turning
                              crossing the dark mountains
In the months of snow
                    turning
                         Los Angeles, San Fran, New York
And return.
           Sustained only by a thin gruel of moonlight
And the knowledge that all was perfection outside my prison of skin.

And perfect there also, although it seemed for a time
That the villain mathematics had sown in the dreaming soul's dark
A sick fancy of number: but there's no number higher
Than One.

All number drowns and dances
                              in still lig●
                                        the great
Aleph of Satori. . .

                    New York, then. . .
                              granite island, mighty
Rock where the spirit gleams and groans in the prison stone:
Held there in black entrapments: soul's Harlems: the steamy
Enchantments of lack and luck: the lonely crucifixions
In the ten thousand endless streets of the megalopolitan dark. . .

And did you come there in summer, toboggoning in the slow sheets
Of earliest love; come there to work your secret name
On the frozen time of a wall; and did you come there riding
The tall and handsome horse whose name's catastrophe?
I came there
            I loved
                    I rebelled with others
                                        I shed my blood
With theirs and we bled a dream alive in the cold streets.
And returned there: after the wars and the years: and colder those iron
Plateaus, and older that dream, and the rapid walls are rusting:
Immortal slogans
                fading
                        that we wrote in fire out of need. . .
Out of need and the generous wish—for love and hunger's the whole
Burden of song. . .

                    And went down there—after years and wars and
                                                        whores
And loaves and fishes: the double-dyed miracles pulled off by Generals
Motors and Moonshine (those gents' act: to starve you while stuffed
With the jawbreaker candy of continual war: the silent American:
Mounted
        automated members of the Hellfire Club
                                        Zombies).
And the talking walls had forgotten our names, down at the Front,
Where the seamen fought and the longshoremen struck the great ships
In the War of the Poor.
                        And the NMU has moved to the deep south
(Below Fourteenth) and built them a kind of a Moorish whorehouse
For a union hall. And the lads who built that union are gone.

Dead. Deep sixed. Read out of the books. Expelled. Members
Of the Ninety-Nine year Club. . .
                              "Business unionism!" says Showboat
(Quinn). "It certainly do hit the spot with the bosses!
Backdoor charters and sweetheart contracts—sell out the workers
And become a by-god proletarian statesmen like Sweet Walter.
Takes a liberal kind of a stiff to make labor-fakin' a *pure* art."
Had swallowed the anchor, that one.
                              And many thousands gone
Who were once the conscience and pride of the cold streets of the
                                                        workers;
Dissolved in numbers is that second Aleph, the Order of Militants,
And the workers defenseless: corralled in the death camps of money
Stoned in a rented dream frozen into a mask
Of false consciousness. . .
                         lip-zipped
                                   the eyes padlocked the ears
Fully transistorized
                    —living a life not their own.
Lost. . .

Still, in the still streets, sometimes, I see them moving—
Sleepwalkers in nightmare, drifting the battlefields of a war
They don't even know is happening—
                              O blessed at the end of a nightstick,
Put to bed in the dark in a painting by Jackson Rauschenberg,
Machined to fit the print in a rack 'n' gawk juke box, stomped
By a runaway herd of Genet fagots, shot full of holes
By the bounty hunters of Mad Avenue, brains drawn off
By the oak-borers of Ivy League schools' mistletoe masters.
Everything's been Los Angelized. . .
                         Alone, now, in the street,
What sign, what blazed tree, what burning lightning of the radical
                                                        Word
Shall write their names on the wall break down that mind-framed
                                                        dark?

Northern lights in winter; in summer the eccentric stairs
The firefly climbs. . .
                    But where is the steering star
                                        where is
The Plow? the Wheel?

Made this song in a bad time. . .
No revolutionary song now, no revolutionary
Party
     sell out
        false consciousness
              yet I *will*
Sing
    for these poor
        for the victory still to come
RSVP

Stone city. . .
        and the dumb struck dim wonders
(Crow voice, hoar head, pig mug)
Citizens of Want County as the Bowery spreads its diseases—
Contemporaries. . .
         An age of darkness has entered that stone
In a few years between wars.   The past holds,
Like a sad dream trapped in granite: what foot can slip free what trail
Blaze in that night-rock where the starry travellers search?

I hear them knock at the far doors of the night I see
Through the haze of marble those shadowy forms. . .
                comrades. . .
                 I'll sing you
Out of the prison stone, I'll pick the lock of your night. . .

But lonesome song, for a fact. History's been put into deep-freeze
In libraries and museums. . .
        those limestone bowers its prisons. . .
But still the wind blows and the stone shakes in the night
Sometimes. . .
     a shrill singing wakes in the granite matrix:
Music of bone flutes, a skeleton harp the wind
Thumbs and fondles. . .
        skull-trumpets. . .
           voices under the ice. . .
The song I hear them singing is the Miseries and the Terrors of New
                York. . .

The misery of morning when the moneyclock turns loose its five loud
                lions

(The lion of the landlord, the lion of bread, the lion of a lone girl
Dying in Cheyenne, and the twin lions of loss and age.)
Terror of morning late dreams like clouds stuffed
With eagles of scrap-iron: sagging over the slow fires
Of anxious beds: those peat-bogs that once held hands with the
                                                            lightning.

The misery of six o'clock and the nightshift oozing like ghosts
Sidereal ectoplasm through hell holes in pavements: a scandal
Of blind birds swelling the clogged sleeve of the dead-lighted
Dayside. . .
                a host burning
                        a nation of smoke. . .

Terror of the time clock mechanical salaams low pressure systems
Blowing out of the nightbound heart's high Saharas,
A muezzin of blood blazing in a cage built out of doves. . .
Terror of the noonday bullhorn pulling its string of sound
Out of the lunch box: time where the tides rage off Hatteras
And the drowned locomotives roll like dream monsters slow in the grip
Of the clashing vast deep: and their bells chime: and the whistle rust
Lights submarine tunnels toward dead harbors, sounding far stations
Closed forever. . .
                retired at sea
                        their circular shoes
Still

    Terror of the quitting hour, the air full of skinning knives
And the damp buffalo falling through the scaly tenement walls.
Thin-fit lives: tamped matrimonial gunpowder, ancestral pistols.

And the terrors and miseries of the arc of darkness extending past
                                                            midnight:
Charismatic lightning of alcohol dead in its chapel of glass,
The harping dream-song in the round ditches of revolving roads
Silent. The last ship sinking on the sea of a wounded brow—
All terror and misery present now in the loud and dying
Parish past midnight—a thousand fast mustangs freezing in juke box
Ice, the little shelters built out of temporal wine
Blowing away in the wind the night-bound death wranglers

Stumbling into the day
                wait.
                    For the angel.
                          Wait.

In New York at five past money, they cut the cord of his sleep.
In New York at the ten past money they mortgaged the road of his
                                tongue,
Slipped past the great church of song and planted a century of silence
On the round hearts' hill where the clocktower the cock and the moon
Sang.
        At a quarter past money in New York a star of ashes
Falls in Harlem and on Avenue C strychnine condenses
In the secret cloisters of the artichoke.
                         At half past money in New York
They seed the clouds of his sleep with explosive carbon of psalms,
Mottoes, prayers in fortran, credit cards.
                       At a quarter to money
In New York the universal blood pump is stuffed full of stock
                              quotations:
And at Money all time is money.
                    False consciousness.
                        Bobbery.
Meanwhile, of course
              —wait for the angel. . .
                      Meanwhile of course. . .

V

   2
      Evening—another evening—and the lights flare
From the farmstead yardlamps far over the blank open
Spread of the prairie night.
                    Renaissance of illumination
Courtesy REA.
            And each lamp beacons and beckons
Across the neighbor and empty fields: *Come ye over.*
But no one comes.
            And the traveller on the worn and improved roads
Goes by in improved darkness not even a barking dog
Lights. . .
         The houses blacked out as if for war, lit only

With random magnesium flashes like exploding bombs (TV
Courtesy REA)
        Cold hellfire
                screams
Tormented, demented, load the air with anguish
                        invisible
Over the sealed houses, dark, a troop of phantoms,
Demonic, rides: the great Indians come in the night like
Santa Claus
        down the electronic chimneys whooping and dead. . .

Still, in the still night from a high hill (if there were one)
In the dark of the moon, with the far and fiery heavensteads blazing—
Huge galaxy-ranches and farm-constellations and solitary starcrofts
                           shining—
On such a night, if one had a hill, he might see, in these lower
And faster fields, the constellations of farmlight: less vast
But moving still, in their hour and season, like the Plough and the Bear
Burning. . .
        impermanent. . .
                companions. . .
                      Having their dignity there.

But from that imagined hill I see also the absence of light—
The abandoned farmhouses, like burnt-out suns, and around them
The planetary out-buildings dead for the lack of warmth, for the
                        obscured
Light that the house once held.
                And where has it gone?
                      And where
Have *they* gone? Those ghosts who warmed these buildings once?

Over the hills and far away. ("Our road"
Is anybody's road now: road that we all went away on.)
Away to the new wars, and the new ways, and the old
Whores of a system that found us expendable; to Work and to Want
In other pressures
        playpens
            —in wilder parts of the sky. . .

Dark, dark the houses lie there.
            The wind of the winter,

Like an animal, tears at the broken roofs,
                              and the rain of spring
Opens the doors sly as a thief;
                              and the fires of summer,
Flare on the broken panes, blister, consume;
                              and autumn
Arranges in those sad parlors, chiefly, the melancholy
Of absent chairs.
                    There, hysteria has entered the wallpaper:
It flaps in the gloom like a trapped bird.

                              In empty kitchens
The rat-turds, hard as beebees, rust.
                              Filth on the stairs
(O grandfather dust!) thick and mousetracked, leads to rooms
Without character: boxes of boxed darkness: birdshit—
(But only the swallow nests here—the daubs of mud over doorways
Are the most live things in the house.)
                              In the downcellar dark
Are nests of Mason jars: crocks; jugs—an entire
Breakable culture abandoned archeological disjecta
Membra lost processes. . .
                    And the attic night trembles
For its terrible treasures
                    its secret histories like deadmen's bones
Unburied in the gapthroated oldfashioned trunks' dark fathoms.

Here, furbearing bibles, inlaid with fake gemstones,
Like sand covered drift-fences of tallies of a winter count,
Record, before Genesis, the early departures and the first begots—
Writ by hand. . .
                    and the letters, packaged in rotting twine,
Talk all dark in a language of leaving and loss
                                        forgotten
Tongues
        foreign
                sounding
                    —words of love and hunger. . .

Finally the aging and ageless photographs, unfixed in time
Or light, mourn: for the abandoned ghosts who no longer
Haunt these frames.
                    And where have they gone?
                                        Through bankruptcy;

To be spiritual props to the interest rate in the Farmers' First
National Bank of West Nowhere Dakota;
                                        to die in the dying
She-towns of the farmlands and the thousand widow-sodalities
Of those depths (the husbands long gone under from working
To assure their wives this final loneliness).
                                        Last, they've gone
Back to the land:
                   in ten thousand little lost graveyards, forgotten:
Before the fashionable collectivity of contemporary death. . .

But you will not find them there, nor even the ruined stone
Maybe, that spelled their fate.
                        (Look for MacCormick reapers,
Look for the brass-tongued Nichols & Shepherd steamer, these dead
Machines are more alive.)
                        And now where the fence lines join,
In deserted coigns and corners abandoned they enter the night rock. . .
In the lilac-choked encampments of the older dead, in a grave plot
(Where in summer the wheat like a bright sea breaks and in winter
                                        the fallow
Encroaches) under the last of the true prairie, the last
Of the wild grass.
              Forgotten.
                        Lost as the last Indian:
Who were good men in their time: a century or a cemetery ago.

                *   *   *   *   *   *

VI

    4
Begun before Easter. . .
                        Sign of the Fish. . .
                                        wind whining
Out of the black north's cold quadrant, the moon
Glistening on the folds of the coulee snow and a far scar
Where the river sings and ceases, locked in its house of ice;
Cold front sliding in: a wisp of high cirrus
Rides over the Indian graves, the barometer drowses, the burning
Clock of midnight turns on its axle of darkness. . .

                                        Had come there,
To that House, first sign in the blessed zodiac

THOMAS McGRATH

Of all my loves and losses. . .
                    —to sing and summon you home.

                    *   *   *   *   *   *

Now: the wind shifts
                    a star
                        falls in the sea.
Skyros
            the statue of Brooke on the citadel.
                                    Time interposes
A discontinuous strata, the sediments of the summer:
What was and what is slide along old fault lines, history
Condenses its marble heros
                        a metamorphic palimpsest
Hardens between the farmhouse and here: and I dive
Into the nightrock
                    terror

                    Now I call you:
                            I call
You:
        from the four Winds and from Fire, come forth now
My thunderbird jawsmiths and soapbox phoenixes;
                                    out of the ice-lined
Rolling coffins of the U.P. Line: rise;
                            I call you
From Water;
            blind marble of those tolling bones
Walk home forever now from the cold dismembering sea;

I call you from holy Earth:
                        boneflower: starform
                                    I call you now:
Goddess, sweet land I love, Old Lady, my darling ones—
Come:
        We'll walk up out of the night together.
                                    It's easy. . .
Only:
        open your eyes. . .
                        slip your foot out of the stone. . .
I'll take you. . .
            my darlings, my dear ones. . .
                                    over the river.
                    North Dakota-Skyros-Ibiza-Agaete-Guadalajara, 1968

ON MY WORK

Someone asks me: "How is *Letter to an Imaginary Friend* like or
unlike other long poems?" And someone has written me: "*Letter* is
the first post-modernist long poem." Someone else: "You have
understood what Whitman meant—that in our time the long poem
has got to be biographical."

I don't know what this means. Aren't all poems now "post-
modernist?" The great poems of the deep past are third person and
"objective." The modernist "long poem" is often not very long, often
essentially lyric, and is usually organized around symbols or themes,
and the poet is usually at pains to establish "esthetic distance." Of
the "long poems" around when I was first at work on *Letter*, Hart
Crane's was the one I loved, but it was so far from what I seemed to
be doing that I never thought about it. It seemed to me then that
there were no models and no theory for the kind of thing that I was
doing. That can be frightening and exhilarating.

The writing of long poems has now become a cottage industry. I
have seen few of these poems of recent years, but there are enough
of them to interest some critic—*something* is going on—even a
bibliography would be valuable. Of the "long poems" critics *do* refer
to (work of Lowell and Berryman)—these seem to me not single
poems at all but collections of related poems. There is nothing wrong
with such collections. What is interesting is that critics seem to *want*
and *need* to regard these collections as *long poems:* as if there were
some unconscious need for the long poem to *exist,* as if the critics
were trying to will it into existence. . .

How is *Letter* unlike other long poems? In part, perhaps, because
it is "pseudo-autobiography." It is *not* simply autobiography. I am
very far from believing that all parts of my life are meaningful enough
to be usable in the poem. But I believe that all of us live twice: once
personally and once as a representative man or woman. I am inter-
ested in those moments when my life line crosses through the
concentration points of the history of my time. *Then* I live both
personally and representatively. I hope to be aware of those mo-
ments, because then, I believe, one may be speaking to and for
many people.

Some other differences from other long poems (perhaps). *Letter*
is not a poem that comes out of the sensibility of the city middle-
class intellectual. The city is in the poem, of course, but there is a
lot, too, of the backlands and of *place*—that "Dakota" which is
central to the poem. There is other material in the poem which seems

to me more or less new. Work, for example, is not something which most poets write about. Also communality or solidarity—feelings which perhaps are more important to us than romantic love—never appear in our poetry. Perhaps I have begun to identify them. The attitudes toward these materials, also, are not those of the petty bourgeois intellectual no matter how alienated.

Finally the poem is *political;* it hopes to invent and restructure the past and the future by using the narrative line of the speaker of the poem and events from personal and political-social history to create the "legend" of these times. I am aware of how arrogant this must sound. But I think perhaps this is the only *long* poem to make the attempt.

*   *   *

I am now working on Part Three. Someone asks: "What kind of materials are in One and Two?"

Part One is a narrative which begins with early childhood on a North Dakota farm, goes on to early work experiences, sex, college, and politics in the north and in Louisiana, hitchhiking journeys, the war, and afterwards. It ends in a kind of satori in Los Angeles. Part Two continues the narrative line, picking up themes from Part One and re-seeing them in the light of new circumstances. My note to the book says that Two "is concerned with the offering of evidences for a revolutionary miracle and with elaborating a ceremony out of these materials to bring such a miracle to pass." Part Two begins by repeating the last line of One, and the two parts are a single whole, Book One of the whole poem. Of Part Three, I know very little. I have written some of it and have some longish passages and some bits and pieces which I think belong in projected sections for which I have notes. I think I begin to see the shape it will take. As to the substance—that will be similar to materials in Parts One and Two, but I think the method will be wilder.

There is an inevitable problem with a poem where one's life provides a main narrative track: since the poem shows no sign of stopping, my death (although I have a Two Hundred Year Plan of work) may leave it unfinished. Someone tells me that this is of no consequence, that, after all, "the paintings of Jackson Pollock are completed in the space beyond the picture surface." Cold comfort. I don't like virtues made from necessity. But perhaps others will complete the poem—it seems, in any case, to have a life independent of me in a way that none of my other poems do.

*   *   *

Methods of work? Do I see the structure of the sections of the poem as a kind of collage? It is a useful metaphor, but I see the structure of the sections and of the poem as a whole as being more analogous to the structures of certain films. It is a question of the use of *time*. In any section there will be a general narrative time—the past. But the poem, like some films, makes use of flash-backs and flashes forward, "replays," "subliminal cuts" (phrases from earlier passages or ones which will be developed later on), etc., etc. It would be easy to push this analogy too far, but there are, I think, equivalents of dissolves, fades, etc. So the narrative line is interrupted by other time-lines right up to the immediate present in which the speaker of the poem is sitting in a particular place writing down the immediate words—because the writing of the poem is *also* a part of the subject of the poem. Thus the immediate landscape, what is "outside this window," enters and qualifies or comments on some landscape or circumstance of the past. Similarly the narrative voice is interrupted: occasionally by a remembered quotation, sometimes by the voice of an identified character. Or the tone or persona of the speaker may change: he may have been narrating something from his childhood from a point of view very close to that of the boy in the past; but then the tone may shift radically, and the passage may move into a satirical or fantastic view of the same material, or may bring in elaborations to the scene, or language that is very distant from the point of view of the telling a few lines back. I think this will seldom confuse if the reader will just go on—the poem will soon be back to the initial narrative line. The same way with words or references: they will be made clear by the context, either in their specific meaning or general intent. As the poem goes on, of course, there are occasional references to earlier passages, the repetitions of phrases or lines from earlier parts. It would be best to know those, but generally, again, the context will make them clear. Or so I hope.

Someone asked Godard if he did not think a film should have a beginning, a middle, and an end. Godard is supposed to have answered: "Yes. But not necessarily in that order." The speaker of *Letter* moves around a bit and is interrupted now and then, time shifts, landscapes dissolve into others, but underneath a surface which is fractured and agitated I think the general movement is clear.

THOMAS McGRATH

W. S. MERWIN

W. S. Merwin was born in 1927 in New York City. Educated at Princeton, he has lived most of his life abroad, chiefly in England, Mexico, Spain, and France. He has earned his living as a translator, perhaps the most prolific and skillful of his time, publishing translations of *The Poem of the Cid, Spanish Ballads, The Satires of Perseus,* and collections of poems by Jean Follain, Antonio Porchia, and Osip Mandelstam. In 1968 he published his *Selected Translations.* Books of his own poems include *A Mask for Janus, The Dancing Bears, Green With Beasts, The Drunk in the Furnace, The Moving Target, The Lice, The Carrier of Ladders,* and *Writings to an Unfinished Accompaniment.*

Douglas Hall

FOR A COMING EXTINCTION

Gray whale
Now that we are sending you to The End
That great god
Tell him
That we who follow you invented forgiveness
And forgive nothing

I write as though you could understand
And I could say it
One must always pretend something
Among the dying
When you have left the seas nodding on their stalks
Empty of you
Tell him that we were made
On another day

The bewilderment will diminish like an echo
Winding along your inner mountains
Unheard by us
And find its way out
Leaving behind it the future
Dead
And ours

When you will not see again
The whale calves trying the light
Consider what you will find in the black garden
And its court
The sea cows the Great Auks the gorillas
The irreplaceable hosts ranged countless
And fore-ordaining as stars
Our sacrifices
Join your word to theirs
Tell him
That it is we who are important

FLY

I have been cruel to a fat pigeon
Because he would not fly
All he wanted was to live like a friendly old man

He had let himself become a wreck filthy and confiding
Wild for his food beating the cat off the garbage
Ignoring his mate perpetually snotty at the beak
Smelling waddling having to be
Carried up the ladder at night content

Fly I said throwing him into the air
But he would drop and run back expecting to be fed
I said it again and again throwing him up
As he got worse
He let himself be picked up every time
Until I found him in the dovecote dead
Of the needless efforts

So that is what I am

Pondering his eye that could not
Conceive that I was a creature to run from

I who have always believed too much in words

FINDING A TEACHER

In the woods I came on an old friend fishing
and I asked him a question
and he said Wait

fish were rising in the deep stream
but his line was not stirring
but I waited
it was a question about the sun

about my two eyes
my ears my mouth
my heart the earth with its four seasons
my feet where I was standing
where I was going

it slipped through my hands
as though it were water
into the river   `
it flowed under the trees
it sank under hulls far away
and was gone without me
then where I stood night fell

I no longer knew what to ask
I could tell that his line had no hook
I understood that I was to stay and eat with him

THE INITIATE

At last a juggler is led out under the stars
tears begin to roll down his cheeks

he catches them
they fly through his hands

he sees the stars swimming up
in his tears
and he feels in his hands his tears
fly trembling through the night

what is that juggler singing
later when the morning star
is dry

he is singing Not a hair
of our head do we need to take with us
into the day

not even a hand do we need
to take with us
not even an eye
do we need to take with us
into the light

THE JUDGMENT OF PARIS

for Anthony Hecht

Long afterwards
the intelligent could deduce what had been offered
and not recognized
and they suggest that bitterness should be confined
to the fact that the gods chose for their arbiter
a mind and character so ordinary
albeit a prince

and brought up as a shepherd
a calling he must have liked
for he had returned to it

when they stood before him
the three
naked feminine deathless
and he realized that he was clothed
in nothing but mortality
the strap of his quiver of arrows crossing
between his nipples
making it seem stranger

and he knew he must choose
and on that day

the one with the gray eyes spoke first
and whatever she said he kept
thinking he remembered
but remembered it woven with confusion and fear
the two faces that he called father

the first sight of the palace
where the brothers were strangers
and the dogs watched him and refused to know him
she made everything clear she was dazzling she
offered it to him
to have for his own but what he saw
was the scorn above her eyes
and her words of which he understood few
all said to him *Take wisdom*
take power
you will forget anyway

the one with the dark eyes spoke
and everything she said
he imagined he had once wished for
but in confusion and cowardice
the crown
of his father the crowns the crowns bowing to him
his name everywhere like grass
only he and the sea
triumphant
she made everything sound possible she was
dazzling she offered it to him
to hold high but what he saw
was the cruelty around her mouth
and her words of which he understood more
all said to him *Take pride*
take glory
you will suffer anyway

the third one the color of whose eyes
later he could not remember
spoke last and slowly and
of desire and it was his
though up until then he had been
happy with his river nymph
here was his mind
filled utterly with one girl gathering
yellow flowers
and no one like her
the words
made everything seem present

almost present
present
they said to him *Take*
her
you will lose her anyway

it was only when he reached out to the voice
as though he could take the speaker
herself
that his hand filled with
something to give
but to give to only one of the three
an apple as it is told
discord itself in a single fruit its skin
already carved
To the fairest

then a mason working above the gates of Troy
in the sunlight thought he felt the stone
shiver

in the quiver on Paris's back the head
of the arrow for Achilles' heel
smiled in its sleep

and Helen stepped from the palace to gather
as she would do every day in that season
from the grove the yellow ray flowers tall
as herself

whose roots are said to dispel pain

VOICE

for Jane Kirstein 1916–1968

By now you will have met
no one
my elder sister
you will have sat

by her breath in the dark
she will have told you I don't know what
in the way she remembers whatever it is
that's how she is
I never see her
but it's you I miss

by now she'll have sat around you
in a circle holding your hand
saying she's listening but
you'll hear you'll hear what she says
to everyone but especially to my friends
is it good what she tells you
is it anything I'd know

her own brother
but I still remember only
afterwards
and we're all like this

by now
more and more I remember
what isn't so
your voice
as I heard it in a dream
the night you died
when it was no longer yours

THE BLACK PLATEAU

The cows bring in the last light
the dogs praise them
one by one they proceed through the stone arch
on the chine of the hill
and their reflections in the little
cold darkening stream
and the man with the pole
then the night comes down to its roads
full of love for them

‎‎‎‎‎‎‎‎‎‎‎‎‎‎‎‎‎‎‎‎‎‎‎‎‎‎‎‎‎‎‎‎‎‎

I go eating nothing so you will be one and clear
but then how could you drown
in this arid country of stone and dark dew
I shake you in your heavy sleep
then the sun comes
and I see you are one of the stones

Like a little smoke in the vault
light for going
before the dogs wake in the cracked barn
the owl has come in from his shift
the water in the stone basin has forgotten
where I touch the ashes they are cold
everything is in order

Kestrel and lark shimmer over the high stone
like two brothers who avoid each other
on the cliff corner I met the wind
a brother

Almost everything you look on great sun
has fallen into itself here
which it had climbed out of like prayers
shadows of clouds
and the clothes of old women blow over the barrens
one apple tree still blossoms for its own sake

The cold of the heights is not the cold of the valleys
the light moves like a wind
the figures are far away walking slowly
in little knots herding pieces of darkness
their faces remote as the plaster above deaths
in the villages

The upper window of a ruin
one of the old faces
many places near here
things grow old where nothing was ever a child

Oh blessed goat live goat blessed rat
and neither of you lost

There is still warmth in the goat sheds years afterwards
in the abandoned fountain a dead branch points
upwards
eaten out from inside as it appears to me
I know a new legend
this is the saint of the place his present form
another blessing in absence
when the last stone has fallen he will rise
from the water
and the butterflies will tell him what he needs to know
that happened while he was asleep

The beginnings and ends of days like the butts of arches
reach for roofs that have fallen
the sun up there was never enough
high in its light
the bird moves apart from his cry

FEBRUARY

Dawn that cares for nobody
comes home
to the glass cliffs
an expression
needing no face
the river flies under cold feathers
flies on
leaving its body
the black streets bare their veins
night
lives on in the uniforms
in the silence of the headlines
in the promises of triumph
in the colors of the flags
in a room of the heart
while the ends and the beginnings
are still guarded
by lines of doors

W. S. MERWIN 273

hand in hand
the dead guarding the invisible
each presenting its message
I know nothing
learn of me

SNOWFALL

for my mother

Some time in the dark hours
it seemed I was a spark climbing
the black road
with my death helping me up
a white self helping me up
like a brother
growing
but this morning
I see that the silent kin I loved as a child
have arrived all together in the night
from the old country
they remembered
and everything remembers
I eat from the hands
of what for years have been junipers
the taste has not changed
I am beginning
again
but a bell rings in some village I do not know
and cannot hear
and in the sunlight snow drops from branches
leaving its name in the air
and a single footprint

brother

BALLADE OF SAYINGS

In spring if there are dogs they will bark
the sieves of the poor grow coarser
even in the dark we wake upward
each flower opens knowing the garden
water feels for water
the law has no face
nowhere are the martyrs more beautiful
the air is clear as though we should live forever

in summer if there are fleas there will be rejoicing
you kill the front of him I'll kill the back
every sieve knows a dance
each soldier is given a little bleached flag
ours are the only parents
the poor do not exist they are just the poor
the poor dream that their flowers are smaller
patience has the stones for a garden
the seer is buried at last in a gooseyard
the air is clear as though we should live forever

in autumn if there are trees eyes will open
one moment of freedom partakes of it all
those who will imitate will betray
the dogs are happy leading the archers
the hunter is hunted the dealer is dealt the listener is heard
the halls of government are the exhibition palaces of fear
anguish rusts
the poor believe that all is possible for others
each fruit hopes to give light
the air is clear as though we should live forever

in winter if there are feet bells will ring
snow falls in the bread of some and in the mouths of others
nobody listens to apologies
when prisoners clasp their hands a door locks
the days are polished with ashes
the cold lie in white tents hoarding sunrise
the poor we have with us always

the old vine stakes smell of the sea
the air is clear as though we should live forever

Prince it is said that night is one of the sieves
there is no end to how fine we shall be
at the names of the poor the eye of the needle echoes
the air is clear as though we should live forever

THE VINEYARD

Going up through the hill called the vineyard
that seems nothing but stone
you come to a tangle of wild plum and hazel bushes
the spring in the cliff like the sex of a green woman
the taste of the water
and of the stone

you come to the fox's cave in the yellow clay
under the foot of the stone
and barely out of reach lime-crusted nests
of swallows
and in the cliff higher up
holes of swifts and bees
solitary grass

all that stone faces southward
and a little to the east
full of crevices
bats and small birds
foxes and wild honey
clear to the top they call it
the vineyard
where earliest the light
is seen that bids the cock crow

ON OPEN FORM

What is called its form may be simply that part of the poem that had directly to do with time: the time of the poem, the time in which it was written, and the sense of recurrence in which the unique moment of vision is set.

Perhaps this is why in much of the poetry of the high Middle Ages the form seems transparent. Both the role of time in the poem and the role of the poem in time doubtless seemed clear and simple to the Arcipreste de Hita, Dante, Guillaume de Lorris and Chaucer. We can be sure of neither, and we cannot even be certain whether the pretense to such certainty that characterizes some later periods of society (in particular certain phases of neoclassicism) is one of the absurd disguises that can help an art to survive, or merely one of the shrouds that are hardly more than wasted efforts to lend decency to its burial.

The invention of a new form of stanza was a matter of genuine poetic importance to the troubadours. To us it would probably seem scarcely a matter for much curiosity. For the troubadours the abstract form (which certainly they did not hear as an abstract thing) was unquestionably related to that part of the poem that was poetic. For us it is hard to remain convinced that the form, insofar as it is abstract, is not merely part of what in the poem is inescapably technical. For us, for whom everything is in question, the making keeps leading us back into the patterns of a world of artifice so intricate, so insidious, and so impressive, that often it seems indistinguishable from the whole of time.

In a world of technique *motions* tend to become methods. But the undependable life that appears on occasion as poetry would rather die, or so it seems, than follow this tendency, and when a poet himself follows it farther than the source of his gift warrants, his gains of technical facility are likely to render him the helpless master of mere confection.

And yet neither technique nor abstract form can be abandoned, finally. And no doubt neither is dangerous in itself as long as each is recognized as no more than a means, and is not made into an idol and loved for itself. (But it seems to be characteristic of a technological age that means come to dwarf and eclipse or destroy their ends.)

And certainly neither of them automatically excludes or implies the other.

* * *

In an age when time and technique encroach hourly, or appear to, on the source itself of poetry, it seems as though what is needed for any particular nebulous unwritten hope that may become a poem is not a manipulable, more or less predictably recurring pattern, but an unduplicatable resonance, something that would be like an echo except that it is repeating no sound. Something that always belonged to it: its sense and its conformation before it entered words.

*   *   *

At the same time I realize that I am a formalist, in the most strict and orthodox sense. For years I have had a recurring dream of finding, as it were in an attic, poems of my own that were as lyrically formal, but as limpid and essentially unliterary as those of Villon.

*   *   *

Much of what appears, or appeared, as great constructive energy in the poetic revolutions of the first half of this century must have been in part energy made available by the decomposition of a vast and finally anti-poetic poetic organism that had become a nuisance even to itself. The original iconoclasts have reared up other anti-poetic poetic monsters that have achieved senility far more quickly since their shapes were less definite and their substance more questionable from the start.

*   *   *

A poetic form: the setting down of a way of hearing how poetry happens in words. The words themselves do not make it. At the same time it is testimony of a way of hearing how life happens in time. But time does not make it.

*   *   *

To recur in its purest forms (whether they are strict, as in Waller's "Go, Lovely Rose," or apparently untrammelled, as in The Book of Isaiah in the King James Version) poetry seems to have to keep reverting to its naked condition, where it touches on all that is unrealized.

Our age pesters us with the illusion that we have realized a great deal. The agitation serves chiefly to obscure what we have forgotten, into whose limbo poetry itself at times seems about to pass.

*   *   *

What are here called open forms are in some concerns the strictest. Here only the poem itself can be seen as its form. In a peculiar sense if you criticize how it happens you criticize what it is.

* * *

Obviously it is the poem that is or is not the only possible justification for any form, however theory runs. The poem is or it is not the answer to 'why that form?' The consideration of the evolution of forms, strict or open, belongs largely to history and to method. The visitation that is going to be a poem finds the form it needs in spite of both.

* * *

The "freedom" that precedes strict forms and the "freedom" that follows them are not necessarily much alike. Then there is the "freedom" that accompanies poetry at a distance and occasionally joins it, often without being recognized, as in some proverbs. ("God comes to see without a bell." "He that lives on hope dances without music.")

W. S. MERWIN

FRANK O'HARA

Kenward Elmslie

Frank O'Hara was born in Baltimore in 1926 and grew up in Massa-
chusetts. After serving in the Navy during World War II, he attended
Harvard University. He lived the rest of his life in New York City,
working for *Art News* and as a curator for the Museum of Modern
Art. In 1966, he was struck and killed by a dune buggy on Fire Island.
His books include *Meditations in an Emergency, Odes,* and *Lunch
Poems.* His *Collected Poems* were published in 1971.

AUTOBIOGRAPHIA LITERARIA

When I was a child
I played by myself in a
corner of the schoolyard
all alone.

I hated dolls and I
hated games, animals were
not friendly and birds
flew away.

If anyone was looking
for me I hid behind a
tree and cried out "I am
an orphan."

And here I am, the
center of all beauty!
writing these poems!
Imagine!

THE HUNTER

He set out and kept hunting
and hunting. Where, he thought
and thought, is the real chamois?
and can I kill it where it is?
He had brought with him only a dish
of pears. The autumn wind soared
above the trails where the drops
of the chamois led him further.
The leaves dropped around him
like pie-plates. The stars fell
one by one into his eyes and burnt.

There is a geography which holds
its hands just so far from the breast
and pushes you away, crying so.

He went on to strange hills where
the stones were still warm from feet,
and then on and on. There were clouds
at his knees, his eyelashes
had grown thick from the colds,
as the fur of the bear does
in winter. Perhaps, he thought, I am
asleep, but he did not freeze to death.

There were little green needles
everywhere. And then manna fell.
He knew, above all, that he was now
approved, and his strength increased.
He saw the world below him, brilliant
as a floor, and streaming with gold,
with distance. There were occasionally
rifts in the cloud where the face
of a woman appeared, frowning. He
had gone higher. He wore ermine.
He thought, why did I come? and then,
I have come to rule! The chamois came.

The chamois found him and they came
in droves to humiliate him. Alone,
in the clouds, he was humiliated.

POEM

to James Schuyler

There I could never be a boy,
though I rode like a god when the horse reared.
At a cry from mother I fell to my knees!
there I fell, clumsy and sick and good,
though I bloomed on the back of a frightened black mare
who had leaped windily at the start of a leaf
and she never threw me.

I had a quick heart
and my thighs clutched her back.

I loved her fright, which was against me
into the air! and the diamond white of her forelock
which seemed to smart with thoughts as my heart smarted with life!
and she'd toss her head with the pain
and paw the air and champ the bit, as if I were Endymion
and she, moonlike, hated to love me.

All things are tragic
when a mother watches!
and she wishes upon herself
the random fears of a scarlet soul, as it breathes in and out
and nothing chokes, or breaks from triumph to triumph!

I knew her but I could not be a boy,
for in the billowing air I was fleet and green
riding blackly through the ethereal night
towards men's words which I gracefully understood,

and it was given to me
as the soul is given the hands
to hold the ribbons of life!
as miles streak by beneath the moon's sharp hooves
and I have mastered the speed and strength which is the armor of the
    world.

FOR JAMES DEAN

    Welcome me, if you will,
    as the ambassador of a hatred
    who knows its cause
    and does not envy you your whim
    of ending him.

    For a young actor I am begging
    peace, gods. Alone
    in the empty streets of New York
    I am its dirty feet and head
    and he is dead.

He has banged into your wall
of air, your hubris, racing
towards your heights and you
have cut him from your table
which is built, how unfairly
for us! not on trees, but on clouds.

I speak as one whose filth
is like his own, of pride
and speed and your terrible
example nearer than the sirens' speech,
a spirit eager for the punishment
which is your only recognition.

Peace! to be true to a city
of rats and to love the envy
of the dreary, smudged mouthers
of an arcane dejection
smoldering quietly in the perception
of hopelessness and scandal
at unnatural vigor. Their dreams
are their own, as are the toilets
of a great railway terminal
and the sequins of a very small,
very fat eyelid.
             I take this
for myself, and you take up
the thread of my life between your teeth,
tin thread and tarnished with abuse,
you still shall hear
as long as the beast in me maintains
its taciturn power to close my lids
in tears, and my loins move yet
in the ennobling pursuit of all the worlds
you have left me alone in, and would be
the dolorous distraction from,
while you summon your army of anguishes
which is a million hooting blood vessels
on the eyes and in the ears
at that instant before death.
                  And
the menials who surrounded him critically,

languorously waiting for a
final impertinence to rebel
and enslave him, starlets and other
glittering things in the hog-wallow,
lunging mireward in their inane
mothlike adoration of niggardly
cares and stagnant respects
paid themselves, you spared,
as a hospital preserves its orderlies.
Are these your latter-day saints,
these unctuous starers, muscular
somnambulists, these stages for which
no word's been written hollow
enough, these exhibitionists in
well-veiled booths, these navel-suckers?

Is it true that you high ones, celebrated
among amorous flies, hated the
prodigy and invention of his nerves?
To withhold your light
from painstaking paths!
your love
should be difficult, as his was hard.

Nostrils of pain down avenues
of luminous spit-globes breathe in
the fragrance of his innocent flesh
like smoke, the temporary lift,
the post-cancer excitement
of vile manners and veal-thin lips,
obscure in the carelessness of your scissors.

Men cry from the grave while they still live
and now I am this dead man's voice,
stammering, a little in the earth.
I take up
the nourishment of his pale green eyes,
out of which I shall prevent
flowers from growing, your flowers.

AVE MARIA

Mothers of America
            let your kids go to the movies!
get them out of the house so they won't know what you're up to
it's true that fresh air is good for the body
                              but what about the soul
that grows in darkness, embossed by silvery images
and when you grow old as grow old you must
                              they won't hate you
they won't criticize you they won't know
                         they'll be in some glamorous country
they first saw on a Saturday afternoon or playing hookey
they may even be grateful to you
                         for their first sexual experience
which only cost you a quarter
                         and didn't upset the peaceful home
they will know where candy bars come from
                              and gratuitous bags of popcorn
as gratuitous as leaving the movie before it's over
with a pleasant stranger whose apartment is in the Heaven on Earth
   Bldg
near the Williamsburg Bridge
                    oh mothers you will have made the little tykes
so happy because if nobody does pick them up in the movies
they won't know the difference
                         and if somebody does it'll be sheer gravy
and they'll have been truly entertained either way
instead of hanging around the yard
                         or up in their room
                                   hating you
prematurely since you won't have done anything horribly mean yet
except keeping them from the darker joys
                         it's unforgivable the latter
so don't blame me if you won't take this advice
                         and the family breaks up
and your children grow old and blind in front of a TV set
                              seeing
movies you wouldn't let them see when they were young

ANSWER TO VOZNESENSKY & EVTUSHENKO

We are tired of your tiresome imitations of Mayakovsky
we are tired
                        of your dreary tourist ideas of our Negro selves
our selves are in far worse condition than the obviousness
of your color sense
                        your general sense of Poughkeepsie is
a gaucherie no American poet would be guilty of in Tiflis
thanks to French Impressionism
                        we do not pretend to know more
than can be known
                        how many sheets have you stained with your semen
oh Tartars, and how many
                        of our loves have you illuminated with
your heart your breath
                        as we poets of America have loved you
your countrymen, our countrymen, our lives, your lives, and
the dreary expanses of your translations
                        your idiotic manifestos
and the strange black cock which has become ours despite your envy

we do what we feel
                        you do not even do what you must or can
I do not love you any more since Mayakovsky died and Pasternak
theirs was the death of my nostalgia for your tired ignorant race
since you insist on race
                        you shall not take my friends away from me
because they live in Harlem
                        you shall not make Mississippi into Sakhalin
you came too late, a lovely talent doesn't make a ball
  I consider myself to be black and you not even part
where you see death
                        you see a dance of death
                                            which is
imperialist, implies training, requires techniques
our ballet does not employ
                        you are indeed as cold as wax
as your progenitor was red, and how greatly we loved his redness
in the fullness of our own idiotic sun! what
"roaring universe" outshouts his violent triumphant sun!

you are not even speaking
                                    in a whisper
Mayakovsky's hat worn by a horse

ODE: SALUTE TO THE FRENCH NEGRO POETS

From near the sea, like Whitman my great predecessor, I call
to the spirits of other lands to make fecund my existence

do not spare your wrath upon our shores, that trees may grow
upon the sea, mirror of our total mankind in the weather

one who no longer remembers dancing in the heat of the moon may
    call
across the shifting sands, trying to live in the terrible western world

here where to love at all's to be a politician, as to love a poem
is pretentious, this may sound tendentious but it's lyrical

which shows what lyricism has been brought to by our fabled times
where cowards are shibboleths and one specific love's traduced

by shame for what you love more generally and never would avoid
where reticence is paid for by a poet in his blood or ceasing to be

blood! blood that we have mountains in our veins to stand off jackals
in the pillaging of our desires and allegiances, Aimé Césaire

for if there is fortuity it's in the love we bear each other's differences
in race which is the poetic ground on which we rear our smiles

standing in the sun of marshes as we wade slowly toward the
    culmination
of a gift which is categorically the most difficult relationship

and should be sought as such because it is our nature, nothing
inspires us but the love we want upon the frozen face of earth

and utter disparagement turns into praise as generations read the
    message
of our hearts in adolescent closets who once shot at us in doorways

or kept us from living freely because they were too young then to know
what they would ultimately need from a barren and heart-sore life

the beauty of America, neither cool jazz nor devoured Egyptian
  heroes, lies in
lives in the darkness I inhabit in the midst of sterile millions

the only truth is face to face, the poem whose words become your
  mouth
and dying in black and white we fight for what we love, not are

A TRUE ACCOUNT OF TALKING
TO THE SUN AT FIRE ISLAND

The Sun woke me this morning loud
and clear, saying "Hey! I've been
trying to wake you up for fifteen
minutes. Don't be so rude, you are
only the second poet I've ever chosen
to speak to personally
                    so why
aren't you more attentive? If I could
burn you through the window I would
to wake you up. I can't hang around
here all day."
                    "Sorry, Sun, I stayed
up late last night talking to Hal."

"When I woke up Mayakovsky he was
a lot more prompt" the Sun said
petulantly. "Most people are up
already waiting to see if I'm going
to put in an appearance."
                    I tried
to apologize "I missed you yesterday."
"That's better" he said. "I didn't
know you'd come out." "You may be
wondering why I've come so close?"
"Yes" I said beginning to feel hot
wondering if maybe he wasn't burning me
anyway.

"Frankly I wanted to tell you
I like your poetry. I see a lot
on my rounds and you're okay. You may
not be the greatest thing on earth, but
you're different. Now, I've heard some
say you're crazy, they being excessively
calm themselves to my mind, and other
crazy poets think that you're a boring
reactionary. Not me.
                    Just keep on
like I do and pay no attention. You'll
find that people always will complain
about the atmosphere, either too hot
or too cold too bright or too dark, days
too short or too long.
                    If you don't appear
at all one day they think you're lazy
or dead. Just keep right on, I like it.

And don't worry about your lineage
poetic or natural. The Sun shines on
the jungle, you know, on the tundra
the sea, the ghetto. Wherever you were
I knew it and saw you moving. I was waiting
for you to get to work.

                    And now that you
are making your own days, so to speak,
even if no one reads you but me
you won't be depressed. Not
everyone can look up, even at me. It
hurts their eyes."
                    "Oh Sun, I'm so grateful to you!"

"Thanks and remember I'm watching. It's
easier for me to speak to you out
here. I don't have to slide down
between buildings to get your ear.
I know you love Manhattan, but
you ought to look up more often.
                             And
always embrace things, people earth

sky stars, as I do, freely and with
the appropriate sense of space. That
is your inclination, known in the heavens
and you should follow it to hell, if
necessary, which I doubt.
                    Maybe we'll
speak again in Africa, of which I too
am specially fond. Go back to sleep now
Frank, and I may leave a tiny poem
in that brain of yours as my farewell."

"Sun, don't go!" I was awake
at last. "No, go I must, they're calling
me."
        "Who are they?"
                    Rising he said "Some
day you'll know. They're calling to you
too." Darkly he rose, and then I slept.

PERSONISM: A MANIFESTO

Everything is in the poems, but at the risk of sounding like the poor wealthy man's Allen Ginsberg I will write to you because I just heard that one of my fellow poets thinks that a poem of mine that can't be got at one reading is because I was confused too. Now, come on, I don't believe in god, so I don't have to make elaborately sounded structures. I hate Vachel Lindsay, always have; I don't even like rhythm, assonance, all that stuff. You just go on your nerve. If someone's chasing you down the street with a knife you just run, you don't turn around and shout, "Give it up! I was a track star for Mineola Prep."

That's for the writing poems part. As for their reception, suppose you're in love and someone's mistreating (*mal aimé*) you, you don't say, "Hey, you can't hurt me this way, I care!" you just let all the different bodies fall where they may, and they always do may after a few months. But that's not why you fell in love in the first place, just to hang onto life, so you have to take your chances and try to avoid being logical. Pain always produces logic, which is very bad for you.

I'm not saying that I don't have practically the most lofty ideas of anyone writing today, but what difference does that make? They're just ideas. The only good thing about it is that when I get lofty enough I've stopped thinking and that's when refreshment arrives.

But how can you really care if anybody gets it, or gets what it means, or if it improves them. Improves them for what? For death? Why hurry them along? Too many poets act like a middle-aged mother trying to get her kids to eat too much cooked meat, and potatoes with drippings (tears). I don't give a damn whether they eat or not. Forced feeding leads to excessive thinness (effete). Nobody should experience anything they don't need to, if they don't need poetry bully for them. I like the movies too. And after all, only Whitman and Crane and Williams, of the Amercian poets, are better than the movies. As for measure and other technical apparatus, that's just common sense: if you're going to buy a pair of pants you want them to be tight enough so everyone will want to go to bed with you. There's nothing metaphysical about it. Unless, of course, you flatter yourself into thinking that what you're experiencing is "yearning."

Abstraction in poetry, which Allen [Ginsberg] recently commented on in *It Is,* is intriguing. I think it appears mostly in the minute particulars where decision is necessary. Abstraction (in poetry, not in painting) involves personal removal by the poet. For instance, the decision involved in the choice between "the nostalgia *of* the infinite" and "the nostalgia *for* the infinite" defines an attitude towards degree of abstraction. The nostalgia *of* the infinite representing the greater degree of abstraction, removal, and negative capability (as in Keats and Mallarmé). Personism, a movement which I recently founded and which nobody knows about, interests me a great deal, being so totally opposed to this kind of abstract removal that it is verging on a true abstraction for the first time, really, in the history of poetry. Personism is to Wallace Stevens what *la poésie pure* was to Béranger. Personism has nothing to do with philosophy, it's all art. It does not have to do with personality or intimacy, far from it! But to give you a vague idea, one of its minimal aspects is to address itself to one person (other than the poet himself), thus evoking overtones of love without destroying love's life-giving vulgarity, and sustaining the poet's feelings towards the poem while preventing love from distracting him into feeling about the person. That's part of Personism. It was founded by me after lunch with LeRoi Jones on August 27, 1959, a day in which I was in love with someone (not Roi, by the way, a blond). I went back to work and wrote a poem for this person. While I was writing it I was realizing that if I wanted to I could use the telephone instead of writing the poem, and so Personism was born. It's a very exciting movement which will undoubtedly have lots of adherents. It puts the poem squarely between the poet and the person, Lucky Pierre style, and the poem is correspondingly gratified. The poem is at last between two persons instead of two pages. In all modesty, I confess that it may be the death of literature as we know it. While I have certain regrets, I am still glad I got there before Alain Robbe-Grillet did. Poetry being quicker and surer than prose, it is only just that poetry finish literature off. For a time people thought that Artaud was going to accomplish this, but actually, for all their magnificence, his polemical writings are not more outside literature than Bear Mountain is outside New York State. His relation is no more astounding than Debuffet's to painting.

What can we expect of Personism? (This is getting good, isn't it?) Everything, but we won't get it. It is too new, too vital a movement to promise anything. But it, like Africa, is on the way. The recent propagandists for technique on the one hand, and for content on the other, had better watch out.

FRANK O'HARA
September 3, 1959

Mary Oppen

GEORGE OPPEN

George Oppen was born in New Rochelle, New York, in 1908. His
family moved to San Francisco while he was still a boy. He describes
his schooling as "minimal." Running a small press in France during
the Depression, he published books by Ezra Pound and W. C.
Williams and *The Objectivist Anthology*. In 1934, the Objectivist Press,
a cooperative of which he was a member, published his first book of
poems, *Discrete Series*, with a preface by Pound. He served in the
U.S. Infantry in the Second World War, and has worked as a tool and
die maker, house builder, and carpenter, and for several years ran
a workshop in Mexico City in which he made and sold furniture. His
books include *The Materials, This in Which,* and *Of Being Numerous*,
which won the Pulitzer Prize in 1969. His most recent book is
Seascape: Needle's Eye. He lives with his wife Mary in San Francisco.

PSALM

Veritas sequitur . . .

In the small beauty of the forest
The wild deer bedding down—
That they are there!

          Their eyes
Effortless, the soft lips
Nuzzle and the alien small teeth
Tear at the grass

          The roots of it
Dangle from their mouths
Scattering earth in the strange woods.
They who are there.

          Their paths
Nibbled thru the fields, the leaves that shade them
Hang in the distances
Of sun

          The small nouns
Crying faith
In this in which the wild deer
Startle, and stare out.

from FIVE POEMS ABOUT POETRY

1 *The Gesture*

The question is: how does one hold an apple
Who likes apples

And how does one handle
Filth? The question is

How does one hold something
In the mind which he intends

To grasp and how does the salesman
Hold a bauble he intends

To sell? The question is
When will there not be a hundred

Poets who mistake that gesture
For a style.

    5   *From Virgil*

I, says the buzzard,
I—

Mind

Has evolved
Too long

If 'life is a search
For advantage.'

'At whose behest

Does the mind think?' Art
Also is not good

For us
Unless like the fool

Persisting
In his folly

It may rescue us
As only the true

Might rescue us, gathered
In the smallest corners

Of man's triumph. *Parve puer* . . . 'Begin,

O small boy,
To be born;

On whom his parents have not smiled

No god thinks worthy of his table,
No goddess of her bed'

THE FORMS OF LOVE

Parked in the fields
All night
So many years ago,
We saw
A lake beside us
When the moon rose.
I remember

Leaving that ancient car
Together. I remember
Standing in the white grass
Beside it. We groped
Our way together
Downhill in the bright
Incredible light

Beginning to wonder
Whether it could be lake
Or fog
We saw, our heads
Ringing under the stars. We walked
To where it would have wet our feet
Had it been water

SARA IN HER FATHER'S ARMS

Cell by cell the baby made herself, the cells
Made cells. That is to say
The baby is made largely of milk. Lying in her father's arms,
        the little seed eyes
Moving, trying to see, smiling for us
To see, she will make a household
To her need of these rooms—Sara, little seed,
Little violent, diligent seed. Come let us look at the world
Glittering: this seed will speak,
Max, words! There will be no other words in the world
But those our children speak. What will she make of a world
Do you suppose, Max, of which she is made.

QUOTATIONS

1
When I asked the very old man
In the Bahamas
How old the village was
He said,
'I found it.'

2
The infants and the animals
And the insects
'stare at the open'

And she said
Therefore they are welcome.

3
'. . . and her closets!
No real clothes—just astounding earrings
And perfumes and bright scarves and dress-up things—

She said she was "afraid," she said she was
"always afraid." '

4
And the child
We took on a trip
Said

'We're having the life of our times'

5
Someone has scrawled
Under an advertisement in the subway
Showing a brassy blond young woman
With an elaborate head-dress:
'Cop's bitch.'

SOME SAN FRANCISCO POEMS

1

*Moving over the hills, crossing the irrigation
canals perfect and profuse in the mountains the
streams of women and men walking under the high-
tension wires over the brown hills*

*in the multiple world of the fly's
multiple eye the songs they go to hear on
this occasion are no one's own*

*Needle's eye   needle's eye   but in the ravine
again and again on the massive spike the song
clangs*

*as the tremendous volume of the music takes
over obscured by their long hair they seem
to be mourning*

A MORALITY PLAY: PREFACE

Lying full length
On the bed in the white room

Turns her eyes to me

Again,

Naked . .

Never to forget her naked eyes

Beautiful and brave
Her naked eyes

Turn inward

Feminine light

The unimagined
Feminine light

Feminine ardor

Pierced and touched

Tho all say
Huddled among each other

'Love'

The play begins with the world

A city street
Leads to the bay

Tamalpais in cloud

Mist over farmlands

Local knowledge
In the heavy hills

The great loose waves move landward
Heavysided in the wind

Grass and trees bent
Along the length of coast in the continual wind

The ocean pounds in her mind
Not the harbor leading inward
To the back bay and the slow river
Recalling flimsy Western ranches
The beautiful hills shine outward

Sunrise   the raw fierce fire
Coming up past the sharp edge

And the hoof marks on the mountain

Shines in the white room

Provincial city
Not alien enough

To naked eyes

This city died young

You too will be shown this

You will see the young couples

Leaving again in rags

3

*So with artists.   How pleasurable
to imagine that, if only they gave
up their art, the children would be
healed, would live.*
        Irving Younger in *The Nation*

'AND THEIR WINTER AND NIGHT IN DISGUISE'

The sea and a crescent strip of beach
Show between the service station and a deserted shack

A creek drains thru the beach
Forming a ditch
There is a discarded super-market cart in the ditch
That beach is the edge of a nation

There is something like shouting along the highway
A California shouting
On the long fast highway over the California mountains

Point Pedro
Its distant life

It is impossible the world should be either good or bad
If its colors are beautiful or if they are not beautiful
If parts of it taste good or if no parts of it taste good
It is as remarkable in one case as the other
                                  As against this
We have suffered fear, we know something of fear
And of humiliation mounting to horror

The world above the edge of the foxhole belongs to the
            flying bullets, leaden superbeings
For the men grovelling in the foxhole danger, danger in
            being drawn to them

These little dumps
The poem is about them

Our hearts are twisted
In dead men's pride

Dead men crowd us
Lean over us

In the emplacements

The skull spins
Empty of subject

The hollow ego

Flinching from the war's huge air

Tho we are delivery boys and bartenders

We will choke on each other

Minds may crack

But not for what is discovered

Unless that everyone knew
And kept silent

Our minds are split
To seek the danger out

From among the miserable soldiers

4

ANNIVERSARY POEM

            'the picturesque
common lot'   the unwarranted light

Where everyone has been

The very ground of the path
And the litter grow ancient

A shovel's scratched edge
So like any other man's

We are troubled by incredulity
We are troubled by scratched things

Becoming familiar
Becoming extreme

Let grief
Be
So it be ours

Nor hide one's eyes
As tides drop along the beaches in the thin wash of
    breakers

And so desert each other

—lest there be nothing

        the Indian girl walking across the desert, the
sunfish under the boat

How shall we say how this happened, these stories, our
    stories

Scope, mere size, a kind of redemption

Exposed still and jagged on the San Francisco hills

Time and depth before us, paradise of the real, we
    know what it is

To find now depth, not time, since we cannot, but depth

To come out safe,   to end well

We have begun to say good bye
To each other
And cannot say it

THE TRANSLUCENT MECHANICS

Combed thru the piers the wind
Moves in the clever city
Not in the doors but the hinges
Finds the secret of motion
As tho the hollow ships moved in their voices,   murmurs
Flaws
In the wind
Fear   fear
At the lumber mastheads
And fetched a message out of the sea again

Say angel   say powers

Obscurely   'things
And the self'

Prosody

Sings

In the stones

        to entrust
To a poetry of statement

At close quarters

A living mind
'and that one's own'

                what then   what spirit

Of the bent seas

                Archangel

of the tide

brimming

in the moon-streak

        comes in whose absence
earth crumbles

6

Silver as
The needle's eye

Of the horizon in the noise
Of their entrance row on row the waves
Move landward   conviction's

Net of branches
In the horde of events the sacred swarm avalanche
Masked in the sunset

Needle after needle more numerous than planets

Or the liquid waves
In the tide rips

We believe   we believe

Beyond the cable car streets
And the picture window

Lives the glittering crumbling night
Of obstructions and the stark structures

That carry wires over the mountain
One writes in the presence of something
Moving close to fear
I dare pity no one
Let the rafters pity
The air in the room
Under the rafters
Pity

In the continual sound
Are chords
Not yet struck
Which will be struck
Nevertheless yes

7

O withering seas
Of the doorstep and local winds unveil

The face of art

Carpenter, plunge and drip in the sea   Art's face
We know that face

More blinding than the sea   a haunted house   a limited

Consensus unwinding

Its powers
Toward the thread's end

In the record of great blows   shocks
Ravishment   devastation   the wood splintered

The keyboard gone in the rank grass swept her hand
Over the strings and the thing rang out

Over the rocks and the ocean
Not my poem   Mr Steinway's

Poem   Not mine   A 'marvelous' object
Is not the marvel of things

            twisting the new
Mouth   forcing the new
Tongue   But it rang

8

THE TASTE

Old ships are preserved
For their queer silence of obedient seas
Their cutwaters floating in the still water
With their cozy black iron work
And Swedish seamen dead   the cabins
Hold the spaces of their deaths
And the hammered nails of necessity
Carried thru the oceans
Where the moon rises grandly
In the grandeur of cause
We have a taste for bedrock
Beneath this spectacle
To gawk at
Something is wrong with the antiques, a black fluid
Has covered them, a black splintering
Under the eyes of young wives
People talk wildly, we are beginning to talk wildly, the wind
At every summit
Our overcoats trip us
Running for the bus
Our arms stretched out
In a wind from what were sand dunes

9

THE IMPOSSIBLE POEM

Climbing the peak of Tamalpais the loose
Gravel underfoot

And the city shining with the tremendous wrinkles
In the hills and the winding of the bay
Behind it, it faces the bent ocean

Streetcars
Rocked thru the city and the winds
Combed their clumsy sides

In clumsy times

Sierras withering
Behind the storefronts

And sanity the roadside weed
Dreams of sports and sportsmanship

In the lucid towns paralyzed
Under the truck tires
Shall we relinquish

Sanity to redeem
Fragments and fragmentary
Histories in the towns and the temperate streets
Too shallow still to drown in or to mourn
The courageous and precarious children

10

BUT SO AS BY FIRE

The darkness of trees
Guards this life
Of the thin ground
That covers the rock ledge

Among the lanes and magic
Of the Eastern woods

The beauty of silence
And broken boughs

And the homes of small animals

The green leaves
Of young plants
Above the dark green moss
In the sweet smell of rot

The pools and the trickle of freshwater

First life, rotting life
Hidden starry life it is not yet

A mirror
Like our lives

We have gone
As far as is possible

Whose lives reflect light
Like mirrors

One had not thought
To be afraid

Not of shadow but of light

Summon one's powers

THE BOOK OF JOB AND A DRAFT
OF A POEM TO PRAISE
THE PATHS OF THE LIVING

in memory of Mickey Schwerner

image   the images   the great games therefore the locked

the half-lit jailwinds

in the veins the lynch gangs

simulate blows   bruise   the bones
breaking   *age*

of the world's deeds this is the young age   age

of the sea's surf   image   image

of the world its least rags
stream among the planets Our
lady of poverty the lever the fulcrum
the cam and the ant
hath her anger and the emmet
his choler the exposed
belly of the land
under the sky
at night and the windy pines unleash
the morning's force what is the form
to say it there is something
to name   Goodman   Schwerner   Chaney
who were beaten not we
who were beaten   children
not our
children   ancestral
children rose in the dark
to their work there grows
there builds there is written
a vividness   there is rawness
like a new sun the flames
tremendous the sun
itself ourselves ourselves
go with us *disorder*

so great the tumult wave

upon wave this traverse

this desert   extravagant
island of light

          • • •

inshore, the rough grasses
rooted on the dry hills or to stand still

like the bell buoy telling

tragedy so wide
spread so

shabby a north sea salt
tragedy 'seeking a statement

of an experience of our own' the bones of my hand

bony   bony   lose me the wind cries find
yourself   I?

this?   the road
and the travelling   always

undiscovered
country forever

savage *the river*
was a rain and flew

with the herons   the sea
flies in the squall

                              .   .   .

            small
and numerous

the windows

look out on the sea's simulacra
of self evidence   meaning's

instant wild
eyes as the cherry
tree blossoms

in that fanatic glass from our own homes our own

rooms we are fetched out we

'the greasers'
says the day's slang
in the path of tornado the words

piled on each other   lean
on each other

dance with the dancing

valve stems   machine-glint
in the commonplace the last words

survivors, will be tame
will stand near our feet
what shall we say   they have lived their lives
they have gone feathery
and askew
in the wind from the beginning   carpenter
mechanic o we
impoverished we hired
hands that turn the wheel   young
theologians of the scantlings   wracked
monotheists of the weather-side sometimes I imagine
they speak

                    .   .   .

luxury, all
said Bill, the fancy things   always

second hand but in extreme
minutes guilt

at the heart
of the thinkable hunger   fear   enemy

world   briefly shame

of loneliness all that has touched
the man

touches him
again arms and dis-

arms him meaning
is the instant

tho we forget the light
shone on her she reflected the light

                    .   .   .

precision of place the rock's place in the fog we suffer
   loneliness painlessly not without fear the common breath
      here at extremity

obsolescent as the breathing
of tribespeople   fingers cold

early in the year cold and windy on the sea the wind still
   blows thru my head in the farmhouse

weather of the camera's click
lonely as the shutter closing
over the glass lens weathered mountains

of the hurrying sea the boat in these squalls sails like
   a sparrow a wind blown
sparrow on the sea some kite string

taut in the wind green
and heavy the masses of the sea weeds move
and move in rock shelters share marvelous games

                        .   .   .

      backward
over the shoulder
now the wave
of the improbable
drains from the beaches the heart of the hollow
tree singing bird note bird rustle we live now
in dreams all
wished to tell him we are locked
in ourselves   That is not
what they dreamed
in any dream they dreamed the morning
of the bird waking mid continent

mid continent iron rails
in the fields and grotesque
metals in the farmers' heartlands a sympathy
across the fields
and down the aisles
of the crack trains

of 1918 the wave
of the improbable
drenches   the galloping carpets in the sharp
edges in the highlights
of the varnished tables we ring
in the continual bell
the undoubtable bell   found music   in itself
of itself speaks the word
actual heart breaking
tone row it is not ended
not ended the intervals
blurred ring
like walls
between floor
and ceiling the taste
of madness in the world   birds
of ice   Pave
the earth o pave
the earth carve
thereon   .   .   .

.   .   .

limited air   drafts
in the treasure house moving and the movements of the living
Things fall   something balanced   move
with all one's force
into the commonplace that pierces or erodes

the mind's structure but nothing
incredible happens
it will have happened to that other
the survivor   the survivor
to him it happened

rooted in basalt
night hums like the telephone dial tone blue gauze
of the forge flames the pulse
of infant
sorrows at the crux

of the timbers
when the middle kingdom

warred with beasts the Middle Things the elves the

magic people in their world
among the plant roots   hopes
which are the hopes
of small self interest called

superstition chitinous
toys of the children wings
of the wasp

IT IS DIFFICULT NOW TO SPEAK OF POETRY—

about those who have recognized the range of choice or those who
have lived within the life they were born to—. It is not precisely a
question of profundity but a different order of experience. One would
have to tell what happens in a life, what choices present themselves,
what the world is for us, what happens in time, what thought is in
the course of a life and therefore what art is, and the isolation of
the actual

I would want to talk of rooms and of what they look out on and of
basements, the rough walls bearing the marks of the forms, the old
marks of wood in the concrete, such solitude as we know—

and the swept floors. Someone, a workman bearing about him,
feeling about him that peculiar word like a dishonored fatherhood
has swept this solitary floor, this profoundly hidden floor—such
solitude as we know.

One must not come to feel that he has a thousand threads
      in his hands,
He must somehow see the one thing;
This is the level of art
There are other levels
But there is no other level of art

                                        GEORGE OPPEN

KENNETH REXROTH

Kenneth Rexroth was born in South Bend, Indiana, in 1905. He grew up in Chicago and New York and was educated at the Chicago Art Institute and the New School for Social Research. He has worked as a horse wrangler, logger, labor organizer, and journalist, and still reviews books for Pacifica Radio. His many volumes of poetry include *The Art of Worldly Wisdom, The Signature of All Things, The Homestead Called Damascus, In Defense of the Earth, Natural Numbers, The Collected Shorter Poems* and *The Collected Longer Poems*. He has done distinguished translation from Greek, Chinese, Japanese, French, and Spanish; among these works are *100 Poems from the Chinese, Poems from the Greek Anthology* and *Pierre Reverdy: Selected Poems*. He is also the author of *An Autobiographical Novel,* a sequence of plays entitled *Beyond the Mountains,* a libretto, and many books of criticism and commentary, including *Bird in the Bush, Assays, The Classics Revisited,* and *The Elastic Retort*. He has won a large number of awards and prizes both here and abroad. He is also a painter and has had one-man shows in Chicago, New York, Paris, and other cities. He has lived most of his life in San Francisco, and now lives and teaches in Santa Barbara.

Margo Moore

from POEMS FROM THE GREEK ANTHOLOGY

Lysidike dedicates
To you, Kypris, her jockey's
Spur, the golden prickle she
Wore on her beautiful leg.
Upside down, she broke many
Horses, yet her own bottom
Was never reddened, she had
Such a skillful seat that she
Always came first in the race.
Now she hangs her weapon in
The midst of your golden gate.

Asklepiades

I used to tell you, "Frances, we grow old.
The years fly away. Don't be so private
With those parts. A chaste maid is an old maid."
Unnoticed by your disdain, old age crept
Close to us. Those days are gone past recall.
And now you come, penitent and crying
Over your old lack of courage, over
Your present lack of beauty. It's all right.
Closed in your arms, we'll share our smashed delights.
It's give and take now. It's what I wanted,
If not what I want.

Ausonius, after *Rufinus*

Here is Klito's little shack.
Here is his little cornpatch.
Here is his tiny vineyard.
Here is his little woodlot.
Here Klito spent eighty years.

Leonidas

Erotion rests here, in the
Hastening shadows, destroyed
By criminal fate in her
Sixth winter. You, whoever
You are, who rule over
This little field after me,
Pay your respects to her small
Ghost each year, that your hearth
May endure, and your family
Be safe, and only this stone,
Out in the fields, ever bring forth a tear.

Martial

You are a stool pigeon and
A slanderer, a pimp and
A cheat, a pederast and
A troublemaker. I can't
Understand, Vacerra, why
You don't have more money.

Martial

I have sworn ten thousand times
To make no more epigrams.
Every ass is my enemy now.
But when I look at your face,
The old sickness overcomes me.

Palladas

I Lais, once an arrow
In the heart of all, am Lais
No longer, but a witness
To the harrying of the years.
I swear by Desire (and what
Is Desire but a swearword?)
Lais can no longer see
Lais in Lais herself.

Sekundos

THE SIGNATURE OF ALL THINGS

My head and shoulders, and my book
In the cool shade, and my body
Stretched bathing in the sun, I lie
Reading beside the waterfall—
Boehme's "Signature of all Things."
Through the deep July day the leaves
Of the laurel, all the colors
Of gold, spin down through the moving
Deep laurel shade all day. They float
On the mirrored sky and forest
For a while, and then, still slowly
Spinning, sink through the crystal deep
Of the pool to its leaf gold floor.
The saint saw the world as streaming
In the electrolysis of love.
I put him by and gaze through shade
Folded into shade of slender
Laurel trunks and leaves filled with sun.
The wren broods in her moss domed nest.
A newt struggles with a white moth
Drowning in the pool. The hawks scream,
Playing together on the ceiling
Of heaven. The long hours go by.
I think of those who have loved me,
Of all the mountains I have climbed,
Of all the seas I have swum in.
The evil of the world sinks.
My own sin and trouble fall away
Like Christian's bundle, and I watch
My forty summers fall like falling
Leaves and falling water held
Eternally in summer air.

      *   *   *

Deer are stamping in the glades,
Under the full July moon.
There is a smell of dry grass
In the air, and more faintly,
The scent of a far off skunk.

As I stand at the wood's edge,
Watching the darkness, listening
To the stillness, a small owl
Comes to the branch above me,
On wings more still than my breath.
When I turn my light on him,
His eyes glow like drops of iron,
And he perks his head at me,
Like a curious kitten.
The meadow is bright as snow.
My dog prowls the grass, a dark
Blur in the blur of brightness.
I walk to the oak grove where
The Indian village was once.
There, in blotched and cobwebbed light
And dark, dim in the blue haze,
Are twenty Holstein heifers,
Black and white, all lying down,
Quietly together, under
The huge trees rooted in the graves.

      *   *   *

When I dragged the rotten log
From the bottom of the pool,
It seemed heavy as stone.
I let it lie in the sun
For a month, and then chopped it
Into sections, and split them
For kindling, and spread them out
To dry some more. Late that night,
After reading for hours,
While moths rattled at the lamp—
The saints and the philosophers
On the destiny of man—
I went out on my cabin porch,
And looked up through the black forest
At the swaying islands of stars.
Suddenly I saw at my feet,
Spread on the floor of night, ingots
Of quivering phosphorescence,
And all about were scattered chips
Of pale cold light that was alive.

FISH PEDDLER AND COBBLER

Always for thirty years now
I am in the mountains in
August. For thirty Augusts
Your ghosts have stood up over
The mountains. That was nineteen
Twenty seven. Now it is
Nineteen fifty seven. Once
More after thirty years I
Am back in the mountains of
Youth, back in the Gros Ventres,
The broad park-like valleys and
The tremendous cubical
Peaks of the Rockies. I learned
To shave hereabouts, working
As cookee and night wrangler.
Nineteen twenty two, the years
Of revolutionary
Hope that came to an end as
The iron fist began to close.
No one electrocuted me.
Nothing happened. Time passed.
Something invisible was gone.
We thought then that we were the men
Of the years of the great change,
That we were the forerunners
Of the normal life of mankind.
We thought that soon all things would
Be changed, not just economic
And social relationships, but
Painting, poetry, music, dance,
Architecture, even the food
We ate and the clothes we wore
Would be ennobled. It will take
Longer than we expected.
These mountains are unchanged since
I was a boy wandering
Over the West, picking up
Odd jobs. If anything they are
Wilder. A moose cow blunders

Into camp. Beavers slap their tails
On their sedgy pond as we fish
From on top of their lodge in the
Twilight. The horses feed on bright grass
In meadows full of purple gentian,
And stumble through silver dew
In the full moonlight.
The fish taste of meadow water.
In the morning on far grass ridges
Above the red rim rock wild sheep
Bound like rubber balls over the
Horizon as the noise of camp
Begins. I catch and saddle
Mary's little golden horse,
And pack the first Decker saddles
I've seen in thirty years. Even
The horse bells have a different sound
From the ones in California.
Canada jays fight over
The last scraps of our pancakes.
On the long sandy pass we ride
Through fields of lavender primrose
While lightning explodes around us.
For lunch Mary catches a two pound
Grayling in the whispering river.
No fourteen thousand foot peaks
Are named Sacco and Vanzetti.
Not yet. The clothes I wear
Are as unchanged as the Decker
Saddles on the pack horses.
America grows rich on the threat of death.
Nobody bothers anarchists anymore.
Coming back we lay over
In Ogden for ten hours.
The courthouse square was full
Of miners and lumberjacks and
Harvest hands and gandy dancers
With broken hands and broken
Faces sleeping off cheap wine drunks
In the scorching heat, while tired
Savage eyed whores paraded the street.

THE BAD OLD DAYS

The summer of nineteen eighteen
I read *The Jungle* and *The
Research Magnificent*. That fall
My father died and my aunt
Took me to Chicago to live.
The first thing I did was to take
A streetcar to the stockyards.
In the winter afternoon,
Gritty and fetid, I walked
Through the filthy snow, through the
Squalid streets, looking shyly
Into the people's faces,
Those who were home in the daytime.
Debauched and exhausted faces,
Starved and looted brains, faces
Like the faces in the senile
And insane wards of charity
Hospitals. Predatory
Faces of little children.
Then as the soiled twilight darkened,
Under the green gas lamps, and the
Sputtering purple arc lamps,
The faces of the men coming
Home from work, some still alive with
The last pulse of hope or courage,
Some sly and bitter, some smart and
Silly, most of them already
Broken and empty, no life,
Only blinding tiredness, worse
Than any tired animal.
The sour smells of a thousand
Suppers of fried potatoes and
Fried cabbage bled into the street.
I was giddy and sick, and out
Of my misery I felt rising
A terrible anger and out
Of the anger, an absolute vow.
Today the evil is clean
And prosperous, but it is

Everywhere, you don't have to
Take a streetcar to find it,
And it is the same evil.
And the misery, and the
Anger, and the vow are the same.

ON THE EVE OF THE PLEBISCITE

The Mistral blows, the plane leaves
Parachute to earth. The Cour
Mirabeau turns from submarine
Green to blue grey and old gold.
When the wind drops it is warm
And drowsy. Glace or pastis
In a sunny chair, the Aixois
Decline to winter. Civic
Calm, the contemplative heart
Of Mediterranean
Civilization throbs with
Its slow, all governing pulse.
Tricolor posters, surcharged
OUI or NON flicker and battle
Like broken film on the screen
Of a malodorous cinema.
The Jeunesse Dorée of the
Law School hunt a sensitive
Overcivilized Algerian
Fellow student between the
Parked cars, around the plane trees,
Like an exhausted fox.
Horror tightens its steel bands
On this land and on every
Heart. Lewd sycophancy and
Brutalized indifference
Rule the highbrow terrasses
And the once militant slums.
Clowns and torturers and cheap
Literary adventurers

Parade like obscene dolls. This
Is no country I ever knew.
And who tightens the screws?
And who pulls these puppets' wires?
Oh, how well I remember
Listening to Chancellor
Bruening's last appeal. Late night,
By the cold green eye of the short-
Wave radio. "You have raised up
Forces from the bottom of
Society. You think they
Will be your willing tools. I
Tell you they will betray you
And destroy you. I beseech
You, bethink yourselves before
It is too late." To whom did
He speak? To the State Department,
The Foreign Office, National City,
Chase, The Bank of England,
Shell, Standard Oil, Krupp, US Steel,
Vickers, Dupont, the same ones
Who are still there—"reducing the heart
Of Europe to the status of a barbaric
Colony." And behind them—to you
By whose indifferent consent they rule.

FOR A MASSEUSE AND PROSTITUTE

Nobody knows what love is anymore.
Nobody knows what happened to God.
After midnight, the lesbians and fairies
Sweep through the streets of the old tenderloin,
Like spirochetes in a softening brain.
The hustlers have all been run out of town.
I look back on the times spent
Talking with you about the idiocies
Of a collapsing world and the brutalities
Of my race and yours,
While the sick, the perverted, the malformed,

Came and went, and you cooked them,
And rolled them, and beat them,
And sent them away with a little taste
Of electric life from the ends of your fingers.
Who could ever forget your amiable body,
Or your unruffled good sense,
Or your smiling sex?
I suppose your touch kept many men
As sane as they could be kept.
Every hour there is less of that touch in the world.

from A BESTIARY

FOX

The fox is very clever.
In England people dress up
Like a movie star's servants
And chase the fox on horses.
Rather, they let dogs chase him,
And they come along behind.
When the dogs have torn the fox
To pieces they rub his blood
On the faces of young girls.
If you are clever do not
Let anybody know it,
But especially Englishmen.

HORSE

It is fun to ride the horse.
If you give him some sugar
He will love you. But even
The best horses kick sometimes.
A rag blowing in the wind
Can cause him to kill you. These
Characteristics he shares
With the body politic.

RACCOON

The raccoon wears a black mask,
And he washes everything
Before he eats it. If you
Give him a cube of sugar,
He'll wash it away and weep.
Some of life's sweetest pleasures
Can be enjoyed only if
You don't mind a little dirt.
Here a false face won't help you.

VULTURE

St. Thomas Aquinas thought
That vultures were lesbians
And fertilized by the wind.
If you seek the facts of life,
Papist intellectuals
Can be very misleading.

WOLF

Never believe all you hear.
Wolves are not as bad as lambs.
I've been a wolf all my life,
And have two lovely daughters
To show for it, while I could
Tell you sickening tales of
Lambs who got their just deserts.

A LETTER TO WILLIAM CARLOS WILLIAMS

Dear Bill,

When I search the past for you,
Sometimes I think you are like

St. Francis, whose flesh went out
Like a happy cloud from him,
And merged with every lover—
Donkeys, flowers, lepers, suns—
But I think you are more like
Brother Juniper, who suffered
All indignities and glories
Laughing like a gentle fool.
You're in the *Fioretti*
Somewhere, for you're a fool, Bill,
Like the Fool in Yeats, the term
Of all wisdom and beauty.
It's you, stands over against
Helen in all her wisdom,
Solomon in all his glory.

Remember years ago, when
I told you you were the first
Great Franciscan poet since
The Middle Ages? I disturbed
The even tenor of dinner.
Your wife thought I was crazy.
It's true, though. And you're "pure," too,
A real classic, though not loud
About it—a whole lot like
The girls of the Anthology.
Not like strident Sappho, who
For all her grandeur, must have
Had endemetriosis,
But like Anyte, who says
Just enough, softly, for all
The thousands of years to remember.

It's a wonderful quiet
You have, a way of keeping
Still about the world, and its
Dirty rivers, and garbage cans,
Red wheelbarrows glazed with rain,
Cold plums stolen from the icebox,
And Queen Anne's lace, and day's eyes,
And leaf buds bursting over
Muddy roads, and splotched bellies
With babies in them, and Cortes

And Malinche on the bloody
Causeway, the death of the flower world.

Nowadays, when the press reels
With chatterboxes, you keep still,
Each year a sheaf of stillness,
Poems that have nothing to say,
Like the stillness of George Fox,
Sitting still under the cloud
Of all the world's temptation,
By the fire, in the kitchen,
In the Vale of Beavor. And
The archetype, the silence
Of Christ, when he paused a long
Time and then said, "Thou sayest it."

Now in a recent poem you say,
"I who am about to die."
Maybe this is just a tag
From the classics, but it sends
A shudder over me. Where
Do you get that stuff, Williams?
Look at here. The day will come
When a young woman will walk
By the lucid Williams River,
Where it flows through an idyllic
News from Nowhere sort of landscape,
And she will say to her children,
"Isn't it beautiful? It
Is named after a man who
Walked here once when it was called
The Passaic, and was filthy
With the poisonous excrements
Of sick men and factories.
He was a great man. He knew
It was beautiful then, although
Nobody else did, back there
In the Dark Ages. And the
Beautiful river he saw
Still flows in his veins, as it
Does in ours, and flows in our eyes,
And flows in time, and makes us

Part of it, and part of him.
That, children, is what is called
A sacramental relationship.
And that is what a poet
Is, children, one who creates
Sacramental relationships
That last always."
    With love and admiration,
    Kenneth Rexroth.

I. from POETRY, REGENERATION, AND D. H. LAWRENCE:

Good cadenced verse is the most difficult of all to write. Any falsity, any pose, any corruption, any ineptitude, any vulgarity, shows up immediately. In this it is like abstract painting. A painting by Mondrian may look impersonal enough to be reduced to code and sent by telegraph. Maybe. But it offers no refuge, no garment, no mask, no ambush, for the person. The painter must stand there, naked, as Adam under the eye of God. Only very great or very trivial personalities dare expose themselves so.

Think of a few typical writers of cadenced verse: Whitman, Sandburg, Wallace Gould, F. M. Ford, F. S. Flint, Aldington, Lola Ridge, and James Oppenheim . . . How the faults stand out! Every little weakness is revealed with glaring cruelty. Whitman's tiresome posturing, Sandburg's mawkishness, Aldington's erotic sentimentality, the overreaching ambition of Lola Ridge and Oppenheim—what a lot of sore thumbs standing out! Yet in many ways these are good poets, and Whitman is a very great one.

Gould, Flint, and Ford were never dishonest, never overreached themselves, did their best to say what they meant and no more, never bargained with art. "The sentimentalist," said Daedalus, "is he who would enjoy, without incurring the immense debtorship for a thing done." They are not prophets, but they are good poets because they rendered a strict accounting with their own souls.

Sentimentality is spiritual realization on the installment plan. Socially viable patterns, like conventional verse, are a sort of underwriting or amortization of the weaknesses of the individual. This is the kernel of sense in the hollow snobbery of Valéry. The sonnet and quatrain are like the national debt, devices for postponing the day of reckoning indefinitely. All artistic conventions are a method of spiritual deficit-financing. If they were abandoned, the entire credit structure of Poets, Ltd., would be thrown into hopeless confusion. It is just as well that the professors have led the young, in my lifetime, away from free verse to something that can be taught. No one could be taught to be Lawrence, but in a world where the led lead the leaders, those who might pretend to do so are sure to be confidence men.

II. from INTRODUCTION TO THE COLLECTED LONGER POEMS

... It is easy to overcome alienation—the net of the cash nexus can simply be stepped out of, but only by the self-actualizing man. But everyone is self actualizing and can realize it by the simplest act—the self unselfing itself, the only act that is actual act. I have tried to embody in verse the belief that the only valid conservation of value lies in the assumption of unlimited liability, the supernatural identification of the self with the tragic unity of creative process. I hope I have made it clear that the self does not do this by an act of will, by sheer assertion. He who would save his life must lose it.

"What endures, what perishes?" The permanent core of thought could perhaps be called a kind of transcendental empiricism—"the 'ineluctable modality' of the invisible." The real objects are their own transcendental meaning. If reality can be apprehended without grasping, the epistemological problem vanishes. The beginning of experience is the same as the end of it. The source or spring of knowing is the same as the fulfillment of it—experience begins and ends in illumination. The holy is in the heap of dust—it is the heap of dust. Beyond the object lies a person—objects are only perspectives on persons. But the experience of either is ultimately unqualifiable. Epistemology is moral. There is no "problem." Visions are problems. Vision is the solution that precedes the problem. It is precisely the thing in itself that we do experience. The rest is reification. So too the I-Thou relationship is primary. The dialogue comes after. Everything else is manipulation—reification again—and so, illusion. It is love and love alone . . . as it says in the old popular song.

"Thus literally living in a blaze of glory." True illumination is habitude. We are unaware that we live in the light of lights because it casts no shadow. When we become aware of it we know it as birds know air and fish know water. It is the ultimate trust.

"If thee does not turn to the Inner Light, where will thee turn?"

KENNETH REXROTH

Thomas Victor

ADRIENNE RICH

Adrienne Rich was born in Baltimore in 1929. While still an under-
graduate at Radcliffe College, she wrote her first book, *A Change of
World*, which was published in 1951 in the Yale Younger Poets series.
She married and had three children and in 1955 published a second
book, *The Diamond Cutters*. She settled in New York City in the
mid-60's, and after her husband's death, raised her children, taught
for a living, and wrote one book after another—*Snapshots of a
Daughter-in-Law, Necessities of Life, Leaflets, The Will to Change,*
and *Diving Into the Wreck*, which won the National Book Award in
1974.

THE STRANGER

Looking as I've looked before, straight down the heart
of the street to the river
walking the rivers of the avenues
feeling the shudder of the caves beneath the asphalt
watching the lights turn on in the towers
walking as I've walked before
like a man, like a woman, in the city
my visionary anger cleansing my sight
and the detailed perceptions of mercy
flowering from that anger

if I come into a room out of the sharp misty light
and hear them talking a dead language
if they ask me my identity
what can I say but
I am the androgyne
I am the living mind you fail to describe
in your dead language
the lost noun, the verb surviving
only in the infinitive
the letters of my name are written under the lids
of the newborn child

FROM THE PRISON HOUSE

Underneath my lids another eye has opened
it looks nakedly
at the light

that soaks in from the world of pain
even when I sleep

Steadily it regards
everything I am going through

and more

it sees the clubs and rifle-butts
rising and falling
it sees

detail not on TV

the fingers of the policewoman
searching the cunt of the young prostitute
it sees

the roaches dropping into the pan
where they cook the pork
In the House of D

it sees
the violence
embedded in silence

This eye
is not for weeping
its vision
must be unblurred
though tears are on my face

its intent is clarity
it must forget
nothing

AUGUST

Two horses in yellow light
eating windfall apples under a tree

as summer tears apart   milkweeds stagger
and grasses grow more ragged

They say there are ions in the sun
neutralizing magnetic fields on earth

Some way to explain
what this week has been, and the one before it!

If I am flesh sunning on rock
if I am brain burning in fluorescent light

if I am dream like a wire with fire
throbbing along it

if I am death to man
I have to know it

His mind is too simple, I cannot go on
sharing his nightmares

My own are becoming clearer, they open
into prehistory

which looks like a village lit with blood
where all the fathers are crying: *My son is mine!*

A PRIMARY GROUND

*"But he must have more than that. It was sympathy
he wanted, to be assured of his genius, first of all,
and then to be taken within the circle of life, warmed
and soothed, to have his sense restored to him, his
barrenness made fertile, and all the rooms of the
house made full of life . . ."*
                    —Virginia Woolf, To the Lighthouse

And this is how you live: a woman, children
protect you from the abyss
you move near, turning on the news
eating Thanksgiving with its pumpkin teeth
drinking the last wine
from the cellar of your wedding

It all seems innocent enough, this sin
of wedlock: you, your wife, your children
leaning across the unfilled plates
passing the salt
down a cloth ironed by a woman
with aching legs
Now they go out to play
in the coarse, rough November air
that smells of soft-coal smoke, the river,
burnt sweet-potato pie.

Sensuality dessicates in words—
risks of the portage, risks of the glacier
never taken
Protection is the genius of your house
the pressure of the steam iron
flattens the linen cloth again
chestnuts puréed with care are dutifully eaten
in every room the furniture reflects you
larger than life, or dwindling

Emptiness
thrust like a batch of letters to the furthest
dark of a drawer
But there is something else:
your wife's twin sister, speechless
is dying in the house
You and your wife take turns
carrying up the trays
understanding her case, trying to make her understand.

THE MIRROR IN WHICH TWO ARE SEEN AS ONE

1
She is the one you call sister.
Her simplest act has glamor,
as when she scales a fish the knife
flashes in her long fingers
no motion wasted or when

rapidly talking of love
she steel-wool burnishes
the battered kettle

Love-apples cramp you sideways
with sudden emptiness
the cereals glutting you, the grains
ripe clusters picked by hand
Love: the refrigerator
with open door
the ripe steaks bleeding
their hearts out in plastic film
the whipped butter, the apricots
the sour leftovers

A crate is waiting in the orchard
for you to fill it
your hands are raw with scraping
the sharp bark, the thorns
of this succulent tree
Pick, pick, pick
this harvest is a failure
the juice runs down your cheekbones
like sweat or tears

2
She is the one you call sister
you blaze like lightning about the room
flicker around her like fire
dazzle yourself in her wide eyes
listing her unfelt needs
thrusting the tenets of your life
into her hands

She moves through a world of India print
her body dappled
with softness, the paisley swells at her hip
walking the street in her cotton shift
buying fresh figs because you love them
photographing the ghetto because you took her there

Why are you crying dry up your tears
we are sisters
words fail you in the stare of her hunger
you hand her another book
scored by your pencil
you hand her a record
of two flutes in India reciting

3
Late summer night the insects
fry in the yellowed lightglobe
your skin burns gold in its light
In this mirror, who are you? Dreams of the nunnery
with its discipline, the nursery
with its nurse, the hospital
where all the powerful ones are masked
the graveyard where you sit on the graves
of women who died in childbirth
and women who died at birth
Dreams of your sister's birth
your mother dying in childbirth over and over
not knowing how to stop
bearing you over and over

your mother dead and you unborn
your two hands grasping your head
drawing it down against the blade of life
your nerves the nerves of a midwife
learning her trade

FROM AN OLD HOUSE IN AMERICA

1
Deliberately, long ago
the carcasses

of old bugs crumbled
into the rut of the window

and we started sleeping here
Fresh June bugs batter this June's

screens, June-lightning batters
the spiderweb

I sweep the wood-dust
from the wood-box

the snout of the vacuum cleaner
sucks the past away

2
Other lives were lived here:
mostly un-articulate

yet someone left her creamy signature
in the trail of rusticated

narcissus straggling up
through meadowgrass and vetch

Families breathed close
boxed-in from the cold

hard times, short growing season
the old rainwater cistern

hulks in the cellar

3
Like turning through the contents of a drawer:
these rusted screws, this empty vial

useless, this box of water-color paints
dried to insolubility—

but this—
this pack of cards with no card missing

still playable
and three good fuses

and this toy: a little truck
scarred red, yet all its wheels still turn

The humble tenacity of things
waiting for people, waiting for months, for years

4
Often rebuked, yet always back returning
I place my hand on the hand

of the dead, invisible palm-print
on the doorframe

spiked with daylilies, green leaves
catching in the screen door

or I read the backs of old postcards
curling from thumbtacks, winter and summer

fading through cobweb-tinted panes—
white church in Norway

Dutch hyacinths bleeding azure
red beach on Corsica

set-pieces of the world
stuck to this house of plank

I flash on wife and husband
embattled, in the years

that dried, dim ink was wet
those signatures

5
If they call me man-hater, you
would have known it for a lie

but the *you* I want to speak to
has become your death

If I dream of you these days
I know my dreams are mine and not of you

yet something hangs between us
older and stranger than ourselves

like a translucent curtain, a sheet of water
a dusty window

the irreducible, incomplete connection
between the dead and living

or between man and woman in this
savagely fathered and unmothered world

6
The other side of a translucent
curtain, a sheet of water

a dusty window, Non-being
utters its flat tones

the speech of an actor learning his lines
phonetically

the final autistic statement
of the self-destroyer

All my energy reaches out tonight
to comprehend a miracle beyond

raising the dead: the undead to watch
back on the road of birth

7
I am an American woman:
I turn that over

like a grassblade pressed in a book
I stop and look up from

into the coals of the stove
or the black square of the window

Foot-slogging through the Bering Strait
jumping from the *Arbella* to my death

chained to the corpse beside me
I feel my pains begin

I am washed up on this continent
shipped here to be fruitful

my body a hollow ship
bearing sons to the wilderness

sons who ride away
on horseback, daughters

whose juices drain like mine
into the *arroyo* of stillbirths, massacres

Hanged as witches, sold as breeding-wenches
my sisters leave me

I am not the wheatfield
nor the virgin forest

I never chose this place
yet I am of it now

In my decent collar, in the daguerrotype
I pierce its legend with my look

my hands wring the necks of prairie chickens
I am used to blood

When the men hit the hobo track
I stay on with the children

my power is brief and local
but I know my power

I have lived in isolation
from other women, so much

in the mining camps, the first cities
the Great Plains winters

Most of the time, in my sex, I was alone

8
Tonight in this northeast kingdom
striated iris stand in a jar with daisies

the porcupine gnaws in the shed
fireflies beat and simmer

caterpillars begin again
their long, innocent climb

the length of leaves of burdock
or webbing of a garden chair

plain and ordinary things
speak softly

the light square on old wallpaper
where a poster has fallen down

Robert Indiana's LOVE
leftover of a decade

9
I do not want to simplify
Or: I would simplify

by naming the complexity
It was made over-simple all along

the separation of powers
the allotment of sufferings

her spine cracking in labor
his plow driving across the Indian graves

her hand unconscious on the cradle, her mind
with the wild geese

his mother-hatred driving him
into exile from the earth

the refugee couple with their cardboard luggage
standing on the ramshackle landing-stage

he with fingers frozen around his Law
she with her down quilt sewn through iron nights

—the weight of the old world, plucked
drags after them, a random feather-bed

10
Her children dead of diphtheria, she
set herself on fire with kerosene

(O Lord I was unworthy
Thou didst find me out)

she left the kitchen scrubbed
down to the marrow of its boards

"The penalty for barrenness
is emptiness

my punishment is my crime
what I have failed to do, is me . . ."

—Another month without a show
and this the seventh year

*O Father let this thing pass out of me
I swear to You*

*I will live for the others, asking nothing
I will ask nothing, ever, for myself*

11
Out back of this old house
datura tangles with a gentler weed

its spiked pods smelling
of bad dreams and death

I reach through the dark, groping
past spines of nightmare

to brush the leaves of sensuality
A dream of tenderness

wrestles with all I know of history
I cannot now lie down

with a man who fears my power
or reaches for me as for death

or with a lover who imagines
we are not in danger

12
If it was lust that had defined us—
their lust and fear of our deep places

we have done our time
as faceless torsos licked by fire

we are in the open, on our way—
our counterparts

the pinyon jay, the small
gilt-winged insect

the Cessna throbbing level
the raven floating in the gorge

the rose and violet vulva of the earth
filling with darkness

yet deep within a single sparkle
of red, a human fire

and near and yet above the western planet
calmly biding her time

13
They were the distractions, lust and fear
but are

themselves a key
Everything that can be used, will be:

the fathers in their ceremonies
the genital contests

the cleansing of blood from pubic hair
the placenta buried and guarded

their terror of blinding
by the look of her who bore them

If you do not believe
that fear and hatred

read the lesson again
in the old dialect

14
But can't you see me as a human being
he said

What is a human being
she said

I try to understand
he said

what will you undertake
she said

will you punish me for history
he said

what will you undertake
she said

do you believe in collective guilt
he said

let me look in your eyes
she said

15
Who is here. The Erinyes.
One to sit in judgment.

One to speak tenderness.
One to inscribe the verdict on the canyon wall.

If you have not confessed
the damage

if you have not recognized
the Mother of reparations

if you have not come to terms
with the women in the mirror

if you have not come to terms
with the inscription

the terms of the ordeal
the discipline   the verdict

if still you are on your way
still She awaits your coming

16
"Such women are dangerous
to the order of things"

and yes, we will be dangerous
to ourselves

groping through spines of nightmare
(*datura* tangling with a simpler herb)

because the line dividing
lucidity from darkness

is yet to be marked out

Isolation, the dream
of the frontier woman

levelling her rifle along
the homestead fence

still snares our pride
—a suicidal leaf

laid under the burning-glass
in the sun's eye

Any woman's death diminishes me

from WHEN WE DEAD AWAKEN:
WRITING AS RE-VISION

Ibsen's *When We Dead Awaken* is a play about the use that the male
artist and thinker—in the process of creating culture as we know it—
has made of women, in his life and in his work; and about a woman's
slow struggling awakening to the use to which her life has been put.
Bernard Shaw wrote in 1900 of this play: "[Ibsen] shows us that no
degradation ever devized or permitted is as disastrous as this
degradation; that through it women can die into luxuries for men
and yet can kill them; that men and women are becoming
conscious of this: and that what remains to be seen as perhaps the
most interesting of all imminent social developments is what will
happen 'when we dead awaken.' "
     It's exhilarating to be alive in a time of awakening consciousness;
it can also be confusing, disorienting, and painful. This awakening of
dead or sleeping consciousness has already affected the lives of
millions of women, even those who don't know it yet. It is also
affecting the lives of men, even those who deny its claims upon them.
The argument will go on whether an oppressive economic class
system is responsible for the oppressive nature of male/female
relations, or whether, in fact, the sexual class system is the original
model on which all the others are based. But in the last few years
connections have been drawn between our sexual lives and our
political institutions which are inescapable and illuminating. The
sleepwalkers are coming awake, and for the first time this awakening
has a collective reality; it is no longer such a lonely thing to open
one's eyes.
     Re-vision—the act of looking back, of seeing with fresh eyes, of
entering an old text from a new critical direction—is for us more
than a chapter in cultural history: it is an act of survival. Until we can
understand the assumptions in which we are drenched we cannot
know ourselves. And this drive to self-knowledge, for woman, is
more than a search for identity: it is part of her refusal of the
destructiveness of male-dominated society. A radical critique of
literature, feminist in its impulse, would take the work first of all as a
clue to how we live, how we have been living, how we have been led
to imagine ourselves, how our language has trapped as well as
liberated us; and how we can begin to see—and therefore live—
afresh. A change in the concept of sexual identity is essential if we

"When We Dead Awaken" was written for the MLA Commission on the Status of Women
in the Profession and was read at the MLA meetings in December 1971.

ADRIENNE RICH 353

are not going to see the old political order reassert itself in every new revolution. We need to know the writing of the past, and know it differently than we have ever known it; not to pass on a tradition but to break its hold over us.

For writers, and at this moment for women writers in particular, there is the challenge and promise of a whole new psychic geography to be explored. But there is also a difficult and dangerous walking on the ice, as we try to find language and images for a consciousness we are just coming into, and with little in the past to support us. I want to talk about some aspects of this difficulty and this danger.

Jane Harrison, the great classical anthropologist, wrote in 1914 in a letter to her friend Gilbert Murray: "By the by, about 'Women,' it has bothered me often—why do women never want to write poetry about Man as a sex—why is Woman a dream and a terror to man and not the other way around? . . . Is it mere convention and propriety, or something deeper?" I think Jane's question cuts deep into the myth-making tradition, the romantic tradition; deep into what women and men have been to each other; and deep into the psyche of the woman writer. Thinking about that question, I began thinking of the work of two twentieth-century women poets, Sylvia Plath and Diane Wakoski. It strikes me that in the work of both Man appears as, if not a dream, a fascination, and a terror; and that the source of the fascination and the terror is, simply, Man's power—to dominate, tyrannize, choose or reject the woman. The charisma of Man seems to come purely from his power over her, and his control of the world by force; not from anything fertile or life-giving in him. And, in the work of both these poets, it is finally the woman's sense of *herself*—embattled, possessed—that gives the poetry its dynamic charge, its rhythms of struggle, need, will and female energy. Convention and propriety are perhaps not the right words, but until recently this female anger, this furious awareness of the Man's power over her, were not available materials to the female poet, who tended to write of Love as the source of her suffering, and to view that victimization by Love as an almost inevitable fate. Or, like Marianne Moore and Elizabeth Bishop, she kept human sexual relationships at a measured and chiselled distance in her poems.

One answer to Jane Harrison's question has to be that historically men and women have played very different parts in each others' lives. Where woman has been a luxury for man, and has served as the painter's model and the poet's muse, but also as comforter, nurse, cook, bearer of his seed, secretarial assistant, and copyist of

JEROME ROTHENBERG

Thomas Victor

Jerome Rothenberg was born in New York City in 1931. He was educated at the University of Michigan and Columbia University and served with the United States Army in Germany. He was editor and publisher of Hawk's Well Press for many years and is currently the editor of *Alcheringa/Ethnopoetics*. He has taught in Germany and at the University of California in San Diego, and last year was awarded a Guggenheim Fellowship. His many books of poetry include *Conversations, Poems 1964–1967, Poems for the Game of Silence, Esther K. Comes to America*, and *Poland/1931*. He has translated extensively from German and several Amerindian languages, and is the editor or co-editor of several brilliant and influential anthologies, among them *Technicians of the Sacred*, and *America: A Prophecy*.

THE BEADLE'S TESTIMONY

The boy who throws the ball
A jewel of a boy
His coat down to his knees
Earlocks flying

He will grow up to sell candles
Will eat a dog
& thrive on fat cigars
He will bless his mother too

Yes we are simple people
Yes we drive carts
& work with shit
Sometimes we study

Sometimes a fish in the hand
Sometimes charity
Eros is the Warsaw banker
Spain is far away

Kansas City is also far away
Where did our love go?
I have two hands & only one wallet
I want to speak to you about it

Cities & Jews
Walls & what is behind a wall
A temple sometimes
Sometimes a shining diesel locomotive

Sometimes charity
A boy's shadow on the wall
A jewel of a boy
He will grow up to sell candles

He will bless his mother too

SOAP (II)

Will the man who gets clean love his neighbor?
Yes the facts are apparent yes the facts
Live on in the mind if the mind lives on
"I have no right to another man's business
& it makes me sick"
When Meyer fell asleep in his chair, his wife shouted
                              DON'T TOUCH MEYER!
The sugar at the bottom of his cup was brown and hard
Twice a month he had the hairs clipped from his nose
& thanked his barber
(He had sold him shaving soap the day before)
Selling soap to the pious
Calling it *zeyf*
Saying: *ah shtick zeyf*
Or saying: *ah shtickeleh zeyf* (dim.)
Theirs was a business between friends
& meant lying
But the tips of his fingers smelt good to him
Women admired it
The books on his shelf were in a language he couldn't
                                              understand

So he began to make little songs
& to stuff his pockets with little bars of soap
"Children, eat omelets
"Children, when the chamberpots are empty the great
                              bear comes at night
"Children, there are other values in this life"
Yes said the voices in his dream yes
Sang the voices to the man who sold soap
& was ticklish
But where will the road end, do the voices
Tell you where the road will end
Do they lead you to a new town where the people
                              aren't clean?
"I have no right to another man's business
& it makes me sick"
There were always towns like that

from THE SEVEN HELLS OF THE JIGOKU ZOSHI

THE FIFTH HELL: of unclean food, for those who served unclean
                         food to others

     The fattened sky
resting at the door of this
     white butchershop
carries the old wounds:
The poor meat stands without skin & streams blood,
it covers flowers & roots in the window
flows in slow rivers under the paws of a cat
The butcher sees me & smiles
     the red steam coating his apron
The breasts of the housewives are heavy with salt

Our looks cross from a distance:
     I feel the grass part
in his smile, the soft paws brushing the earth
Why should this butcher concern me?
Why should I want to run or cry out
     to rise like a river of teeth?
Why should I look so long at those rows of sweet flesh,
the flanks black with flies, the white tiles?

His breath is stirring the hair of these women,
like dry smoke it moves down the aisle
     past the register
     comes to rest on the scales:
Salt & fire, dismemberment, blood, old commitments
marigolds stuffed into jars in the sun
the flesh caving in, the warm center
     Now they come in small groups
to watch the skulls behind glass
the gouged eyes, the hills of flayed bones
the blue despair of the sinews
the soft hairy flesh

The butcher prods the young leaves:
     Someday
when the dawn has grown old

we will face each other across the wet roofs
(like the priests of Xipe watching the Spaniards draw in)
And the bones will tell us that life eats life & grows fat
      that we claw at each other
(Have I said enough now? Are you sick enough of this meat?)

      Sitting at tables
stuffing our skulls with the tag-ends of life
we will go on as before
      forgetting
changing flesh into words, words into paper
lying in wait for each other
eating ourselves on this miserable earth
      And if sometimes
we should pass a window
      strewn with flowers & flesh
& the old memory of the old wounds should begin
& the sweet smell stick to our throats:
We will know again
      that image of a dark bull
bathed in its entrails
      a shroud of wild heavy flowers
that draws us to worship in silence
the sorrow of all this poor meat

THE SIXTH HELL: of women pursued by fire-breathing monsters

Because she breathed too wildly in the sun
Because the sun·had risen for her because it fell into her lap
Because she held a bird between her legs, eyeless, but the face still
    warm, still tender
They have left her

Because sand was covering the factories
Because the wind wiped out the traces of a bridge
Because their throats bled spiders & poppy seeds & wheels
They have left her

Because it was raining when she got there
Because the houses overflowed with broken tiles
Because horses grazed along the river & in the cities fires burned in
    empty stalls
They have left her

When it was over a rain of salamanders washed the suburbs
Magnetos burned her eyelids & the fibers growing from her spine
When it was over blue milk bathed the beaches
They have left her

When it was over the living room smelled of submarines & death
When it was over her eyes closed to crazy throbbings underneath the
    moon
When it was over the trolleys shattered glass in front of convents
They have left her

Sorrow ran down the hills where she bled
Sorrow older than the stones lining the highways older than the sea
Sorrow of lions crying from before her birth
They have left her

In the rain in the unlit places where the morning waits on its dead
In cemeteries overlooking monstrous cities
In the granular darkness of her womb with its cry of raw beginnings
They have left her

In the wake of autos speeding over sunless roads
On anguished nights in resorts in casinos overrun by a chimera
At the blind center of a sundial
They have left her

Now dawn rides the restless ferries out of town
Dawn swallows a city in its hunger, waiting with new blood across
    its lips
Dawn grovels in the minds of those who wait, the lately risen
They have left her

They have left her in the rain where her voice was sleeping
They have sucked the moon & stars from her veins
& have left her, to return to empty offices with windows high above
    the sea
They have left her

They have left her bathed with water-guts & lymph
They have left her with bandages that cry & teeth & open sores
With her shadow eyeless on the shores of Hell
They have left her

Oh shadow risen from an ocean without boats
Oh shadow of lost roads & comets lonely shadow sleeping in the
    wind
Oh shadow of the silence's deep echoes
They have left her

Oh rain of hair oh flower without roots
Oh dark flower of death oh rose of desperation
Oh virgin without fingers oh hands I cannot touch oh to whom
    should I turn?
They have left her

There is no one nothing I can hold: the rain against the steps
This room oppressing me with love, old wounds, the fear beginning
Rising, till I cannot stand or walk
They have left her

Till I reach for her: a hairpin on the floor, a shawl
& all the doors are closing where she sleeps
These long mornings without hope or rest, this fever as the sunlight
    falters, as the rain falls down
They have left her

ESTHER K. COMES TO AMERICA: 1931

The Wilderness: but otherwise
name of a cafeteria
where the two lovers drink tea
not speaking to each other
but sharing a world through separation:
1931: Esther K.
& Leo Levy
have met here at the end of a short life:
nothing begins as painfully
as the first step outside the glass door
the first sight of traffic

even the rumblings of the new subway under Houston Street:
all this happened in the course of ages
the priest tormented her & that was one
the governor broke into sighs and that was another
her mother became incontinent & that was the third
other events followed: fourth was the birth
of a child dead at childbirth
she massaged its hands but had to suck her own breasts:
stale odors: Leo Levy
going every morning to the chicken market
pursues his dream of power
Esther K. wonders: how was I ever trapped
inside this body?
in another life she would have been
a playgirl: not she
but someone else threw roses
in the Dnieper
danced on the drifting icefloe
to America
not someone else but she
opened the fly of the Shanghai dog-merchant
& greased his cock:
flesh erupting in the tropics
bewildering parrots
bathed in the mind of Esther K.
the traveler who crossed the Ganges
found Harlem
on the other side
the man with six fingers on one hand
had four on the other:
thus history repeated itself with marked rapidity
leading her to first meet
& then lose
Leo Levy: leading him
to polish his fingernails
with eggwhite
leading them both to read fortunes in earwax
to sell candy in turkish baths
& cotton in Canada
to remake "1931" as a talking movie:
what lovely dreams the world will have of Esther K.
said Leo Levy

I will make dreams for the world to have of Esther K.
& garments to wear in her image
I will comb her hair out until it reaches to Nicaragua
then will climb its length
& let it carry me to the top of a windy boat
sailing for Jerusalem: farewell!
the next price of almonds is a fair price
the poor under your window & the poor
around your table
will always be there: the bicylists will too
but peddling backwards stumbling
against churches they will pretend
to drop behind: a crisis
the good life of the timid
beckons: it is a value
to be learned: a source of fortune
only too distant without refinement
both will grow sick & die
much later: separate beds
wait for them
chimeras dressed as chorus girls
to direct & love: his name
changed to Ben Messiah
hers to his: an aged couple
smelling of wet sheets
they will sometimes be holding hands
feeling how small the palms are: the Wilderness
has shrunk them: tomorrow
morning
was a lie:
a glass of tea:
maybe a bun with onions:
a suck:
two bitter almonds:
three half-chewed jelly slices:
a lemon
a lemon
a lemon
a lemon
a lemon
a lemon
etc

PORTRAIT OF A JEW OLD COUNTRY STYLE

visitor to warsaw
        old man with open fly
    flesh girls could suck
        mothers would die to catch sight of
sometimes would pass your door
        his song was
    a generation is a day, time floweth
coldly he blew his nose
reached a hand around his high round waist
        money was pinned to caftan
        aches & pains
a jew's a jew he says
love brings him to the words he needs
        but sadly
    no
        I cannot stay
        for breakfast loving
        the taste of duck eggs loving
        little rolls & butter
        loving cereals in metal pans
he tells them
        all we touch is love
        & feeds us
        this is a portrait of a jew old country style
        the gentile will fail to understand
        the jew come on better days will run from it
        how real
        the grandfathers become
        my grandfather the baker son of bakers
        YOSEL DOVID ben SHMIEL
        who was a hasid at the court in Rizhyn
        came to U.S.A. circa 1913
        but found the country godless
        tho he worked in leather
        shoes were the craft all our friends
        got into first
        e.g. his brother-in-law we called
        THE UNCLE
        I remember in a basement shop
        somewhere "downtown"

bent over shoes he stitched
how many years would pass
till nineteen-fifty maybe
when I saw him last
his lungs gone in east bronx tenement
he slept behind a curtain
seeing me he thought
I was my brother   old & crazy
he was the oldest jew I knew
my grandfather had died
in nineteen-twenty
on the night my parents
ran to warsaw
to get married   my father
left for U.S.A. the next day
no one told him of his father's death
he would never be a talmudist
would go from shoes
to insurance
from insurance back to shoes
later an entrepreneur & bust
he was always clean
shaven   my grandmother
the religious one I mean
saw the first beard
I'd ever grown   got angry
"jews don't wear beards"
(she said) no
not in golden U.S.A.
the old man had fled from
to his Polish death

for which reason I deny autobiography
or that the life of a man
matters more or less
          "We are all one man"
          Cezanne said
I count the failures of these jews
as proof of their election
they are divine because they all die
                    screaming

                    like the first
          universal jew
                    the gentiles
                    will tell you had some special deal

COKBOY, Part Two

comes a brown
wind curling from
tense tissues sphincter
opened over the whole continental
divide & shot the people up
plop plop a little girl emergeth
she with the beaver tits nose furry
eyes of the Redman's
Sabbath
gropes down the corridor
(sez) hallo doctor
got a hand to spare?
doctor sez hokay
—yas doctor
—hev ah suck
—yas doctor
hand up her bush
he pulls
a baby   howling
in lamplight a little Moses
now the Cacique's daughter laugheth
—oh doctor not so-o hard
so hard America is born
so hard the Baal Shem dreams about it
200 years later
in Vitebsk
(he was in correspondence with Wm Blake
appeared on Peckham Rye
—yes fully clothed!—
& was his angel)
angel says his mother
smiling proud

she sees his little foot
break through
her crotch an itching
races up her ribs
America is born
the Baal Shem is a beaver
(happened while the Indian talked
chanted behind Cody
the mad Jew slid to life
past pink styrofoam snow of her body's
channels
the freaky passageways
unlit unloved
like gums of an old woman
teeth were ripped from
ages gone) into
another kind of world
he hurtles
does reawaken in the female swamp
a beaver amongst the rushes
—momma!—calls the Baal Shem
—mommeleh!
vot em I doink here
I hev become mine beard
(he sez) the blind world shines on him
water runs through his mouth
down belly it is dark
a darkness (fur is dark
& hides the skin & blood
a universal fur
but leaves one hole
to open from the body's
darkness pushing
into light)
erupts
like great cock of the primal beings
red & smooth like copper
of the sun's red eye at night
old Beaver lugs it in his hand
I am myself   my grandfather
(he sings) my name is Cokboy
—COKBOY, understand?

I leave my grandmother in the female swamp
will be the Great Deliverer someday yuh-buh-bum
even might find a jar of honey might stick my prick in my prick
    might tingle might it not tickle me the bees find out about it &
    sting the knob it grows a second a dozen or so knobs along its
    length are maybe 30 knobs
so what's the use I ask maybe will try again I drag it red & sore
    behind me so vulnerable I have become in this hot climate
    shitting & farting shooting marbles was opening my mouth &
    coming in it
the blackbird shits o not so fast love into my hat eyes turn white
    wood-lilies are growing from them a slavic birth I can't deny so
    tender in my eyes tender the native turds come floating
& across America in an outrage uselessly I shout against the Sun you
    are no longer my father Moon you are no longer my mother I have
    left you have gone out jaunty with cock slung over shoulder this is
    the journey your young men will take
(says Beaver) makes it to the hut where that old woman lives apron
    over her belly carp in oven maybe fried bread fat fat little mother
    don't mind if I drop a stone onto your brains your daughters be
    back later little hot girls I ride on pretending I was you I suck
    their ears & scream o put me lower down love o my cock inside
& have to cool it
I cool it
in waters where a princess
daughter of a chief
went bathing
lethal & innocent the cock
has found its mark
(his train has reached Topeka
Custer is dead)
& enters the bridegroom's quarters
darkness her flesh prepared for it
by new moon
in her abdomen a sliver
grows
a silver dollar over Barstow
lighting the Marriage of America
in kabbalistic time
(say Cokboy) you are the daughter of
the mountain
now will I take thee to my father's tribe

to do the snake dance
o jewish feet of El go crazy
in his mind
o
El
o
Him
I carry in my knapsack
dirty pictures land grants
(but further back her people
gun for him
how should they feel
seeing their daughter in arms of
Cokboy
—C—O—C—K, understand?—)
thou art become my Father's bride
are wedded to (ugh) Christian god
forever
bye bye I got to run now
engagements await us in Salt Lake City
industry riseth everywhere
arrows strike concrete
never shall bruise my sweetie's flesh
(says Cokboy) on horse
up river he makes his way
past mining camps Polacks were panning gold in
& other pure products of America
o prospectors o Anglo Saxons
baby-faced dumplings who pacified the west
with gattling guns with bounties for hides of babes
mothers' vulvas made baseballs to their lust
o bringers of civilization heros heros
I will fight my way past you who guard the sacred border
last frontier village of my dreams
with shootouts tyrannies
(he cries) who had escaped the law
or brought it with him
how vass I lost tzu get here
(dot dot dot) was luckless
on a mountain & kept from
true entry to the west true paradise
like Moses in the Rockies who stares at California spooky in
                                        the jewish light

of horns atop my head great orange freeways of the mind
America disaster
America disaster
America disaster
America disaster
where he can watch sun go down
in desert
Cokboy asleep? (they ask)
awake (cries Cokboy)
only his beard has left him
like his own his grandfather's
ghost of Ishi was waiting on the crest
looked like a Jew
but silent
was silent in America
guess I got nothing left to say

PERSONAL MANIFESTO

I think of myself as making poems that other poets haven't provided for me, & for the existence of which I feel a deep need.

I look for new forms & possibilities, but also for ways of presenting in my own language the oldest possibilities of poetry going back to the primitive & archaic cultures that have been opening up to us over the last hundred years.

I believe that everything is possible in poetry, & that our earlier "Western" attempts at definition represent a failure of perception we no longer have to endure.

I have recently been translating American Indian poetry (including the "meaningless" syllables, word distortions, & music) & have been exploring ancestral sources of my own in the world of Jewish mystics, thieves, & madmen.

My personal manifesto reads:
   (1) I will change your mind.
   (2) Any means (=methods) to that end.
   (3) To oppose the "devourers" = bureaucrats, system-makers, priests, etc. (W. Blake).
   (4) "& if thou wdst understand that wch is me, know this: all that I have sd I have uttered playfully—& I was by no means ashamed of it." (J.C. to his disciples, *The Acts of St. John*).

JEROME ROTHENBERG

MURIEL RUKEYSER

Muriel Rukeyser was born in 1913 in New York City. Educated at Vassar and Columbia, she was a political activist in the early Thirties and was arrested in Alabama during the second Scottsboro trial. She attended Roosevelt Aviation School; out of that experience came her first book, *Theory of Flight,* which won publication in the Yale Younger Poets Series. She travelled widely in Europe, working for various magazines. Her many books of poems include *A Turning Wind, U.S. 1, The Green Wave, Beast in View, Selected Poems, Body of Waking, Waterlily Fire* and *Breaking Open.* She has also written several plays, novels, and children's books, translated Octavio Paz and Gunnar Ekelof, and written the scripts for three films. She has taught at Columbia, Sarah Lawrence, New York University, and San Francisco State and has held a Guggenheim Fellowship. She lives in New York City.

Thomas Victor

GAULEY BRIDGE

Camera at the crossing sees the city
a street of wooden walls and empty windows,
the doors shut handless in the empty street,
and the deserted Negro standing on the corner.

The little boy runs with his dog
up the street to the bridge over the river where
nine men are mending road for the government.
He blurs the camera-glass fixed on the street.

Railway tracks here and many panes of glass
tin under light, the grey shine of towns and forests:
in the commercial hotel (Switzerland of America)
the owner is keeping his books behind the public glass.

Postoffice window, a hive of private boxes,
the hand of the man who withdraws, the woman who reaches
    her hand
and the tall coughing man stamping an envelope.

The bus station and the great pale buses stopping for food;
April-glass-tinted, the yellow-aproned waitress;
coast-to-coast schedule on the plateglass window.

The man on the street and the camera eye:
he leaves the doctor's office, slammed door, doom,
any town looks like this one-street town.

Glass, wood, and naked eye: the movie-house
closed for the afternoon frames posters streaked with rain,
advertise "Racing Luck" and "Hitch-Hike Lady."

Whistling, the train comes from a long way away,
slow, and the Negro watches it grow in the grey air,
the hotel man makes a note behind his potted palm.

Eyes of the tourist house, red-and-white filling station,
the eyes of the Negro, looking down the track,
hotel-man and hotel, cafeteria, camera.

MURIEL RUKEYSER 377

And in the beerplace on the other sidewalk
always one's harsh night eyes over the beerglass
follow the waitress and the yellow apron.

The road flows over the bridge,
Gamoca pointed at the underpass,
opposite, Alloy, after a block of town.

What do you want—a cliff over a city?
A foreland, sloped to sea and overgrown with roses?
These people live here.

GEORGE ROBINSON: BLUES

Gauley Bridge is a good town for Negroes, they let us stand
      around, they let us stand
around on the sidewalks if we're black or brown.
Vanetta's over the trestle, and that's our town.

The hill makes breathing slow, slow breathing after you
      row the river,
and the graveyard's on the hill, cold in the springtime blow,
the graveyard's up on high, and the town is down below.

Did you ever bury thirty-five men in a place in back of your
      house,
thirty-five tunnel workers the doctors didn't attend,
died in the tunnel camps, under rocks, everywhere, world
      without end.

When a man said I feel poorly, for any reason, any weakness
      or such,
letting up when he couldn't keep going barely,
the Cap and company come and run him off the job surely.

I've put them
DOWN from the tunnel camps
to the graveyard on the hill,
tin-cans all about—it fixed them!—

TUNNELITIS
hold themselves up
at the side of a tree,
I can go right now
to that cemetery.

When the blast went off the boss would call out, Come, let's
     go back,
when that heavy loaded blast went white, Come, let's go back,
telling us hurry, hurry, into the falling rocks and muck.

The water they would bring had dust in it, our drinking water,
the camps and their groves were colored with the dust,
we cleaned our clothes in the groves, but we always had the
     dust.

Looked like somebody sprinkled flour all over the parks and
     groves,
it stayed and the rain couldn't wash it away and it twinkled
that white dust really looked pretty down around our ankles.

As dark as I am, when I came out at morning after the tunnel
     at night,
with a white man, nobody could have told which man was white.
The dust had covered us both, and the dust was white.

NUNS IN THE WIND

As I came out of the New York Public Library
you said your influence on my style would be noticed
and from now on there would be happy poems.
          It was at that moment
the street was assaulted by a covey of nuns
going directly toward the physics textbooks.

Tragic fiascos shadowed that whole spring.
The children sang streetfuls, and I thought:
O to be the King in the carol
kissed and at peace;   but recalling Costa Brava
the little blossoms in the mimosa tree

and later, the orange cliff, after they sent me out,
I knew there was no peace.
                            You smiled, saying : Take it easy.

That was the year of the five-day fall of cities.
              First day, no writers. Second, no telephones. Third
              no venereal diseases. Fourth, no income tax. And on
              the fifth, at noon.
The nuns blocked the intersections, reading.
I used to go walking in the triangle of park,
seeing that locked face, the coarse enemy skin,
the eyes with all the virtues of a good child,
but no child was there, even when I thought, Child!
The 4 a.m. cop could never understand.
You said, not smiling, You are the future for me,
but you were the present and immediate moment
and I am empty-armed without, until to me is given
two lights to carry : my life and the light of my death.

If the wind would rise, those black throbbing umbrellas
fly downstreet, the flapping robes unfolding,
my dream would be over, poisons cannot linger
when the wind rises. . . .

All that year, the classical declaration of war was lacking.
There was a lot of lechery and disorder.
And I am queen on that island.

Well, I said suddenly in the tall and abstract room,
time to wake up.
Now make believe you can help yourself alone.
And there it was, the busy crosstown noontime
crossing, peopled with nuns.

                    Now, bragging now,
the flatfoot slambang victory,
                            thanks to a trick of wind
will you see faces blow, and though their bodies
by God's grace will never blow,
cities shake in the wind, the year's over,
calendars tear, and their clothes blow. O yes!

AJANTA

1. THE JOURNEY

Came in my full youth to the midnight cave
Nerves ringing; and this thing I did alone.
Wanting my fulness and not a field of war,
For the world considered annihilation, a star
Called Wormwood rose and flickered, shattering
Bent light over the dead boiling up in the ground,
The biting yellow of their corrupted lives
Streaming to war, denying all our words.
Nothing was left among the tainted weather
But world-walking and shadowless Ajanta.
Hallucination and the metal laugh
In clouds, and the mountain-spectre riding storm.
Nothing was certain but a moment of peace,
A hollow behind the unbreakable waterfall.
All the way to the cave, the teeming forms of death,
And death, the price of the body, cheap as air.
I blessed my heart on the expiation journey
For it had never been unable to suffer:
When I met the man whose face looked like the future,
When I met the whore with the dying red hair,
The child myself who is my murderer.
So came I between heaven and my grave
Past the serene smile of the *voyeur*, to
This cave where the myth enters the heart again.

2. THE CAVE

Space to the mind, the painted cave of dream.
This is not a womb, nothing but good emerges:
This is a stage, neither unreal nor real,
Where the walls are the world, the rocks and palaces
Stand on a borderland of blossoming ground.
If you stretch your hand, you touch the slope of the world
Reaching in interlaced gods, animals, and men.
There is no background.   The figures hold their peace
In a web of movement.   There is no frustration,

Every gesture is taken, everything yields connections.
The heavy sensual shoulders, the thighs, the blood-born flesh
And earth turning into color, rocks into their crystals,
Water to sound, fire to form; life flickers
Uncounted into the supple arms of love.
The space of these walls is the body's living space;
Tear open your ribs and breathe the color of time
Where nothing leads away, the world comes forward
In flaming sequences.   Pillars and prisms.   Riders
And horses and the figures of consciousness,
Red cow grows long, goes running through the world.
Flung into movement in carnal purity,
These bodies are sealed—warm lip and crystal hand
In a jungle of light.   Color-sheeted, seductive
Foreboding eyelid lowered on the long eye,
Fluid and vulnerable.   The spaces of the body
Are suddenly limitless, and riding flesh
Shapes constellations over the golden breast,
Confusion of scents and illuminated touch—
Monster touch, the throat printed with brightness,
Wide outlined gesture where the bodies ride.
Bells, and the spirit flashing.   The religious bells,
Bronze under the sunlight like breasts ringing,
Bronze in the closed air, the memory of walls,
Great sensual shoulders in the web of time.

3. LES TENDRESSES BESTIALES

A procession of caresses alters the ancient sky
Until new constellations are the body shining:
There's the Hand to steer by, there the horizon Breast,
And the Great Stars kindling the fluid hill.
All the rooms open into magical boxes,
Nothing is tilted, everything flickers
Sexual and exquisite.
The panther with its throat along my arm
Turns black and flows away.
Deep in all streets passes a faceless whore
And the checkered men are whispering one word.
The face I know becomes the night-black rose.
The sharp face is now an electric fan
And says one word to me.

The dice and the alcohol and the destruction
Have drunk themselves and cast.
Broken bottle of loss, and the glass
Turned bloody into the face.
Now the scene comes forward, very clear.
Dream-singing, airborne, surrenders the recalled,
The gesture arrives riding over the breast,
Singing, singing, tender atrocity,
The silver derelict wearing fur and claws.
O love, I stood under the apple branch,
I saw the whipped bay and the small dark islands,
And night sailing the river and the foghorn's word.
My life said to you : I want to love you well.
The wheel goes back and I shall live again,
But the wave turns, my birth arrives and spills
Over my breast the world bearing my grave,
And your eyes open in earth.   You touched my life.
My life reaches the skin, moves under your smile,
And your throat and your shoulders and your face and your
        thighs
Flash.
            I am haunted by interrupted acts,
Introspective as a leper, enchanted
By a repulsive clew,
A gross and fugitive movement of the limbs.
Is this the love that shook the lights to flame?
Sheeted avenues thrash in the wind,
Torn streets, the savage parks.
I am plunged deep.   Must find the midnight cave.

4. BLACK BLOOD

A habit leading to murder, smoky laughter
Hated at first, but necessary later.
Alteration of motives.   To stamp in terror
Around the deserted harbor, down the hill
Until the woman laced into a harp
Screams and screams and the great clock strikes,
Swinging its giant figures past the face.
The Floating Man rides on the ragged sunset
Asking and asking.   Do not say, Which loved?

Which was beloved? Only, Who most enjoyed?
Armored ghost of rage, screaming and powerless.
Only find me and touch my blood again.
Find me.　　A girl runs down the street
Singing Take me, yelling Take me Take
Hang me from the clapper of a bell
And you as hangman ring it sweet tonight,
For nothing clean in me is more than cloud
Unless you call it.　　—As I ran I heard
A black voice beating among all that blood:
"Try to live as if there were a God."

5. THE BROKEN WORLD

Came to Ajanta cave, the painted space of the breast,
The real world where everything is complete,
There are no shadows, the forms of incompleteness.
The great cloak blows in the light, rider and horse arrive,
The shoulders turn and every gift is made.
No shadows fall.　　There is no source of distortion.
In our world, a tree casts the shadow of a woman,
A man the shadow of a phallus, a hand raised
The shadow of a whip.
Here everything is itself,
Here all may stand
On summer earth.
Brightness has overtaken every light,
And every myth netted itself in flesh.
New origins, and peace given entire
And the spirit alive.
In the shadowless cave
The naked arm is raised.
Animals arrive,
Interlaced, and Gods
Interlaced, and men
Flame-woven.
I stand and am complete.
Crawls from the door,
Black at my two feet
The shadow of the world.

World, not yet one,
Enters the heart again.
The naked world, and the old noise of tears,
The fear, the expiation and the love,
A world of the shadowed and alone.

The journey, and the struggles of the moon.

FIELDS WHERE WE SLEPT

Fields where we slept
Lie underwater now
Clay meadows of nightmare
Beneath the shallow wave.

A tremor of speech
On all lips and all mirrors;
Pink sweater and tornado
Announce dawn's littoral.

South lies evocative
On the fine Negro mouth.
Play of silver in streams
Half lake under.

High on the unplowed red
The waterweeds respond,
Where Sheriff Fever
Ordered me to trial.

Where once hatred and fear
Touched me the branch of death,
I may float waves of making
Hung above my lost field.

Remember they say and Incarnatus Est,
The fire-tailed waves, never forget the eyes
Or the distorted jailers or their kindness
Even while they were torturing Mr. Crystal.

Psalms awake and asleep, remember the manmade
Lake where those barren treecrowns rode.
Where air of curses hung, keel of my calm
Rides our created tide.

"NO ONE EVER WALKING THIS
OUR ONLY EARTH"

No one ever walking this our only earth, various, very clouded,
    in our forests, in all the valleys of our early dreams,
No one has ever for long seen any thing in full, not live
As any one river or man has run his changes, child
Of the swarms and sowings.   Death nor the woman, seed
Of the born, all growing, going through the grass.
However deep you have looked into the well of the cradle
Or into any dream or open eyes the grave
While the soul, many-leaved and waiting,
Began to assume another exact flower.
Smoke and smell in the wind, a single life!
However true you tell, you never have told.
And even that is not altogether true.   It changes, we say,
    changes, for yes,
Indeed we all know this, any, any of us, there are secrets known
    to all.

Was it indeed shown you in a flash of journey, the flicker along
    change?
In the fine shadow between the curve of lips, shadow of days
    lengthening,
In the flicker of meaning revealed by many windows;
In the form of the eye, the form of words, of the word;   mean-
    ing that formed
These marvelous genitals, nameless as God;
Or in the informing light behind his dream, and he was dreaming
    of you.
Did his own self escape him, now to reach us, reaving the edge
    of cloud?

Has a gift then been given, each other giving our lives?
As air is given to the mouth of all?

LOOKING AT EACH OTHER

Yes, we were looking at each other
Yes, we knew each other very well
Yes, we had made love with each other many times
Yes, we had heard music together
Yes, we had gone to the sea together
Yes, we had cooked and eaten together
Yes, we had laughed often day and night
Yes, we fought violence and knew violence
Yes, we hated the inner and outer oppression
Yes, that day we were looking at each other
Yes, we saw the sunlight pouring down
Yes, the corner of the table was between us
Yes, bread and flowers were on the table
Yes, our eyes saw each other's eyes
Yes, our mouths saw each other's mouth
Yes, our breasts saw each other's breasts
Yes, our bodies entire saw each other
Yes, it was beginning in each
Yes, it threw waves across our lives
Yes, the pulses were becoming very strong
Yes, the beating became very delicate
Yes, the calling   the arousal
Yes, the arriving   the coming
Yes, there it was for both entire
Yes, we were looking at each other

WAITING FOR ICARUS

He said he would be back and we'd drink wine together
He said that everything would be better than before
He said we were on the edge of a new relation
He said he would never again cringe before his father
He said that he was going to invent full-time
He said he loved me that going into me
He said was going into the world and the sky
He said all the buckles were very firm

He said the wax was the best wax
He said Wait for me here on the beach
He said Just don't cry

I remember the gulls and the waves
I remember the islands going dark on the sea
I remember the girls laughing
I remember they said he only wanted to get away from me
I remember mother saying : Inventors are like poets,
                                            a trashy lot
I remember she told me those who try out inventions are
    worse
I remember she added : Women who love such are the
    worst of all

I have been waiting all day, or perhaps longer.
I would have liked to try those wings myself.
It would have been better than this.

MYTH

Long afterward, Oedipus, old and blinded, walked the
roads.   He smelled a familiar smell.   It was
the Sphinx.   Oedipus said, "I want to ask one question.
Why didn't I recognize my mother?"   "You gave the
wrong answer," said the Sphinx.   "But that was what
made everything possible," said Oedipus.   "No," she said.
"When I asked, What walks on four legs in the morning,
two at noon, and three in the evening, you answered,
Man.   You didn't say anything about woman."
"When you say Man," said Oedipus, "you include women
too. Everyone knows that."   She said, "That's what
you think."

ALONG HISTORY

Along history, forever
    some woman dancing,
    making shapes on the air;
    forever a man
    riding a good horse,
    sitting the dark horse well,
    his penis erect with
        fantasy

BOYS OF THESE MEN FULL SPEED

for Jane Cooper

Boys of these men
    full speed across free,
    my father's boyhood eyes.
    Sail-skating with friends
    bright on Wisconsin ice
    those years away.

Sails strung across their backs
    boys racing toward
    fierce bitter middle-age
    in the great glitter of
    corrupted cities.
    Father, your dark mouth
    speaking its rancor.

Alive not yet, the girl
    I would become
    stares at that ice
    stippled with skaters,
    a story you tell.

Boys of those men
 call across winter
 where I stand and shake,
 woman of that girl.

DON BATY, THE DRAFT RESISTER

I Muriel stood at the altar-table
The young man Don Baty stood with us
I Muriel fell away in me
in dread but in a welcoming
I am Don Baty then I said
before the blue-coated police
ever entered and took him.

I am Don Baty, say we all
we eat our bread, we drink our wine.
Our heritage has come, we know,
your arrest is mine. Yes.
Beethoven saying Amen Amen Amen Amen Amen
and all a singing, earth and eyes,
strong and weaponless.

There is a pounding at the door;
now we bring our lives entire.
I am Don Baty. My dear, my dear,
in a kind of welcoming,
here we meet, here we bring
ourselves. They pound on the wall of time.
The newborn are with us singing.

from THE LIFE OF POETRY

The form of a poem is much more organic, closer to other organic
form, than has been supposed. D'Arcy Wentworth Thompson, whose
book *On Growth and Form* is a source and a monument, says that
organic form is, mathematically, a function of time. There is, in the
growth of a tree, the story of those years which saw the rings being
made: between those wooden rippled rings, we can read the wetness
or dryness of the years before the charts were kept. But the tree is
in itself an image of adjustment to its surroundings. There are many
kinds of growth: the inorganic shell or horn presents its past and
present in the spiral; the crocus grows through minute pulsations,
each at an interval of twenty seconds or so, each followed by a
partial recoil.

A poem moves through its sounds set in motion, and the reaction
to these sounds, their rhymes and repetitions and contrast, has a
demonstrable physical basis which can be traced as the wave-length
of the sounds themselves can be traced. The wave-length is
measurable; the reaction, if you wish such measurements, could be
traced through heartbeat and breath, although I myself do not place
much value on such measurement.

The impact of the images, and the tension and attraction between
meanings, these are the clues to the flow of contemporary poetry.
Baudelaire, Lawrence, Eliot have been masters here, and well have
known the effects and the essences they offered. But to go on, to
recognize the energies that are transferred between people when a
poem is given and taken, to know the relationships in modern life
that can make the next step, to see the tendencies in science which
can indicate it, that is for the new poets.

In the exchange, the human energy that is transferred is to be
considered.

Exchange is creation; and the human energy involved is conscious-
ness, the capacity to produce change from the existing conditions.

Into the present is flung naked life. Life is flung into the present
language. The new forms emerge, with their intensive properties,
or potentials—their words and images; and their extensive properties,
existing in time: sound, forms, subjects, content, and that last includes
all the relations between the words and images of the poem.

When the poem arrives with the impact of crucial experience,
when it becomes one of the turnings which we living may at any
moment approach and enter, then we become more of our age and
more primitive. Not primitive as the aesthetes have used the term,

MURIEL RUKEYSER 391

but complicated, fresh, full of dark meaning, insisting on discovery, as the experience of a woman giving birth to a child is primitive.

I cannot say what poetry is; I know that our sufferings and our concentrated joy, our states of plunging far and dark and turning to come back to the world—so that the moment of intense turning seems still and universal—all are here, in a music like the music of our time, like the hero and like the anonymous forgotten; and there is an exchange here in which our lives are met, and created.

*　　*　　*

Tonight I will try again for the music of truth.*

MURIEL RUKEYSER

* Ms. Rukeyser wishes us to say that this statement comes from a book written some time ago, and she has appended the last line from a recent poem.—Ed.

CHARLES SIMIC

Charles Simic was born in Yugoslavia in 1938 and came to this country at an early age. He was educated at New York University. His books of poetry are *What the Grass Says, Somewhere Among Us a Stone Is Taking Notes, Dismantling the Silence, White,* and *Return to a Place Lit by a Glass of Milk.* He has translated from French and Russian and has published three volumes of translations of Yugoslavian poetry. He teaches at the University of New Hampshire and lives nearby with his wife and children.

POEM

Every morning I forget how it is.
I watch the smoke mount
In great strides above the city.
I belong to no one.

Then, I remember my shoes,
How I have to put them on,
How bending over to tie them up
I will look into the earth.

BUTCHER SHOP

Sometimes walking late at night
I stop before a closed butcher shop.
There is a single light in the store
Like the light in which the convict digs his tunnel.

An apron hangs on the hook:
The blood on it smeared into a map
Of the great continents of blood,
The great rivers and oceans of blood.

There are knives that glitter like altars
In a dark church
Where they bring the cripple and the imbecile
To be healed.

There is a wooden slab where bones are broken,
Scraped clean:—a river dried to its bed
Where I am fed,
Where deep in the night I hear a voice.

THE SPOON

An old spoon
Bent, gouged,
Polished to an evil
Glitter.

It has bitten
Into my life—
This kennel-bone
Sucked thin.

Now, it is a living
Thing: ready
To scratch a name
On a prison wall—

Ready to be passed on
To the little one
Just barely
Beginning to walk.

HUNGER

We are old friends.
She put my father to bed
When he was little.

Her stories are like lace
The girls from the last century
Wore against their thighs.

There are dogs
Who want to bite her throat.
No use. There isn't a grain
Of salt in it.

The old lady
Makes jams.

For recipe she takes the palm
From a newborn child.

Take it as a medicine,
A teaspoon at a time, and remember:
You are a Saint turned over on a spit,
You are a roach caught by the convicts.

When you can't get out of bed
She'll come visiting
In her white bonnet
Tapping her cane.

With a tiny silver spoon
She'll part the bark of your lips.
She's a bee, you are her flower.
That's all the explanation I find necessary.

PASTORAL

I came to a field
Where the grass was silence
And flowers
Words

I saw they were both
Of flesh and blood
And that they sense and fear
The wind like a knife

So I sat between the word *obscure*
And the word *gallows*
Took out my small cauldron
And ladle

Whistled to the word *fire*
And she answered me
From her sleep

Spat in the palm of my hand
To catch the stars
Behind my back
And light her way

POEM WITHOUT A TITLE

I say to the lead
Why did you let yourself
Be cast into a bullet?
Have you forgotten the alchemists?
Have you given up hope
Of turning into gold?

Nobody answers.
Lead. Bullet. With names
Such as these
The sleep is deep and long.

BROOMS*

1
Only brooms
Know the devil
Still exists

That the snow grows whiter
After a crow has flown over it
That a dark dusty corner
Is the place of dreamers and children

That a broom is also a tree
In the orchard of the poor
That a roach there
Is a mute dove.

* This is an earlier and shorter version of the poem by the same name which appears
in *Thank You and Other Poems* and is printed here by permission of the author.—Ed.

2
Brooms appear in dreambooks
As omens of approaching death.
This is their secret life.
In public they act like flat-chested old maids
Preaching temperance.

They are sworn enemies of lyric poetry.
In prison they accompany the jailer,
Enter cells to hear confessions.
Their short-end comes down
When you least expect it.

Left alone behind a door
Of a condemned tenement
They mutter to no one in particular
Words like *virgin wind moon-eclipse*
And that most sacred of all names:
Hieronymus Bosch.

3
And then of course there's my grandmother
Sweeping the dust of the nineteenth century
Into the twentieth and my grandfather plucking
A straw out of the broom to pick his teeth.

Long winter nights.
Dawns thousand years deep.
Kitchen-windows like heads
Bandaged for toothache.

The broom beyond them sweeping
Tucking in the lucent grains of dust
Into neat pyramids
That have tombs in them

Already sacked by robbers
Once, long ago.

ELEMENTARY COSMOGONY

How to the invisible
I hired myself to learn
Whatever trade it might
Consent to teach me.

How the invisible
Came out for a walk
On a certain evening
Casting the shadow of a man.

How I followed behind
Dragging my body
Which is my tool box,
Which is my sustenance,

For a long apprenticeship
That has as its last
And seventh rule:
The submission to chance.

NOTHING

I want to see it face to face,
And then, I intend to raise hell.
No, I don't have anything prepared.
I will rely entirely on inspiration,
Also on my ancestors who just now
Begin to laugh their heads off.

In all probability I'll make a fool of myself,
Turn away grinning stupidly,
Light a cigarette with trembling fingers,
Ask about the weather, about that cloud
Shaped like a medicine bundle, hovering
So still, in the windless sky.

BREASTS

I love breasts, hard
Full breasts, guarded
By a button.

They come in the night.
The bestiaries of the ancients
Which include the unicorn
Have kept them out.

Pearly, like the east
An hour before sunrise,
Two ovens of the only
Philosopher's stone
Worth bothering about.

They bring on their nipples
Beads of inaudible sighs,
Vowels of delicious clarity
For the little red schoolhouse of our mouths.

Elsewhere, solitude
Makes another gloomy entry
In its ledger, misery
Borrows another cup of rice.

They draw nearer: Animal
Presence. In the barn
The milk shivers in the pail.

I like to come up to them
From underneath, like a kid
Who climbs on a chair
To reach a jar of forbidden jam.

Gently, with my lips,
Loosen the button.
Have them slip into my hands
Like two freshly poured beer-mugs.

I spit on fools who fail to include
Breasts in their metaphysics,
Star-gazers who have not enumerated them
Among the moons of the earth . . .

They give each finger
Its true shape, its joy:
Virgin soap, foam
On which our hands are cleansed.

And how the tongue honors
These two sour buns,
For the tongue is a feather
Dipped in egg-yolk.

I insist that a girl
Stripped to the waist
Is the first and last miracle,

That the old janitor on his deathbed
Who demands to see the breasts of his wife
For one last time
Is the greatest poet who ever lived.

O my sweet, my wistful bagpipes.
Look, everyone is asleep on the earth.
Now, in the absolute immobility
Of time, drawing the waist
Of the one I love to mine,

I will tip each breast
Like a dark heavy grape
Into the hive
Of my drowsy mouth.

THE STORY

About a fly
Which is not
A fly

About its swift
Powerful wings
Which do not exist

About its eyes
Which remain behind
In winter

Its eggs which
The epicureans
Consider a delicacy

Its bite which
Is painful
And equally imaginary

The art of plucking
Its nonexistent legs
One by one

Fortune-telling
With a sugar-cube
As its bait

How I drank
Its corpse
In a glass of milk

And caught
Its shadow
On the flypaper of my tongue.

STRICTLY FOR POSTERITY

Brothers, my teeth hurt
And I've no money to have them pulled.
If you know a way, tell me.

The collection man knocks on my window.
My wife sleeps with her thighs bare.
In my time I attempted a few prayers.
If you know a way, tell me.

No special identifying marks.
My coat is torn.
The wind's cold even for a dog.
My coat is still torn.

What next? I make journeys
(mostly in my thoughts),
I go back to 1942.
There's no money there either.

Here, I'll pour one shot for me,
One for this snowy night.
If I get through my 33rd year,
I'll live forever.

ERRATA

Where it says snow
read teeth-marks of a virgin
Where it says knife read
you passed through my bones
like a police-whistle
Where it says table read horse
Where it says horse read my migrant's bundle
Apples are to remain apples
Each time a hat appears
think of Isaac Newton
reading the Old Testament

Remove all periods
They are scars made by words
I couldn't bring myself to say
Put a finger over each sunrise
it will blind you otherwise
That damn ant is still stirring
Will there be time left to list
all errors to replace
all hands guns owls plates
all cigars ponds woods and reach
that beer-bottle my greatest mistake
the word I allowed to be written
when I should have shouted
her name

STATEMENT

Poetry is the orphan of silence. Maternal silence. That in you which belongs to the Universe. The mother's voice calls its name at dusk over the roofs of the world. Whoever hears it, turns towards his ancestral home.

For a devastating simplicity. Only that which we all share, convinces. When my silence meets yours, what strange bread is broken. The gifts I bring sing. The answer is Yes if your spirit is moved to joy.

There is a need here, an obsession with purity. Kinnell calls it in a poem, "tenderness towards all existence." Basho said: "A poet does not make a poem—something in him naturally becomes a poem." It's a labor of monks, an order that prays to life on earth. What is a poem if it doesn't equal a bowl of hot soup on a cold winter day?

All my caution is based on the suspicion that edifices which leave the earth far behind do not get nearer to the stars. I prefer huts with floors of dirt. Still, I cannot help dreaming of a house which would guard the smell of the earth as it rises higher and higher—call it a long poem or a vast vision.

In the end, I am always at the beginning. Poverty—an endless condition. I think of explorers setting out over an unknown ocean. I remember the prince in a fairy tale stealing the miraculous white steed from the old hag who lives in the forest. I love beginnings. They restore mystery and youth to a weary world.

CHARLES SIMIC

LOUIS SIMPSON

Louis Simpson was born in Jamaica, British West Indies, in 1923. After serving in the 101st Airborne Division in World War II, he earned advanced degrees at Columbia University. Author of several books of poetry, including *Good News of Death, A Dream of Governors, At the End of the Open Road,* and *Adventures of the Letter I,* he has also written *Introduction to Poetry* and a novel, *Riverside Drive.* He teaches at the State University of New York at Stony Brook.

Thomas Victor

THE MORNING LIGHT

In the morning light a line
Stretches forever. There my unlived life
Rises, and I resist,
Clinging to the steps of the throne.

Day lifts the darkness from the hills,
A bright blade cuts the reeds,
And my life, pitilessly demanding,
Rises forever in the morning light.

THE LAUREL TREE

In the clear light that confuses everything
Only you, dark laurel,
Shadow my house,

Lifting your arms in the anguish
Of nature at the stake.
And at night, quivering with tears,

You are like the tree called Tasso's.
Crippled, and hooped with iron,
It stands on Peter's hill.

When the lovers prop their bicycles
And sit on the high benches
That look across to eternity,

That tree makes their own torsion
Seem natural. And so, they're comforted.

2
One of the local philosophers . . .
He says, "In California
We have the old anarchist tradition."

What can he mean? Is there an anarchist tradition?
And why would an anarchist want one?
O California,

Is there a tree without opinions?
Come, let me clasp you!
Let me feel the idea breathing.

I too cry O for a life of sensations
Rather than thoughts—
"The sayling Pine, the Cedar proud and tall."

Like the girls in our neighborhood,
They're beautiful and silent.

3
As I was digging in the back yard
I thought of a man in China.
A lifetime, it seemed, we gazed at each other.

I could see and hear his heart-beats
Like a spade hurling clods.
He pointed behind him, and I saw

That the hills were covered with armed men,
And they were all on the other side
Of the life that I held dear.

He said, "We are as various
As the twigs of a tree,
But now the tree moves as one man.

It walks. And the earth trembles
When a race of slaves is leaving."

4
I said, "Yet, all these people
Will fall down as one man
When the entrails of a bomb are breathing.

When we came down from Chosin
Carrying the guns in dainty snow-wear
And all the dead we had to,

It was a time of forgetfulness,
Like a plucked string.
It was a river of darkness.

Was it not so on your side, when you came
To the sea that was covered with ships?
Let us speak to each other,

Let the word rise, making dark strokes in the air.
That bird flies over the heads of the armed men."

5
One part of the tree grows outward.
The other I saw when, with a light,
I explored the cellar—shattering roots.

They had broken through the wall,
As though there were something in my rubbish
That life would have at last.

I must be patient with shapes
Of automobile fenders and ketchup bottles.
These things are the beginning

Of things not visible to the naked eye.
It was so in the time of Tobit—
The dish glowed when the angel held it.

It is so that spiritual messengers
Deliver their meaning.

A STORY ABOUT CHICKEN SOUP

In my grandmother's house there was always chicken soup
And talk of the old country—mud and boards,
Poverty,
The snow falling down the necks of lovers.

Now and then, out of her savings
She sent them a dowry. Imagine
The rice-powdered faces!
And the smell of the bride, like chicken soup.

But the Germans killed them.
I know it's in bad taste to say it,
But it's true. The Germans killed them all.

                    *   *   *

In the ruins of Berchtesgaden
A child with yellow hair
Ran out of a doorway.

A German girl-child—
Cuckoo, all skin and bones—
Not even enough to make chicken soup.
She sat by the stream and smiled.

Then as we splashed in the sun
She laughed at us.
We had killed her mechanical brothers,
So we forgave her.

                    *   *   *

The sun is shining.
The shadows of the lovers have disappeared.
They are all eyes; they have some demand on me—
They want me to be more serious than I want to be.

They want me to stick in their mudhole
Where no one is elegant.
They want me to wear old clothes,
They want me to be poor, to sleep in a room with many others—

Not to walk in the painted sunshine
To a summer house,
But to live in the tragic world forever.

STUMPFOOT ON 42ND STREET

A Negro sprouts from the pavement like an asparagus.
One hand beats a drum and cymbal;
He plays a trumpet with the other.

He flies the American flag;
When he goes walking, from stump to stump,
It twitches, and swoops, and flaps.

Also, he has a tin cup which he rattles;
He shoves it right in your face.
These freaks are alive in earnest.

He is not embarrassed.
It is for you to feel embarrassed,
Or God, or the way things are.

Therefore he plays the trumpet
And therefore he beats the drum.

2
I can see myself in Venezuela,
With flowers, and clouds in the distance.
The mind tends to drift.

But Stumpfoot stands near a window
Advertising cameras, trusses, household utensils.
The billboards twinkle. The time
Is 12:26.

O why don't angels speak in the infinite
To each other? Why this confusion,
These particular bodies—
Eros with clenched fists, sobbing and cursing?

The time is 12:26.
The streets lead on in burning lines
And giants tremble in electric chains.

3

I can see myself in the middle of Venezuela
Stepping in a nest of ants.
I can see myself being eaten by ants.

My ribs are caught in a thorn bush
And thought has no reality.
But he has furnished his room

With a chair and table.
A chair is like a dog, it waits for man.
He unstraps his apparatus,

And now he is taking off his boots.
He is easing his stumps,
And now he is lighting a cigar.

It seems that a man exists
Only to say, Here I am in person.

DOUBTING

I remember the day I arrived.
In the dawn the land seemed clear
and green and mysterious.

I could see the children of Adam
walking among the haystacks;
then, over the bay, a million sparkling windows.

Make room, let me see too!
Let me see how the counters are served
and move with the crowd's excitement the way it goes.

*   *   *

Since then so much has changed;
as though Washington, Jefferson, Lincoln
were only money and we didn't have it.

As though the terrible saying of Toqueville
were true: 'There is nothing so sordid . . .
as the life of a man in the States.'

I would like to destroy myself, or failing that,
   my neighbors;
to run in the streets, shouting 'To the wall!'
I would like to kill a hundred, two hundred, a thousand.

I would like to march, to conquer foreign capitals.

           *   *   *

And there's no end, it seems, to the wars of democracy.
What would Washington, what would Jefferson say
of the troops so heavily armed?

They would think they were Hessians,
and ride back into the hills
to find the people that they knew.

THE TAILOR'S WEDDING

The room was divided by a curtain.
There was a space on the other side
Where the tailor lived and you waited.

There was a bed, a table, a basin.
The wall was covered with pictures of women—
Blondes, brunettes—a tailor's dreams—

And privation is shameless.
He had cut them out of the magazines
Carefully with a scissors.

At last the suit was altered.
When I counted out the *lire*
He was as silent as death.

The work was perfect—and cheap, considering
That the man's life came with it.

2
The interior of the room was as clear
As a glimpse of brain surgery.
I walked out, stunned, in the Italian sunlight.

And when I look back, the hero
Who lifts Medusa's head
Must yield to the tailor's scissors.

For he reminds me of days
When I was a student, and life
Out there—the light that hurt the eyes.

All day it was cutting and stitching
Ideas by a dim light—
Handwork, in an age of machinery;

While the streets belonged to the rich—
The people with strong teeth.

3
And women went with the rich—
With the smell of new car upholstery,
A wind, white tablecloths.

For the poor there are moving pictures,
From which the young man emerges
Drugged, to the harsh light.

The wires and boards of the electric signs
Are like the pallid structure
Of his own mind laid bare.

Yet, over the roofs of the city
The moon hangs, faithful to the last,
Revealing her amorous craters.

Muse of the city, hope of the insane,
What would he do without you?

4

Yet once, perhaps, in his wandering
He rooms with a poor family,
And there's a girl, the household drudge

With mop and bucket, always in a clatter.
She's always entering with "Please
Excuse me." It is she who penetrates

His disguise—he's not a student, but a hero!
On a cold night she brings him
A bowl of soup.

Her body is rancid and thin.
When he leaves for another town, she stands
At the door, convulsed in a handkerchief.

Dear heart, I have bestowed
Your hand on a skillful tailor.

5

Lightly I've gone through life, accepting
Their services—a soup bowl
And a suit of clothes.

In the door a handkerchief waves,
And the tailor turns away
Thinking—the thoughts that tailors have.

And so my real life, my feelings
Are left on the cutting-room floor
And swept away with a broom.

And I've come to the end of a street
That is full of strangers.
And still, a spot is gleaming—

Something like a handkerchief
Or a pair of scissors.

DVONYA

In the town of Odessa
there is a garden
and Dvonya is there,
Dvonya whom I love
though I have never been in Odessa.

I love her black hair, and eyes
as green as a salad
that you gather in August
between the roots of alder,
her skin with an odor of wildflowers.

We understand each other perfectly.
We are cousins twice removed.
In the garden we drink our tea,
discussing the plays of Chekhov
as evening falls and the lights begin to twinkle.

But this is only a dream.
I am not there
with my citified speech,
and the old woman is not there
peering between the curtains.

We are only phantoms, bits of ash,
like yesterday's newspaper
or the smoke of chimneys.
All that passed long ago
on a summer night in Odessa.

A NIGHT IN ODESSA

Grandfather puts down his tea-glass
and makes his excuses
and sets off, taking his umbrella.
The street-lamps shine through a fog
and drunkards reel on the pavement.

One man clenches his fists in anger,
another utters terrible sobs. . . .
And women look on calmly.
They like those passionate sounds.
He walks on, grasping his umbrella.

His path lies near the forest.
Suddenly a wolf leaps in the path,
jaws dripping. The man strikes
with the point of his umbrella. . . .
A howl, and the wolf has vanished.

Go on, grandfather, hop!
It takes brains to live here,
not to be beaten and torn
or to lie drunk in a ditch.
Hold on to your umbrella!

He's home. When he opens the door
his wife jumps up to greet him.
Her name is Ninotchka,
she is young and dark and slender,
married only a month or so.

She hurries to get his supper.
But when she puts down the dish
she presses a hand to her side
and he sees that from her hand
red drops of blood are falling.

ISIDOR

Isidor was always plotting
to overthrow the government.
The family lived in one room. . . .
A window rattles,
a woman coughs,
snow drifts over the rooftops . . .
despair. An intelligent household.

One day, there's a knock at the door. . . .
The police! A confusion. . . .
Isidor's wife throws herself
on the mattress . . . she groans
as though she is in labor.
The police search everywhere,
and leave. Then a leg comes out . . .
an arm . . . then a head with spectacles.
Isidor was under the mattress!

When I think about my family
I have a feeling of suffocation.
Next time . . . how about the oven?

The mourners are sitting around
weeping and tearing their clothes.
The inspector comes. He looks in the oven . . .
there's Isidor, with his eyes
shut fast . . . his hands are folded.
The inspector nods, and goes.
Then a leg comes out, and the other.
Isidor leaps, he dances . . .

'Praise God, may His Name be exalted!'

A FRIEND OF THE FAMILY

Once upon a time in California
the ignorant married the inane
and they lived happily ever after.

But nowadays in the villas
with swimming-pools shaped like a kidney
technicians are beating their wives.
They're accusing each other of mental cruelty.

And the children of those parents
are longing for a rustic community.
They want to get back to the good old days.

Coming toward me . . . a slender
sad girl dressed like a sailor . . .
she says, 'Do you have any change?'

One morning when the Mother Superior
was opening another can of furniture polish
Cyd ran for the bus
and came to San Francisco.
Now she drifts from pad to pad. 'Hey mister,'
she says, 'do you have any change?
I mean, for a hamburger. Really.'

2
Let Yevtushenko celebrate the construction
of a hydroelectric dam.
For Russians a dam that works is a miracle.

Why should we celebrate it?
There are lights in the mountain states,
sanatoriums, and the music of Beethoven.

Why should we celebrate the construction
of a better bowling-alley?
Let Yevtushenko celebrate it.

A hundred, that's how ancient it is
with us, the rapture of material conquest,
democracy 'draining a swamp,
turning the course of a river.'

The dynamo howls
but the psyche is still, like an Indian.

And those who are still distending the empire
have vanished beyond our sight.
Far from the sense of hearing
and touch, they are merging
with Asia . . .

expanding the war on nature
and the old know-how to Asia.

Nowadays if we want that kind of excitement—
selling beads and whiskey to Indians,
setting up a feed-store,
a market in shoes, tires, machineguns,
material ecstasy, money with hands and feet
stacked up like wooden Indians . . .

we must go out to Asia,
or rocketing outward in space.

3
What are they doing in Russia
these nights for entertainment?

In our desert where gaspumps shine
the women are changing their hair—
bubbles of gold and magenta . . .

and the young men yearning to be off
full speed . . . like Chichikov

in a troika-rocket, plying
the whip, while stars go flying
(Too bad for the off-beat horse!)

These nights when a space-rocket rises
and everyone sighs 'That's Progress!'
I say to myself 'That's Chichikov.'

As it is right here on earth—
osteopaths on Mars,
actuaries at the Venus-Hilton . . .
Chichikov talking, Chichikov eating,
Chichikov making love.

'Hey Chichikov, where are you going?'

'I'm off to the moon,' says Chichikov.

'What will you do when you get there?'

'How do I know?' says Chichikov.

4
Andrei, that fish you caught was my uncle.
He lived in Lutsk, not to be confused
with Lodz which is more famous.

When he was twenty he wrote to Chekhov,
and an answer came—'Come to us.'
And there it was, signed 'Chekhov.'

I can see him getting on the train.
It was going to the great city
where Jews had been forbidden.

He went directly to Chekhov's house.
At the door he saw a crowd . . .
they told him that Chekhov had just died.

So he went back to his village.
Years passed . . . he danced at a wedding
and wept at a funeral. . . .

Then, when Hitler sent for the Jews
he said, 'And don't forget Isidor . . .
turn left at the pickle-factory.'

Andrei, all my life I've been haunted
by Russia—a plain,
a cold wind from the *shtetl*.

I can hear the wheels of the train.
It is going to Radom,
it is going to Jerusalem. . . .

In the night where candles shine
I have a luminous family . . .
people with their arms round each other

forever.

5
I can see myself getting off the train.
'Say, can you tell me how to get. . . .'

To Chekhov's house perhaps?

That's what everyone wants, and yet
Chekhov was just a man . . . with ideas,
it's true. As I said to him once,
Where on earth do you meet those people?

Vanya who is long-suffering
and Ivanov who is drunk.

And the man, I forget his name,
who thinks everything is forbidden . . .
that you have to have permission
to run, to shout. . . .

And the people who say, 'Tell us,
what is it you do exactly to justify your existence?'

These idiots rule the world,
Chekhov knew it, and yet
I think he was happy, on his street.
People live here . . . you'd be amazed.

THE MIDDLEAGED MAN

There is a middleaged man, Tim Flanagan,
whom everyone calls 'Fireball.'
Every night he does the rocket-match trick.
'Ten, nine, eight . . .' On zero
p f f t! It flies through the air.

Walking to the subway with Flanagan . . .
He tells me that he lives out in Queens
on Avenue Street, the end of the line.
That he 'makes his home' with his sister
who has recently lost her husband.

What is it to me?
Yet I can't help imagining what it would be like

to be Flanagan. Climbing the stairs
and letting himself in . . .
I can see him eating in the kitchen.

He stays up late watching television.
From time to time he comes to the window.
At this late hour the streets are deserted.
He looks up and down. He looks right at me,
then he steps back out of sight.

*   *   *

Sometimes I wake in the middle of the night
and I have a vision of Flanagan.
He is wearing an old pair of glasses
with a wire bent around the ear
and fastened to the frame with tape.

He is reading a novel by Morley Callahan.
Whenever I wake he is still there . . .
with his glasses. I wish he would get them fixed.
I cannot sleep as long as there is wire
running from his eye to his ear.

TO MAKE WORDS DISAPPEAR

Emotional intensity—this, as far as I can tell, is what poetry consists of. A poem will move from one moment of intensity to another, and there will be a connection. This, I suppose, is where I part company with surrealism and with some of my contemporaries— they don't care about the connection, don't feel a need to get a narrative line into their work. They seem to think that it is enough to say that they are having a feeling—but they do not try to convey it in an image or a narrative line. I'd rather not read such poetry—I don't care about writing that merely tells me that the writer is having a feeling. I want to be able to experience the feeling—I want lyric or narrative poetry.

As for poetry that preaches, I can do without it entirely. I don't want to listen to a poet berating people for their shortcomings—for example, for not being as 'politically aware' as he is. It would be better to give them some pleasure rather than make them feel inferior. The most pleasurable poetry I know is lyric or narrative, and sometimes it's a poetry of ideas, but the ideas are transformed into emotion, as images, so that the reader can experience them.

None of this is new, but it seems to have been forgotten in recent years. There is a lot of hard breathing going on—you see the poet straining to say something important, and you may feel sympathetic, but it doesn't do a thing for your life. It would be better if he were less self-absorbed and told you something that was interesting. To be interesting is an act of love—it may be the best thing we can do for each other.

I would like to write poems that made people laugh or made them want to cry, without their thinking that they were reading poetry. The poem would be an experience—not just talking about life, but life itself.

I think that the object of writing is to make words disappear.

LOUIS SIMPSON

GARY SNYDER

Gary Snyder was born in San Francisco in 1930 and grew up in
Oregon. He attended Reed College and afterward studied at Berkeley.
He has worked as a logger, seaman, and forest ranger, and has
traveled widely in Europe and the Orient. He studied Zen Buddhism
for many years in Kyoto, Japan. His books of poems include *Riprap,
Myths & Texts, The Back Country, Mountains and Rivers Without
End,* and *Collected Poems.* He is also the author of a collection of
essays, *Earth House Hold.* He lives with his wife and sons in the
Sierra Nevadas, near Nevada City, California.

FOUR POEMS FOR ROBIN

SIWASHING IT OUT ONCE IN SIUSLAW FOREST

I slept under   rhododendron
All night   blossoms fell
Shivering on   a sheet of cardboard
Feet stuck   in my pack
Hands deep   in my pockets
Barely   able   to   sleep.
I remembered   when we were in school
Sleeping together   in a big warm bed
We were   the youngest lovers
When we broke up   we were still nineteen.
Now our   friends are married
You teach   school back east
I dont mind   living this way
Green hills   the long blue beach
But sometimes   sleeping in the open
I think back   when I had you.

A SPRING NIGHT IN SHOKOKU-JI

Eight years ago this May
We walked under cherry blossoms
At night in an orchard in Oregon.
All that I wanted then
Is forgotten now, but you.
Here in the night
In a garden of the old capital
I feel the trembling ghost of Yugao
I remember your cool body
Naked under a summer cotton dress.

AN AUTUMN MORNING IN SHOKOKU-JI

Last night watching the Pleiades,
Breath smoking in the moonlight,
Bitter memory like vomit
Choked my throat.
I unrolled a sleeping bag
On mats on the porch
Under thick autumn stars.
In dream you appeared
(Three times in nine years)
Wild, cold, and accusing.
I woke shamed and angry:
The pointless wars of the heart.
Almost dawn. Venus and Jupiter.
The first time I have
Ever seen them close.

DECEMBER AT YASE

You said, that October,
In the tall dry grass by the orchard
When you chose to be free,
"Again someday, maybe ten years."

After college I saw you
One time. You were strange.
And I was obsessed with a plan.

Now ten years and more have
Gone by: I've always known
                 where you were—

I might have gone to you
Hoping to win your love back.
You still are single.

I didn't.
I thought I must make it alone. I
Have done that.

Only in dream, like this dawn,
Does the grave, awed intensity
Of our young love
Return to my mind, to my flesh.

We had what the others
All crave and seek for;
We left it behind at nineteen.

I feel ancient, as though I had
Lived many lives.

And may never now know
If I am a fool
Or have done what my
        karma demands.

WHAT DO THEY SAY

The glimpse of a once-loved face
            gone into a train.
Lost in a new town, no one knows the name.
    lone man sitting in the park
Chanced on by a friend
            of thirty years before,
            what do they say.
Play chess with bottle caps.
    "for sale" sign standing in the field:
            dearest, dearest,
Soot on the sill,
    a garden full of weeds

LOOKING AT PICTURES
TO BE PUT AWAY

Who was this girl
In her white night gown
Clutching a pair of jeans

On a foggy redwood deck.
She looks up at me tender,
Calm, surprised,

What will we remember
Bodies thick with food and lovers
After twenty years.

AUGUST WAS FOGGY

for Sally

August was foggy,
September dry.
October grew too hot.
Napa and Sonoma grasslands,
            brushlands,
        burned.

In November
        then,
We all set back the clock,
        and suddenly it rained.

The first green shoots of grass.
            you
        like some slender
        fresh young plant
turn smooth and cool across me
        in the night.

touch, and taste, and interlace
deep in the ground.
new rain.
as we begin our life.

AFTER WORK

The shack and a few trees
float in the blowing fog

I pull out your blouse,
warm my cold hands
on your breasts.
you laugh and shudder
peeling garlic by the
hot iron stove.
bring in the axe, the rake,
the wood

we'll lean on the wall
against each other
stew simmering on the fire
as it grows dark
drinking wine.

OUT WEST

In the cross field
all day a new gas cultivator
cough cough   down each row
frizzing the soil, fine chopper "friable"

before it was cucumber,
the boy in a straw hat
clumsily turns at the end of a run
shifting levers,

through deodar limbs come the gas fumes
    cucumber vines
    poles and straw ropes
    torn down, two crops a summer,

last year the family
was out there with hoes.
the old woman dead now?

one-eyed chop tongue rotary
bucks and wheezes,

    that straw hat shaped like a stetson
        wearing those tight blue jeans.
                                    Kyoto

BURNING THE SMALL DEAD

    Burning the small dead
            branches
    broke from beneath
        thick spreading
                whitebark pine.

                a hundred summers
    snowmelt   rock   and air

    hiss in a twisted bough.

        sierra granite;
                mt. Ritter—
            black rock twice as old.

    Deneb, Altair

    windy fire

FOR JOHN CHAPPELL

Over the Arafura sea, the China sea,
    Coral sea, Pacific
chains of volcanoes in the dark—
you in Sydney where it's summer;
I imagine that last ride outward
late at night.
                stiff new gears—tight new engine
up some highway I have never seen
too fast—too fast—
    like I said at Tango
        when you went down twice on gravel—

Did you have a chance to think
o *shit I've fucked it now*
instant crash and flight and sudden death—

    Malaya, Indonesia
    Taiwan, the Philippines, Okinawa
        families sleeping—reaching—
        humans by the millions
        world of breathing flesh.

me in Kyoto.   You in Australia
wasted in the night.
black beard, mad laugh, and sadly serious brow.
    earth lover;   shaper and maker.
        potter, cooker,

    now be clay in the ground.

                                1964

THE TRUTH LIKE THE BELLY
OF A WOMAN TURNING

for Ali Akbar Khan

The truth
like the belly of a woman turning,
    always passes by.
    is always true.

throat and tongue—
    do we all feel the same?
    sticky hair curls

quivering throat
pitch of jaw
      strung pull
    skinnd turn, what will
  be the wrack
        of all the old—

who
cares.
    CRYING
all these passt,
        losst,
            years.

    "It always changes"
      wind child
      wound child

MOTHERS AND DAUGHTERS
  live oak and madrone.

WHAT HAPPENED HERE BEFORE

300,000,000
First a sea: soft sands, muds, and marls
  —loading, compressing, heating, crumpling,
   crushing, recrystallizing, infiltrating,
several times lifted and submerged.
intruding molten granite magma
  deep-cooled and speckling,
    gold quartz fills the cracks—

80,000,000
sea-bed strata raised and folded,
  granite far below.
warm quiet centuries of rains
  (make dark red tropic soils)
  wear down two miles of surface,
lay bare the veins and tumble heavy gold
  in streambeds
    slate and schist rock-riffles catch it—
volcanic ash floats down and dams the streams,
  piles up the gold and gravel—

3,000,000
flowing north, two rivers joined,
  to make a wide long lake.
and then it tilted and the rivers fell apart
  all running west
   to cut the gorges of the Feather,
    Bear, and Yuba.
Ponderosa pine, manzanita, black oak, mountain yew.
  deer, coyote, bluejay, gray squirrel,
  ground squirrel, fox, blacktail hare,
  ringtail, bobcat, bear,
    all came to live here.

35,000
And human people came with basket hats and nets
  winter-houses underground
  yew bows painted green,
  feasts and dances for the boys and girls
    songs and stories in the smoky dark.

Then came the white man: tossed up trees and
   boulders with big hoses,
   going after that old gravel and the gold.
horses, apple-orchards, card games,
   pistol-shooting, churches, county jail.

§

We asked, who the land belonged to.
   and where one pays tax.
(two gents who never used it twenty years,
and before them the widow
   of the son of the man
   who got a patented deed
   on a worked-out mining claim,)
laid hasty on land that was deer and acorn
   grounds of the Nisenan?
   branch of the Maidu?
(they never had a chance to speak, even,
   their name.)
(and who remembers the Treaty of Guadalupe Hidalgo.)

   the land belongs to itself.
   "no self in self; no self in things"
     Turtle Island swims
     in the ocean-sky swirl-void
     biting her tail while the worlds go
       on-and-off
        winking

& Mr. Tobiassen, a Cousin Jack,
   assesses the county tax.
(the tax is our body-mind, guest at the banquet
   Memorial and Annual, in honor
   of sunlight grown heavy and tasty
   while moving up food-chains
in search of a body with eyes and a fairly large
   brain—
   to look back at itself
     on high.)
        now,

we sit here near the diggins
in the forest, by our fire, and watch
the moon and planets and the shooting stars—

my sons ask, who are we?
drying apples picked from homestead trees,
drying berries, curing meat,
shooting arrows at a bale of straw.

military jets head northeast, roaring, every dawn.

my sons ask, who are they?

> WE SHALL SEE
> WHO KNOWS
> HOW TO BE

Bluejay screeches from a pine.

FOR NOTHING

Earth a flower
A phlox on the steep
slopes of light
hanging over the vast
solid spaces
small rotten crystals;
salts.

Earth a flower
by a gulf where a raven
flaps by once
a glimmer, a color
forgotten as all
falls away.

A flower
for nothing;
an offer;
no taker;

Snow-trickles, feldspar, dirt.

THE BATH

Washing Kai in the sauna,
The kerosene lantern set on a box
    outside the ground-level window,
Lights up the edge of the iron stove and the
    washtub down on the slab
Steaming air and crackle of waterdrops
    brushed by on the pile of rocks on top
He stands in warm water
Soap all over the smooth of his thigh and stomach
    "Gary don't soap my hair!"
    —his eye-sting fear—
    the soapy hand feeling
    through and around the globes and curves of his body,
    up in the crotch,
And washing-tickling out the scrotum, little anus,
    his penis curving up and getting hard
    as I pull back skin and try to wash it
Laughing and jumping, flinging arms around,
    I squat all naked too,
                is this our body?

Sweating and panting in the stove-steam hot-stone
    cedar-planking wooden bucket water-splashing
    kerosene lantern-flicker wind-in-the-pines-out
    sierra forest ridges night—
Masa comes in, letting fresh cool air
    sweep down from the door
    a deep sweet breath
And she tips him over gripping neatly, one knee down
    her hair falling hiding one whole side of
    shoulder, breast, and belly,
Washes deftly Kai's head-hair
    as he gets mad and yells—
The body of my lady, the winding valley spine,
    the space between the thighs I reach through,
    cup her curving vulva arch and hold it from behind,
    a soapy tickle   a hand of grail
The gates of Awe

That open back a turning double-mirror world of
        wombs in wombs, in rings,
        that start in music,
                    is this our body?

The hidden place of seed
The veins net flow across the ribs, that gathers
        milk and peaks up in a nipple—fits
        our mouth—
The sucking milk from this our body sends through
        jolts of light; the son, the father,
        sharing mother's joy
That brings a softness to the flower of the awesome
        open curling lotus gate I cup and kiss
As Kai laughs at his mother's breast he now is weaned
        from, we
        wash each other,
                    this our body

Kai's little scrotum up close to his groin,
        the seed still tucked away, that moved from us to him
In flows that lifted with the same joys forces
        as his nursing Masa later,
        playing with her breast,
Or me within her,
Or him emerging,
                    this is our body:

Clean, and rinsed, and sweating more, we stretch
        out on the redwood benches hearts all beating
Quiet to the simmer of the stove,
        the scent of cedar
And then turn over,
        murmuring gossip of the grasses,
        talking firewood,
Wondering how Gen's napping, how to bring him in
        soon wash him too—
These boys who love their mother
        who loves men, who passes on
        her sons to other women;

The cloud across the sky.   The windy pines.
      the trickle gurgle in the swampy meadow

this is our body.

Fire inside and boiling water on the stove
We sigh and slide ourselves down from the benches
      wrap the babies, step outside,

black night & all the stars.

Pour cold water on the back and thighs
Go in the house—stand steaming by the center fire
Kai scampers on the sheepskin
Gen standing hanging on and shouting,

"Bao!   bao!   bao!   Bao!   bao!"

This is our body. Drawn up crosslegged by the flames
      drinking icy water
      hugging babies, kissing bellies,

Laughing on the Great Earth

Come out from the bath.

            WHY LOG TRUCK DRIVERS
            RISE EARLIER THAN
            STUDENTS OF ZEN

            In the high seat,
                before-dawn dark,

            Polished hubs gleam
            And the shiny diesel stack
            Warms and flutters
            Up the Tyler Road grade
            To the logging on Poorman
                              Creek.
            Thirty miles of dust.

            There is no other life.

WHAT YOU SHOULD KNOW TO BE A POET

all you can about animals as persons.
the names of trees and flowers and weeds.
names of stars, and the movements of the planets
                    and the moon.

your own six senses, with a watchful and elegant mind.

at least one kind of traditional magic:
divination, astrology, the *book of changes*, the tarot;

dreams.
the illusory demons and illusory shining gods;

kiss the ass of the devil and eat shit;
fuck his horny barbed cock,
fuck the hag,
and all the celestial angels
                    and maidens perfum'd and golden—

& then love the human: wives   husbands   and friends.

childrens' games, comic books, bubble-gum,
the weirdness of television and advertising.

work, long dry hours of dull work swallowed and accepted
and livd with and finally lovd.   exhaustion,
                    hunger, rest.

the wild freedom of the dance, *extasy*
silent solitary illumination, *enstasy*

real danger.   gambles.   and the edge of death.

GARY SNYDER

WILLIAM STAFFORD

William Stafford was born in Hutchinson, Kansas, in 1914. He has
worked for the Forest Service and for Church World Service, and was
Consultant in Poetry for the Library of Congress in 1970–71. He
teaches at Lewis and Clark College, where he is chairman of the
English Department. His books of poetry include *West of Your City*,
Traveling Through the Dark, *The Rescued Year*, *Allegiances*, and
Someday, Maybe. He won the National Book Award for *Traveling
Through the Dark*.

Thomas Victor

BESS

Ours are the streets where Bess first met her
cancer. She went to work every day past the
secure houses. At her job in the library
she arranged better and better flowers, and when
students asked for books her hand went out
to help. In the last year of her life
she had to keep her friends from knowing
how happy they were. She listened while they
complained about food or work or the weather.
And the great national events danced
their grotesque, fake importance. Always

Pain moved where she moved. She walked
ahead; it came. She hid; it found her.
No one ever served another so truly;
no enemy ever meant so strong a hate.
It was almost as if there was no room
left for her on earth. But she remembered
where joy used to live. She straightened its flowers;
she did not weep when she passed its houses;
and when finally she pulled into a tiny corner
and slipped from pain, her hand opened
again, and the streets opened, and she wished all well.

STRANGERS

Brown in the snow, a car with a heater
in it searches country roads all yesterday afternoon
for our farm. At crossroads the car stops
and over the map the two people bend.
They love how the roads go on, how the heater
hums. They are so happy they can be
lost forever that afternoon.

They will probably live.
They may die. The roads go on. On the
checkered map they find themselves, and their
car is enough audience, their eyes enough
to know. If the state breaks off they will
burrow at the edge, or fall. I thought of
them yesterday, and last night sang by the
fire, thinking of them.

They are something of us, but I think better
lost back there in our old brown car.

A STORY

After they passed I climbed
out of my hole and sat
in the sun again. Loose rocks
all around make it safe—I can
hear anyone moving. It often
troubles me to think how others
dare live where stealth is possible,
and how they can feel safe, considering
all the narrow places,
without whiskers.

Anyway, those climbers were a puzzle—
above where I live nothing lives.
And they never came down. There is no
other way. The way it is,
they crawl far before they die.
I make my hole the deepest one
this high on the mountainside.

A SOUND FROM THE EARTH

Somewhere, I think in Dakota,
they found the leg bones—just the
big leg bones—of several hundred
buffalo, in a gravel pit.

Near there, a hole in a cliff
has been hollowed so that
the prevailing wind
thrums a note so low and persistent
that bowls of water placed in that
cave will tremble to foam.

The grandfather of Crazy Horse
lived there, they say, at the last,
and his voice like the thrum of the hills
made winter come as he sang, "Boy,
where was your buffalo medicine?
I say you were not brave enough, Boy.
I say Crazy Horse was too cautious."

Then the sound he cried out for his grandson
made that thin Agency soup that they
put before him tremble. The whole
earthen bowl churned into foam.

THINGS THAT HAPPEN

Sometimes before great events a person will try,
disguised, at his best, not to be a clown:
he feels, "A great event is coming, bow down."
And I, always looking for something anyway,
always bow down.

Once, later than dawn but early,
before the lines of the calendar fell,
one of those events turned an unseen corner

and came near, near, sounding before it
something the opposite from a leper's bell.

We were back of three mountains called
"Sisters" along the Green Lakes trail
and had crossed a ridge when that
one little puff of air touched us,
hardly felt at all.

That was the greatest event that day;
it righted all wrong.
I remember it, the way the dust moved there.
Something had come out of the ground
and moved calmly along.

No one was ahead of us, no one
in all that moon-like land.
Oh, I thought, how hard the world has tried
with its wind, its miles, its blundering
stumbling days, again and again, to find my hand.

HUMANITIES LECTURE

Aristotle was a little man with
eyes like a lizard, and he found a streak
down the midst of things, a smooth place for his feet
much more important than the carved handles
on the coffins of the great.

He said you should put your hand out
at the time and place of need:
strength matters little, he said,
nor even speed.

His pupil, a king's son, died
at an early age. That Aristotle spoke of him
it is impossible to find—the youth was
notorious, a conqueror, a kid with a gang,
but even this Aristotle didn't ever say.

Around the farthest forest and along
all the bed of the sea, Aristotle studied
immediate, local ways. Many of which
were wrong. So he studied poetry.
There, in pity and fear, he found Man.

Many thinkers today, who stand low and grin,
have little use for anger or power, its palace
or its prison—
but quite a bit for that little man
with eyes like a lizard.

THESE DAYS

Hurt people crawl as if they
suddenly love each part of themselves
again, after years of neglect,
as if the next place they might find
could bring a new sun in its hand,
or a mist they could separate and follow.

As if any time a bird might call and it
will be day, or from a ditch a cousin
or a lover will sing, hurt people
curiously turn their heads,
as if their duty, in a democracy, if
we are to have peace, is quickly
to crawl away over the horizon.

THE ESCAPE

Now as we cross this white page together
people begin to notice us, and we
cut back and pretend indifference,
but all the time we pick up and lay
down our tracks cunningly, farther

and farther down the page. If we zig-
zagged or jumped a few times we could
make it, but even better would be
to take hands and perform a dance, our eyes
locked onto understanding, while our shadows
tell us which way to go. Those others
glare on our trail; they know what
is happening, and they certainly do not
approve. Remember, we are each other's: do not
look away. Every life is like this,
carried on while some inane plot
tries to intrude. How lucky we were
to find each other and make our escape
down the page and on out like this over the edge.

THE WHOLE STORY

1

When we shuddered and took into ourselves
the cost of the way we had lived,
I was a victim, touched by the blast.
Death! I have death in me!
No one will take me in from the cold.

Now among leaves I approach, and I
am afraid that pain and anger
have crept their fire into my bones,
but the slaver around my mouth is drying.
I hope that the light on the hills can
pass open woods and slide
easily around slopes, hold my eyes
before they search their way to an enemy:
I have to contain all this anger, but with luck
it can pass directly into the sky.

2

I am the sky. After everything ends
and even while the story goes on
I accept all that is left over. When all
the signals finally die, they still find

their way everywhere, meaning the same
as ever: they can't get away. I hold
them for something that approaches through winter.

3
Though I am winter, through the light on the hills
I let children approach. In a pale straw slant
the sun angles down. Maybe the children will not see
the victims, will somehow survive. The sun touches
along and goes away, and while the stars
come out the sky waits and wherever they look
it is now and there is still time.

4
I am time. When you look up
from this page I will be waiting to go
with you to the end of the story.

THE MOMENT

It happens lonely—no one,
then sky. Where is it?
Yorkshire? Wyoming? It doesn't
matter: lonely. Tremendous.
Anywhere. Suddenly.

Is it just you, Wind?
Maybe. But it is Now;
it is what happens, the moment,
the stare of the moon, an
opening birds call out of,
anything true. We have it.

That's what the rich old
shepherd meant, pointing
through the storm at
the blowing past wind
passing nothing:

"Those who have gone
and those who never existed,
they don't have it."

NOW

Where we live, the teakettle whistles out
its heart. Fern arrives to
batter the window. Every day gets lost
in a stray sunset and little touches of air.
Someone opens a door. It is this year.

We hear crickets compute their brittle
almanac. A friend or a stranger
comes to the door; it is always "Hello" again,
but just a friend or a stranger.
We get up and look out: a good year?

God knows. People we meet look older.
They ask how we are. It is this year.

LATE AT NIGHT

Driving, I come for a while
into my father's town, to swim in his
day when leaves could swim and my mother's
careless body had found a man.
On their farm with cottonwood trees, if I
go back, some of the people can tell
what happened, though the landscape drank
the survivors, and years have worn scuffling
shoes. The grove is there. They all
come swimming into the light.

"Work is such an uncompromising friend,"
my father said, "be kind or be an artist

and let them all live." And I follow him.
Now the family intertwine, and I
disengage gently to come back,
let them drift quietly away,
secure in their still grove,
along the dark road I drive.

AMONG STRANGERS

Remember when
we both had
simple motives?

You and I would
disguise ourselves as
part of the world;

Our motions would be
like theirs,
like their life.

And at the last,
carefully watching
people's ways,

We would even die.

THE STRANGER NOT OURSELVES

We pass a stranger. He glances
a gift look—it says many fortunes, if we
had been other, but now only one,
since we became what we have become.

After that look, a million pictures
not in our album throb in their unfound
mine, and we by a childhood glance
arrive all the way back where we first
heard the doves in the morning, and we
stop there, wringing our hands this time.

BROKEN HOME

Here is a cup left empty in their
kitchen, a-brim of that silent air
all the cold mornings, all the cold years.

And here is an old jacket that held a scared
    heart
too loud for this house, hurt
in its pocket, wanting out.

How alone is this house!—an unreeled
phone dangling down a hall
that never really led to tomorrow.

AT THE EDGE OF TOWN

Sometimes when clouds float
their shadows make dark fields,
wings that open. Just by looking
we become them. Is there a kingdom
where only the soundless have honor?
Some days, yes. We look up and follow.

THESE LEAVES

Somewhere a forest, every
leaf still, far but clear.
Somewhere staggering pines
making it over a pass.

And somewhere a wind
ready to find far lost men
and cover their tracks.
We walk on, leaves blow past.

CAPTURING "PEOPLE OF THE SOUTH WIND"

Thoughts, statements, implications are much more various, unaccountable, and free-flowing than most intentional people would lead us to assume. The appearance, or the sound, or the whole feel, of the world can be changed at will. Set free, the mind discovers shortcuts and arabesques through and over and around all purposes.

Now—what would happen if you ventured into a sequence of these arabesques and shortcuts, straying from conscious intention but staying true to the immediate *feel* of what is happening? Would a pattern emerge? Yes, it would. Do you have to be careful to make a meaningful pattern emerge? No. And could that pattern that naturally emerges become a poem? Of course.

Instead of presenting such a poem and then explaining it, I would like to present some speculations and impulses and from them climb outward farther and farther toward one of the possible poems where those impulses begin to vibrate right, out there at what I could call their "periphery of justice." So—suppose a landscape that hints at the presence of people you do not meet. They could be quiet, withdrawn, infinitely wise. I imagine such people, and call them "People of the South Wind," after a tribe that used to live on the prairies. Now, these people would inhabit a world in which natural events could come about in terms of a big story behind everything. Maybe the sun, for instance, is staring around because it is hunting something. I imagine a statement about such a scene: "One day Sun found a new canyon"—and then I let my speculations link forward from that one assertion based on the presumed lives of an extraordinary people. Whether I really believe my hunch or tentative pattern is not the point. I enter the sequence, turn the world a little to one side, and then discover the results of a sustained sequence, adventuring along into a developing pattern that grows from accepting opportunities that come along, not from following a plan or a conviction.

Here's the poem—a periphery of justice—that resulted from this kind of adventure into the crystalizing potential of a people, the people of the south wind:

PEOPLE OF THE SOUTH WIND

1

One day Sun found a new canyon.
It hid for miles and ran far away,
then it went under a mountain. Now Sun
goes over but knows it is there. And that
is why Sun shines—it is always looking.
Be like the sun.

2

Your breath has a little shape—
you can see it cold days. Well,
every day it is like that, even in summer.
Well, your breath goes, a whole
army of little shapes. They are living
in the woods now and are your friends.
When you die—well, you go with
your last breath and find the others.
And in open places in the woods
all of you are together and happy.

3

Sometimes if a man is evil his breath
runs away and hides from him. When he
dies his last breath cannot find the others,
and he never comes together again—
those little breaths, you know, in the autumn
they scurry the bushes before snow.
They never come back.

4

You know where the main river
runs—well, for five days below is
No One, and out in the desert
on each side his children live.
They have their tents that echo dust
and give a call for their father
when you knock for acquaintance:
"No One, No One, No One."

When you cross that land the sandbars
have his name in little tracks
the mice inscribe under the bushes,
and on pools you read his wide, bland
reply to all that you ask. You wake
from dreams and hear the end of things:
"No One, No One, No One."

So much for my poem. It is possible for me to dismantle the lines and reduce them to patterns of apparently rigged opportunities. For example, it might occur to me to have an extreme line: "No One, No One, No One." Then why not build a setting to justify such a line? Or it might be fun to assert something outrageous and then give yourself and your audience a jab of a sudden justification—not an adequate justification perhaps, but the quick excitement of a beginning belief. For example this: "Your breath has a little shape—you can see it cold days." It might be fun to smuggle many cousin sounds so closely together that a reader would miss recognition but still be influenced—for example, this: "One day Sun found a new canyon." It might be fun to sequence along with the reader and then shift perspective and make an extreme demand—for example, this: "Be like the sun."

It might even be fun to stumble along through wording that would ordinarily be considered awkward, but make that very awkwardness be itself a part of the effect—for example, this: "Well, every day it is like that, even in summer. Well, your breath goes. . . ." These extra syllables—"well, well, well"—that would ordinarily be cluttering up the talk could become some kind of meaningful part of the sequence.

If you have indulged me through this pattern of speculation, you have become like those people of the south wind, and have experienced a wild visioning. I now ask you to accept something even wilder. Someone asks you how you write a poem, and you begin to explain. You send forth many speculations and reasons; you watch them go. No matter how fast and how far they go, it is never enough. They never catch the actual poem, and they never come back. . . .

You see, if I try to witness adequately about how it feels to enter the creative trance, I have to put quite a test on ordinary explanations, the kind of explaining we can do when we are doing the usual planning, assembling of parts, arriving at an objective, and then assessing how well we have accomplished what we set out to do. I want, instead of that usual way of explaining things, to make a clear witness for a wilder, unplanned, utterly trustworthy process. I'll try several blunt statements about that process, always realizing that it is too odd for neat formulation.

First—intention endangers creation. True, intention seems to work well in some kinds of project, where we want to prevail in a hurry, where we are competing. But I want to raise the question of whether creation isn't something other than the putting together of materials into the service of a pre-selected goal. Hence—intention endangers creation.

Second—let me worry around that "periphery of justice" phrasing. It's like this: how you feel can lead to a closure not related to any other end than its own satisfaction. I'm not sure the phrasing is helpful, but "periphery of justice" is my groping attempt to establish some kind of terminology for that feeling you have when you go along accepting what occurs to you and finding your way out somewhere to the rim where you are ready to abandon that sequence and come back and start all over again.

Third—when I said that I would go back and dismantle the lines of my poem, it might sound as if I was discrediting what the lines said. No, I feel that I was somehow affirming those lines, discovering their real, internal source. What might sound like reducing the importance of the language in which something is said—this could really be just discovering something about the feeling in a statement, what validates it for both speaker and hearer. The dance of syllables in "One day Sun found a new canyon" is part of what makes it *stick*.

The spirit back of all I've said is this: an intentional person is too effective to be a good guide in the tentative activity of creating. I think it takes a certain amount of irresponsibility, to create. And now I find a paradox in my present role. I'm supposed to be responsible in what I am saying, and of course in a way I *am* being responsible. But I'm being responsible in a pretty reckless way, because this is an odd activity, creating.

WILLIAM STAFFORD

Nancy Crampton

JAMES WRIGHT

James Wright was born in Martin's Ferry, Ohio, in 1927 and grew up on a small farm in the Ohio Valley. He was educated at Kenyon College, the University of Washington, and the University of Vienna. He served in the United States Army during the occupation of Japan. Besides his books of poetry, which include *The Green Wall, Saint Judas, The Branch Will Not Break, Shall We Gather at the River,* and *Two Citizens,* among his works are several volumes of translation from Spanish and German. His *Collected Poems* won the Pulitzer Prize in 1972. He and his wife live in New York City, where he teaches at Hunter College.

IN OHIO

White mares lashed to the sulky carriages
Trot softly
Around the dismantled fairgrounds
Near Buckeye Lake.

The sandstone blocks of a wellspring
Cool dark green moss.

The sun floats down, a small golden lemon dissolves
In the water.
I dream, as I lean over the edge, of a crawdad's mouth.

The cellars of haunted houses are like ancient cities,
Fallen behind a big heap of apples.

A widow on a front porch puckers her lips
And whispers.

LIVING BY THE RED RIVER

Blood flows in me, but what does it have to do
With the rain that is falling?
In me, scarlet-jacketed armies march into the rain
Across dark fields. My blood lies still,
Indifferent to cannons on the ships of imperialists
Drifting offshore.
Sometimes I have to sleep
In dangerous places, on cliffs underground,
Walls that still hold the whole prints
Of ancient ferns.

LATE NOVEMBER IN A FIELD

Today I am walking alone in a bare place,
And winter is here.
Two squirrels near a fence post
Are helping each other drag a branch
Toward a hiding place; it must be somewhere
Behind those ash trees.
They are still alive, they ought to save acorns
Against the cold.
Frail paws rifle the troughs between cornstalks
    when the moon
Is looking away.
The earth is hard now,
The soles of my shoes need repairs.
I have nothing to ask a blessing for,
Except these words.
I wish they were
Grass.

A PRAYER TO THE LORD RAMAKRISHNA

1
The anguish of a naked body is more terrible
To bear than God.
And the rain goes on falling.

2
When I stand up to cry out,
She laughs.
On the window sill, I lean
My bare elbows.
One blue wing, torn whole out of heaven,
Soaks in the black rain.

3
Blind, mouth sealed, a face blazes
On my pillow of cold ashes.

4
No!
I kneel down, naked, and ask forgiveness.
A cold drizzle blows into the room,
And my shoulders flinch to the bone.
You have nothing to do with us.
Sleep on.

LIFTING ILLEGAL NETS BY FLASHLIGHT

The carp are secrets
Of the creation: I do not
Know if they are lonely.
The poachers drift with an almost frightening
Care under the bridge.
Water is a luminous
Mirror of swallows' nests. The stars
Have gone down.
What does my anguish
Matter? Something
The color
Of a puma has plunged through this net, and is gone.
This is the firmest
Net I ever saw, and yet something
Is gone lonely
Into the headwaters of the Minnesota.

WILLY LYONS

My uncle, a craftsman of hammers and wood,
Is dead in Ohio.
And my mother cries she is angry.
Willy was buried with nothing except a jacket
Stitched on his shoulder bones.
It is nothing to mourn for.

It is the other world.
She does not know how the roan horses, there,
Dead for a century,
Plod slowly.
Maybe they believe Willy's brown coffin, tangled heavily
      in moss,
Is a horse trough drifted to shore
Along that river under the willows and grass.
Let my mother weep on, she needs to, she knows of cold winds.
The long box is empty.
The horses turn back toward the river.
Willy planes limber trees by the waters,
Fitting his boat together.
We may as well let him go.
Nothing is left of Willy on this side
But one cracked ball-peen hammer and one suit,
Including pants, his son inherited,
For a small fee, from Hesslop's funeral home;
And my mother,
Weeping with anger, afraid of winter
For her brothers' sake:
Willy, and John, whose life and art, if any,
I never knew.

OUTSIDE FARGO, NORTH DAKOTA

Along the sprawled body of the derailed
      Great Northern freight car,
I strike a match slowly and lift it slowly.
No wind.

Beyond town, three heavy white horses
Wade all the way to their shoulders
In a silo shadow.

Suddenly the freight car lurches.
The door slams back, a man with a flashlight
Calls me good evening.
I nod as I write good evening, lonely
And sick for home.

OLD AGE COMPENSATION

There are no roads but the frost,
And the pumpkins look haggard.
The ants have gone down to the grave, crying
God spare them one green blade.
Failing the grass, they have abandoned the grass.
All creatures who have died today of old age
Have gone more than ten miles already.
All day I have slogged behind
And dreamed of them praying for one candle,
Only one.
Fair enough. Only, from where I stand,
I can see one last night nurse shining in one last window
In the Home for Senior Citizens.
The white uniform flickers, the town is gone.
What do I do now? I have one candle,
But what's the use?
If only they can catch up with twilight,
They'll be safe enough.
Their boats are moored there, among the cattails
And the night-herons' nests.
All they have to do now
Is to get one of those lazy birds awake long enough
To guide them across the river.
Herons fly low, too.
All it will take is one old man trawling one oar.
Anybody can follow a blue wing,
They don't need my candle.
But I do.

IN RESPONSE TO A RUMOR THAT THE OLDEST
WHOREHOUSE IN WHEELING, WEST VIRGINIA,
HAS BEEN CONDEMNED

I will grieve alone,
As I strolled alone, years ago, down along
The Ohio shore.

I hid in the hobo jungle weeds
Upstream from the sewer main,
Pondering, gazing.

I saw, down river,
At Twenty-third and Water Streets
By the vinegar works,
The doors open in early evening.
Swinging their purses, the women
Poured down the long street to the river
And into the river.

I do not know how it was
They could drown every evening.
What time near dawn did they climb up the other shore,
Drying their wings?

For the river at Wheeling, West Virginia
Has only two shores:
The one in hell, the other
In Bridgeport, Ohio.

And nobody would commit suicide, only
To find beyond death
Bridgeport, Ohio.

TO THE MUSE

It is all right. All they do
Is go in by dividing
One rib from another. I wouldn't
Lie to you. It hurts
Like nothing I know. All they do
Is burn their way in with a wire.
It forks in and out a little like the tongue
Of that frightened garter snake we caught
At Cloverfield, you and me, Jenny
So long ago.

I would lie to you
If I could.
But the only way I can get you to come up
Out of the suckhole, the south face
Of the Powhatan pit, is to tell you
What you know:

You come up after dark, you poise alone
With me on the shore.
I lead you back to this world.

Three lady doctors in Wheeling open
Their offices at night.
I don't have to call them, they are always there.
But they only have to put the knife once
Under your breast.
Then they hang their contraption.
And you bear it.

It's awkward a while. Still, it lets you
Walk about on tiptoe if you don't
Jiggle the needle.
It might stab your heart, you see.
The blade hangs in your lung and the tube
Keeps it draining.
That way they only have to stab you
Once. Oh Jenny,

I wish to God I had made this world, this scurvy
And disastrous place. I
Didn't, I can't bear it
Either, I don't blame you, sleeping down there
Face down in the unbelievable silk of spring,
Muse of black sand,
Alone.

I don't blame you, I know
The place where you lie.
I admit everything. But look at me.
How can I live without you?
Come up to me, love,
Out of the river, or I will
Come down to you.

SMALL FROGS KILLED ON THE HIGHWAY

Still,
I would leap too
Into the light,
If I had the chance.
It is everything, the wet green stalk of the field
On the other side of the road.
They crouch there, too, faltering in terror
And take strange wing. Many
Of the dead never moved, but many
Of the dead are alive forever in the split second
Auto headlights more sudden
Than their drivers know.
The drivers burrow backward into dank pools
Where nothing begets
Nothing.

Across the road, tadpoles are dancing
On the quarter thumbnail
Of the moon. They can't see,
Not yet.

A WAY TO MAKE A LIVING

from an epigram by Plato

When I was a boy, a relative
Asked for me a job
At the Weeks Cemetery.
Think of all I could
Have raised that summer,
That money, and me
Living at home,
Fattening and getting
Ready to live my life
Out on my knees, humming,
Kneading up docks
And sumac from

Those flawless clerks-at-court, those beautiful
Grocers and judges, the polished
Dead of whom we make
So much.

I could have stayed there with them.
Cheap, too.
Imagine, never
To have turned
Wholly away from the classic
Cold, the hill, so laid
Out, measure by seemly measure clipped
And mown by old man Albright
The sexton. That would have been a hell of
A way to make a living.

OHIO VALLEY SWAINS

The granddaddy longlegs did twilight
And light.

Oh here comes Johnny Gumball.

Guido?
Bernoose got Lilly deVecchis.
Guido don't give a diddly damn.

Up on my side of the river
The cocksmen ramp loose.

The bad bastards are fishing.
They catch condoms.

What are you doing here, boy,
In cherry lane?

Leave her alone. I love her.

They knocked me down.

So I walked on up the river,
Outside the Jesus Jumpers' tent,

Oh God our help in ages past,
Our hope for years to come.

Here comes Johnny Gumball.

It took me many years to understand
Just what happened to her that evening.

I walked, stiff and lonely, up the long river.
The railroad dick asked me
Very politely what
I was doing there.

They're hurting a girl down there, I said.
Well, he said, you go on home,
And get out of this.

Johnny Gumball,
You and your gang caught up with my brother,
And beat him up. But that was no terror of mine.
My brother has his own life.

But I heard you and Guido cackling down below
That tent where the insane Jesus Jumpers
Spoke in their blind tongues,
And you laughed and laughed.

You thought that was funny, didn't you, to mock a girl?
I loved her only in my dreams,
But my dreams meant something
And so did she,
You son of a bitch,
And if I ever see you again, so help me in the sight of God,
I'll kill you.

THE OLD DOG IN THE RUINS OF
THE GRAVES AT ARLES

I have heard tell somewhere,
Or read, I forget which,
That animals tumble along in a forever,
A little dream, a quick longing
For every fine haunch that passes,
As the young bitches glitter in their own light.

I find their freedom from lonely wisdom
Hard to believe.
No matter the brief skull fails to contain,
The old bones know something.

Almost indistinguishable from the dust,
They seek shadow, they limp among the tombs.
One stray mutt, long since out of patience,
Rises up, as the sunlight happens to strike,
And snaps at his right foreleg.

When the hurrying shadow returns
He lies down in peace again,
Between the still perfectly formed sarcophagi
That have been empty of Romans or anybody
Longer than anybody remembers.
Graves last longer than men. Nobody can tell me
The old dogs don't know.

SIMON AND THE TARANTULA

Have I spent all my life turning
My face away?
Not all of it, not all of my faces.
I have had a good secret friendship with a horse
Who liked me, and three dogs.
One of them got drunk with me more than once.

And one dog, my beloved Simon,
Sat down with me on a Christmas evening.
We sang out of key.

He used to vanish into the five-foot snow
Of western Minnesota at thirty degrees below only
Because he was in love with someone
Miles away on the prairie.
If Simon was in love with a dog,
I wish I knew.
At thirty degrees below he came home.

Thirty degrees.
Five feet of snow.
The seeds of cockleburrs snarled into his ears,
And seeds I could never identify clung between his beautiful
And shameless toes.
Simon was not a cat, but for some reason
He kept his mustache clean, and I loved him
For his brotherliness.

Now I have seen the tarantula's nest on the desert,
I wonder.
I wonder about Simon's secret friend on the prairie.

I have never been drunk with a tarantula.
But may even my drunk friends
Have secrets.

Maybe the tarantula was asleep
And lying down drunk with the elf owl.

Maybe the tarantula, the cholla cactus,
And the diamondback rattler
Think I am beautiful.

Simon, you shaggy airedale, your shoulders were larger
And braver than an airplane's. Seed-bringer and lover,
You got lost in that snow.
I weep for you in secret. Where have you gone?
The shaggy burdocks of Minnesota
Owe their lives to you, somewhere
Somewhere, I owe my life.
I will not pester your grave.

Will you grow on mine?

VERONA

optima dies prima fugit

First, the two men stand pondering
The square stone block sunk in the earth.
It must weigh five hundred pounds. The best
Days are the first
To flee. The taller man has gray hair
And long thin arms, the other
Squat with young shoulders, his legs
Slightly bowed already, a laborer
With the years, like a tree.

One works the edge
Of his steel claw subtly
Between the stones.
The other waits for the right instant,
A dazzle of balance, and slips the blade
Of his cold chisel into the crack.

Balancing the great weight of this enormous
And beautiful floorstone laid by the Romans,
Holding a quarter-ton of stone lightly
Between earth and air,
The tall man with the gray hair reaches
Around the corner of stone
And most delicately eases
A steel pipe beneath.
The best days are the first
To flee. Now both men
Can stand upright, then gradually,
Their fine hands sure, they can ease
The stone from its place.

I look beneath.
It does not look like a grave.
The earth smells fresh, like the breath
Of an animal just born.

When I look up,
The tall old man with the slender arms, the young

With the frail bulging shoulders
Are gone for some wine. Work hard, and give
The body its due of rest, even at noon.
The best days are first to flee,
And the underside of the stone
Is pink marble
From Verona where the poet found shelter,
The intelligent friendship of daylight, and kindness,
And a little peace.

MANTOVA

optima dies prima fugit

The first thing I saw in the morning
Was a huge golden bee ploughing
His burly right shoulder into the belly
Of a sleek yellow pear
Low on a bough.
Before he could find that sudden black honey
That squirms around in there
Inside the seed, the tree could not bear any more.
The pear fell to the ground,
With the bee still half alive
Inside its body.
He would have died had I not knelt down
And sliced the pear gently
A little more open.
The bee shuddered, and returned.
Maybe I should have left him alone there
Drowning in his own delight.
The best days are the first
To flee.

REDWINGS

It turns out
You can kill them.
It turns out
You can make the earth absolutely clean.

My nephew has given my younger brother
A scientific report while they both flew
In my older brother's small airplane
Over the Kokosing River, that looks

Secret, it looks like the open
Scar turning gray on the small
Of your spine.

Can you hear me?

It was only in the evening I saw a few redwings
Come out and dip their brilliant yellow
Bills in their scarlet shoulders.
Ohio was already going to hell.
But sometimes they would sit down on the creosote
Soaked pasture fence posts.
They used to be few, they used to be willowy and thin.

One afternoon, along the Ohio, where the sewer
Poured out, I found a nest.
The way they build their nests in the reeds,
So beautiful,
Redwings and solitaries,
And the skinny girl I fell in love with
In late autumn married
A strip miner in late autumn.
Her five children are still alive,
Floating near the river.

Somebody is on the wing, somebody
Is wondering right at this moment
How to get rid of us, while we sleep.

Together among the dead gorges
Of highway construction, while we flare

Across highways and drive
Motorists crazy, while we fly
Down home to the river.

Where, one summer evening, a dirty man
Gave me a nickel and a potato
And fell asleep by a fire.

NAMES IN MONTERCHI: TO RACHEL

We woke early
Because we had to wake.
What is that country
To me?

The spider in Anghiari is a brilliant
In the dust. I am going to find my way
To Anghiari, because on the way
The earth is a warm diamond.
Anghiari is a true place on the earth.
But that is one last true name I will tell.

On the way to Anghiari
We mounted the true frightening
Mountains, and there
The slim bus driver the messenger
Set us down and said,
Go find her.

I hurried you and my beloved
(Both you beloved)
To a secret place.

On the mile way there the tiny grapes
Glazed themselves so softly in the soft tuft
Of butterflies, it was hard to name
Which vine, which insect, which wing,
Which of you, which of me.

In the little graveyard there,
We are buried, Rachel, Annie, Leopoldo, Marshall,
The spider, the dust, the brilliant, the wind.

Our name is Piero, and the rest of
Piero's name is a secret.

POSTSCRIPT

One of my favorite passages from Dante's *De Vulgari Eloquentia:*
"... each one ought to take up a subject of such weight as to be a
fair burden for his own shoulders, so that their strength may not be
too heavily taxed and he be forced to tumble into the mud. This is the
advice our master Horace gives us when he says, in the beginning of
his *Art of Poetry,* 'Ye who write, take up a subject suited to your
strength.' "

JAMES A. WRIGHT